AN INTRODUCTION TO TOWN AND COUNTRY PLANNING

JOHN RATCLIFFE
Principal Lecturer, Polytechnic of Central London

 HUTCHINSON EDUCATIONAL

Hutchinson Educational Ltd
3 Fitzroy Square, London W1

London Melbourne Sydney Auckland
Wellington Johannesburg Cape Town
and agencies throughout the world

First published 1974
© John Ratcliffe 1974

Set in Monotype Garamond
Printed in Great Britain by
R. J. Acford Ltd, Chichester, Sussex
and bound by Wm. Brendon of
Tiptree, Essex

ISBN 0 09 116760 4 (cased)
      0 09 116761 2 (paperback)

Contents

Preface

The principal purpose of this book is to provide an introductory text for students preparing for the examinations of the Royal Institution of Chartered Surveyors, especially the Town and Country Planning syllabus, although certain aspects of the Urban Economics syllabus have been included where appropriate to the general theme. It has also been compiled with a view to fulfilling the same function for the various diploma and degree courses in Estate Management that qualify for exemption from the Institution's examinations. It is further hoped that it will serve as preliminary reading for both undergraduate and postgraduate town planning courses. In addition, it has been conceived with a view to catering for the recent development in modular unit degree courses, specifically those which offer some aspect of town planning within their range of options. At the present time this includes certain science, social science, engineering, cartography and construction courses. Having been actively involved in the teaching and preparation of courses in town planning for both planners and estate managers I am only too aware that no single publication currently satisfies these respective syllabus demands.

An attempt has been made to produce a simple and economic review that encompasses the historical development of town planning, its recent emergence, the existing organisation and management, some modern trends, certain popular techniques and predominant problems. This general objective is on the one hand ambitious, aiming to cover in a comparatively comprehensive manner a wide range of subjects falling within the broad sphere of planning, on the other it is relatively modest, seeking merely to introduce the selected topics, forsaking any pretence at great depth or special authority in particular areas. Naturally in such an ever changing and increasingly all-embracing discipline the contents of a text as restricted as this one are bound to be somewhat arbitrary in their selection and from time to time inevitably reflect the author's own views, limitations, and prejudices. In seeking to draw together the many elements and aspects that together constitute the history, development, and practice of planning this book cannot hope to rival in chosen fields more specialist publications, and for the interested reader further detailed references are supplied. The choice of the title itself presented certain difficulties epitomising the inherent problems surrounding a subject which can mean all things to all men. I opted for An Introduction to Town and Country Planning purely for its simplicity, fully recognising that strong and cogent arguments can be advanced for adopting any one of a number of other descriptions as valid alternatives.

Part One seeks to define the indefinable and explain the nature and context of present-day town planning, at the same time outlining the professions that practise or participate within it. It also sets out to describe the emergence and development of the subject, highlighting the most illustrious personalities and summarising the most salient occurrences. Particular attention is paid to the legislative framework that supports the planning system and the way in which the various agencies at different scales attempt to implement policy.

The implicit complexity of the planning process has predicated the need for a variety of methods with which to comprehend and predict the forces at play in determining the quality and performance of the environment. Part Two outlines some of the most popularly applied techniques of appraisal. Because the book is not intended for practitioners, or even for advanced study, the detailed mechanics of the surveys and techniques reviewed, the scope of which is by no means exhaustive, is not set out. The various selected approaches are merely introduced. A separate chapter, however, is devoted to explaining the need for the evaluation of alternative strategies, a much neglected field of study.

Town planning frequently appears in the form of contentious or controversial public issues such as the topical debates concerning pollution, public participation, conservation, and traffic congestion. Part Three sets out to explore a number of these problems and attempts to indicate the role of the town planner in tackling respective solutions. With a growing emphasis being placed upon the social, economic, and political aspects of urban and regional affairs it has become strangely *passé* to devote much attention to the regulatory, physical and legislative facets of the planning spectrum. Part Four tries to recognise their continuing relevance in allocating land between competing uses and controlling the impact of resultant development.

Although every effort has been taken to ensure that the incorporated material is accurate and up-to-date the usual *apologia* has to be made for the effluxion of time, the inadequacies of authorship and the speed of change. Writing on town planning has been repeatedly likened to painting the Forth Bridge, and as I watch the introduction of new techniques, the floating of new ideas and the pursuit of fresh strategies, I am only too aware how apt is the analogy.

Throughout my studies and my career to date I have been exceptionally fortunate in both my teachers and my colleagues. It would be inappropriate, not to mention invidious, to single out the many individuals who have on different occasions contributed the necessary advice and stimulus. I must, however, acknowledge the debt I owe to Dr. Gerald Burke, who first instilled in me an interest in town planning, and to Michael Bruton whose experience, guidance and encouragement has proved invaluable during the course of preparation. A book of this kind is actually written by innumerable people whose contribution is recognised, albeit inadequately, by the copious references throughout the text and without whom the task would have been utterly impossible.

Finally I would like to thank my wife Vivien, to whom I dedicate the book, which is little enough repayment for the patience and understanding she has constantly shown me in all my work.

JOHN RATCLIFFE

PART ONE

The Nature and Development of Town Planning

1 The Need to Plan

What is town planning?

The persisting process of urbanisation, the worst excesses of an industrial society, and the explosion in population growth and car ownership, have all contributed towards a heightened awareness, and ultimate acceptance, for the introduction of some form of regulation regarding the distribution of land between competing uses. The expression, profession and practice of town planning, with its multi-disciplinary nature, comprehensive perspective, changing character and continued self-questioning, is extremely difficult to define. It has been variously described as 'the art and science of ordering the use of land and siting of buildings and communication routes so as to secure the maximum practicable degree of economy, convenience, and beauty'[1] and as 'an attempt to formulate the principles that should guide us in creating a civilised physical background for human life'[2] whose main impetus is thus '. . . foreseeing and guiding change'.[3] Put another way, however, it is concerned with providing the right site, at the right time, in the right place, for the right people.

Control over the layout and design of urban settlement has been exercised since time immemorial. The early civilisations that congregated in the valleys of the Tigres and Euphrates demonstrated an ability to impose order upon comparatively high-density community living, and established an elementary

3

system for the provision of services and facilities, as did the Inca and Maya cultures of South and Central America. Hippodamus of Miletus is generally accredited the accolade of being the first town planner with his 'chequerboard' or gridiron layout of Piraeus nearly 2500 years ago in Greece. The distinctive hallmark of Roman colonial expansion was the dispersion throughout their empire of standardised uniform town plans. Not only has planning a long history, however, it can also be said that to some extent all development is planned. The individual dwelling is constructed so as to maximise efficiency in terms of function, daylight, outlook, and convenience. Similarly a block of offices is designed to facilitate movement, management, and servicing. There is little difference between the planning of separate dwellings and that of whole towns, it is only the scale and the interests involved that vary.

Perhaps the most important single justification of a formal system of town planning concerns these very interests, for planning is a reconciliation of social and economic aims, of private and public objectives. It is the allocation of resources, particularly land, in such a manner as to obtain maximum efficiency, whilst paying heed to the nature of the built environment and the welfare of the community. In this way planning is therefore the art of anticipating change, and arbitrating between the economic, social, political, and physical forces that determine the location, form, and effect of urban development. In a democracy it should be the practical and technical implementation of the people's wishes operating within a legal framework, permitting the manipulation of the various urban components such as transport, power, housing, and employment, in such a way as to ensure the greatest benefit to all.

Town planning aims at securing a sensible and acceptable blend of conservation and exploitation of land, as the background or stage for human activity. This involves the process of establishing the desires of the community, formulating them in a manner that facilitates comprehension and discussion, preparing a policy for their adoption, regulating the degree and proportion of public and private investment, guiding the provision of public services, initiating action where necessary, and contin-

4

ually examining the effect of the adopted policy, making adjustments if required.[4]

Planning and the market

In the absence of town planning land would be apportioned between competing uses by the price mechanism and the interaction of demand and supply. In this free-market situation land would be used for the purpose which could extract the largest net return over a foreseeable period of time, but experience has shown that, unfettered, the market can consume resources in an ill-conceived and short-sighted way, creating almost insurmountable problems for generations to come. Moreover, the competition engendered in the private sector where *laissez-faire* conditions prevail can all too often breed waste. The private sector developer seeking to maximise his personal profit frequently neglects the provision of both social services and public utilities. The very need for planning arose out of the inequality, deprivation and squalor caused by the interplay of free-market forces and lack of social concern prevalent during the nineteenth century. Furthermore, unplanned, these forces combine to produce the fluctuating booms and slumps that epitomise private sector instability.

The market, operating alone, does not provide the most appropriate location for what are generally described as the non-profit-making uses of land, such as transport terminii, gasworks, roads, fire stations, and sewerage plants. Nevertheless, the correct siting of these non-profit-making uses of land can render the profit-making uses of land more profitable. Proximity and accessibility to these various services and activities are often essential to commercial viability. Thus planning assists the market in becoming more efficient.

At a time of ever-accelerating social, technological, and political change, planning seeks to direct and control the nature of the built environment in the interests of society as a whole. In doing so it is unlikely to please all the people all of the time. There can be little doubt, however, about the need for some degree of intervention in private sector decision making, despite occasional frustration, fault, and delay. Although there exist violent political and philosophical schisms regarding the ownership, management, and return from land, the needs of traffic management, for example, demand far wider comprehensive layout and design than can be provided by the private sector. Central area reconstruction is another instance where large-scale corporate acquisition is more effective than fragmentary private purchase. Despite the obvious merits implicit in some form of control and guidance over the nature and function of the built environment, ensuring economic efficiency, social justice and physical quality, the application of comprehensive land use planning does not always meet with universal acclaim. Strong undercurrents, favouring a great deal less formal planning and a freer interplay of market forces, exist in a number of quarters. Planning and planners are often accused of setting themselves up as arbiters of public taste, frequently in blissful ignorance of consumer demand. The model or plan that they produce, which aims to achieve balance, symmetry, and order among the various elements and systems of urban organisation, does not always cater for changes in taste, habit, or preference. A case in point is the recent trend towards out-of-town retailing, extremely attractive to the shopping public, but not popular, it appears, with the planner. Their intransigent policy, with its innate conservatism, can lead to the charge of social engineering of the kind least befitting the spirit and purpose of town planning. It is possible that the restriction of residential development, and the control of densities against prevailing demand even when adequate services are available, could preserve the social status and property values of current residents, without due consideration being given to the welfare of potential future residents. In this way, the planner becomes the protector of existing social class structure on a selective basis, as opposed to being the guardian of the well-being of society at large. Furthermore, the reactionary nature of the planning process is said to stifle initiative, and the conformity that is introduced lacks the incentives required to stimulate experimentation and change. One can scarcely imagine a proposal to build the equivalent of a latter-day Brighton Pavilion or Albert Memorial endearing itself to a modern town planning committee, let alone meeting the

6

many building regulations and planning standards imposed. In a similar vein, the machinery of town planning is criticised for being excessively preoccupied with the trivia of urban development such as advertisement control, the siting of vending machines, the design of private houses, and the provision of car parking. It is a matter of regret that in the minds of many the term 'town planning' has become synonymous with 'development control'. Planning in all spheres of life, and throughout all professional activities, can easily become obsessed with scrutinising the detail of every tree in the wood, and lose sight of the shape, size, and significance of the wood itself.

Another aspect that detracts from the total success, and complete acceptance, of comprehensive land use planning is the inadequacy of the statutory system providing the legal framework within which it is forced to operate. Often, by its very nature, a particular plan or policy will depreciate the value of certain individual interests. This might be caused by the construction of a nearby urban motorway, airport, or school. The law of the land is at present incompetent to recompense this loss or blight.

Despite the above deficiencies it can be said that the twin forces of the free market and the planning process tend to act as a beneficial corrective, one of the other. The planner has to operate alongside of the market, directly influencing, and frequently assisting, its functioning, but in a manner that takes account of both public and private interests. Increasingly he depends upon private sector development for the implementation of a large proportion of planning proposals, not only city centre redevelopment where high costs virtually prohibit public investment alone, but also residential, industrial, and commercial undertakings of all kinds. Moreover, there is a tendency towards the use of free-market methods by planning agencies, such as the introduction of parking charges to ease the congestion of traffic in towns. Compromise solutions and joint developments are becoming the order of the day.

Categories of planning

At different times and by different people the organisation and management of the human environment has been variously described as town and country planning, town planning, physical land use planning, development planning, social and environmental planning, and even simply planning. Distinctions have been drawn between economic, physical, and social planning. In essence planning is merely a process which evolves a method for doing something, economics is the science of the management of resources, physical means pertaining to the world of material things, and social is concerned with the condition of people. The stewardship of the environment is all these. The dominance of one aspect above another is essentially one of scale rather than method. The construction of a new urban motorway, or the establishment of a new university, within a town, obviously affects the environment and has economic, physical, and social repercussions. The degree of importance or consideration given to each respective element largely depends upon the level of planning, whether it is national, regional or local.

Economic planning, for example, is often considered to be a national and regional approach, calculating and controlling the allocation of resources, ignoring physical and social implications, and primarily concerned with facilitating the working of the market. Physical planning is more closely associated with the regional and local scale, intervening in, and controlling, the market mechanism, reconciling public and private objectives, and directed towards the spatial qualities and relationships of development. Although divorced from any particular scale, social planning is commonly held to suggest some form of idealistic or Utopian engineering detached from practical feasibility and economic sense, but is more appropriately seen as the organisation of resources to combat problems such as poverty, discrimination, or deprivation. The endless comparing and contrasting of these supposedly separate subjects is both invidious and fruitless. Without the framework of national policy, which is after all meant to be the political expression of the community, the distribution of resources to geographical regions, public and private sectors, selected industries, and social groups, could not be contrived and co-ordinated in such a way as to permit realistic regional and local planning. Thus social considerations should determine the nature of national economic policy whilst physical planning is very much the material expression of that policy at the local scale. The different elements cannot, therefore, be separated, they are part of the same process, interrelated and interacting. This does not mean to say that they always attract the attention they deserve, but if one element, be it economic, physical, or social, is neglected, it is not necessarily planning that is bad, but merely bad planning. It is evident that national economic policies such as the location of industry, office decentralisation, housing subsidy, education and hospital expansion programmes are bound to be put into practice within the local context, having an inevitable reaction upon all other local activities, which in turn may require treatment in a physical or social planning sense. The barriers between these different areas, so strong in the 1950's, are at last breaking down. It has finally been recognised that it is impossible to prepare a plan for a community without the assistance of a number of contributory disciplines. The role of the town planner cannot be confined to land use allocation alone, it must also include consideration and co-ordination of associated activities bearing upon the human and physical environment. This synoptic view is succinctly put by Gordon Cherry who describes the purpose of town planning as being 'to promote a physical environment which is harmonious, pleasing, and convenient; a related social objective is to assist in securing for man some of the means of individual personal satisfaction and happiness. This is a wide field, but the interrelated aspects of total planning practice as at present conducted fall into place: for example, determination of land use and a communications pattern to secure order and convenience; the planned provision of distribution and facilities design to secure aesthetic qualities in the physical environment; regional planning to promote effective growth patterns in the national interest and to equalise economic opportunity, and so on. The role of social planning is the third part of the total planning trilogy, supporting the other fields of physical and economic planning.'[5]

Concepts of town planning

There are probably as many concepts of planning as there are planners, possibly more. Most would accept, however, that

9

planning is concerned with taking an objective and rational view of future conditions, assessing what society desires its destiny to be, forecasting the amount of change, estimating the degree of control required, and formulating a policy to take account of this destiny, change, and control. Where any conscious attempt to undertake this task exists, two extreme forms can be distinguished; these are sometimes described as Blueprint Planning and Process Planning.

Blueprint planning

This adopts a comprehensive approach towards planning and is ideally portrayed in the system employed since 1947 in the United Kingdom. It has developed from the technical professions architecture, surveying, and engineering, and has consequently produced solutions to urban problems that are predominantly physical in character, such as land-use maps, zoning, density controls, building regulations and planning standards. It acts through the medium of a 'master plan', hence the description 'blueprint', and operates upon a rigorous established administrative structure. The overall desires of the community, otherwise known as the goals and objectives, are given, having been previously decided by the political representatives, and do not therefore form part of the procedure of planning. Although it attempts to influence or direct all the activities connected with the physical environment, and is founded upon the notion of public benefit and amenity, it is singularly ill-equipped to deal with the majority of social issues and at times incompatible with economic expediency. Whilst exercising great control over the environment it is subject to considerable delays between the political decision, the preparation of the plan, its implementation, and any subsequent review and amendment. The exact nature of the problems encountered in this country are discussed later.[6]

Process planning

In contrast this concept sees planning as a continuous process, distinct from a static policy prepared at one particular point in time. Great premium is placed upon the incorporation of social and economic planning within the physical framework. Constant review is maintained regarding the performance of the plan and adjustments made whenever necessary, thus reducing delays to a minimum and preserving the relevance of the policy in the light of prevailing circumstances. Although in theory this approach is the tendency in the United States, being of a more *ad-hoc* nature, better geared towards a market economy, and with a more flexible relationship towards fluctuating public interest, the lack of coercive legislation and the degree of local autonomy has precluded the effectiveness there of almost any planning system. The realisation of recent years, in this country, that the complex problems of urban structure and organisation require an approach more akin to process planning has led to fundamental changes in both the theory and practice of town planning. This again is described in later sections.[7]

The practice and problems of town planning

In practice the town planner is expected to be able to 'operate to secure adequately related activity in the various parts of the framework of a comprehensive town and country planning system involving the local, urban, metropolitan, regional, rural and natural resource fields'.[8] Furthermore, his traditional role of controlling and allocating the use of land among competing activities has been substantially enlarged to take account of social and economic factors. In addition to which he is expected to assist in the selection of overall goals for the welfare of the community at the policy-making level of local government, and assist in the organisation and management of local government itself.

These wide terms of reference call for peculiar skills and present many problems. Firstly, on the one hand the professional town planner attempts to direct, guide and influence the formulation of a plan and exert pressure to gain its acceptance and implementation. He theorises on bigger and better ways of planning. He seeks to establish policy, co-ordinate departments, set goals, outline objectives and control development. On the other he is charged with discovering, examining, and acting upon the wishes of the local community, translating their dictates into a feasible plan through the application of professional skills, techniques, and judgement. He is thus faced with a situation where he is both master and servant.

Secondly, he is expected to undertake a comprehensive appraisal and detailed analysis of all problems related to the physical environment. He must grapple at the same time with transport, housing, education, commerce and recreation; and consider them in their economic, social, and physical contexts, bearing in mind their national and regional, as well as local connotations. With each component, in each context, and at every level he is attributed with exceptional proficiency. Thus the planner is made both generalist and specialist.

Thirdly, he is repeatedly confronted with the problems of poverty, deprivation, loneliness, old age, discrimination and unemployment. Yet all too often he is forced to reconcile these contentious and controversial long-term aspects of town planning with short-term financial and political expediency. He is thus asked to provide both social and economic planning expertise.

Fourthly, the town planner is presumed to possess taste and judgement in aesthetic and environmental matters. Being vested with powers of conservation and protection he is taken to be the guardian of heritage and the arbiter of architectural and historic interest. Increasingly, however, he is placed in situations which require a methodical and scientific approach, based upon a thorough training in numerate disciplines. In this way he is asked to bridge the gulf between the arts and the sciences.

Fifthly, one of the planner's principal accredited skills is that of communication. Communication between the planner and the planned, the professional and the politician, one department and another, and from one scale of operation to another. Despite this there is a marked tendency towards the excessive use of 'jargon' which inclines to confuse what is otherwise clear and over-sophisticate what might well be straightforward. The theories and expressions involved are not only often 'lifted' from other disciplines, but also used inaccurately and out of context. He is therefore portrayed as both articulate and esoteric.

Lastly there are a number of other areas of practice where the town planner is placed in a difficult and frequently conflicting position. He is assumed, for example, to reconcile the impact of private and public costs and benefits, whilst at the same time it is often necessary, in order to secure the proper performance of the plan, in the short-run to stimulate the degree of private investment and therefore entrepreneurial reward, sometimes at a long-run loss to the community. These days he is also charged with ensuring that full consultation and liaison with the public take place at all stages of the planning process even though this very participation and discussion of alternative strategies can spread blight like a great plague over the face of the land.

From the all-embracing nature of the complex task relating to the organisation and management of the physical environment, it can be seen that it is impossible for the town planner to tackle all aspects, cater for all attitudes and deal with all dimensions involved. He must be appreciative and selective; where he specialises he must consider the wider repercussions of his decisions; where he acts on behalf of one group, sector, or agency he must be aware of the interests of others, and all the time he must direct himself towards the study of uncertainty and the consequences of change—the very essence of planning.

The professions in planning

The process of planning is an extremely complex and comprehensive operation and therefore demands a variety of skills on the part of the people who participate within it. If any one person attempts to master all these diverse disciplines, and practise what is loosely described as 'general planning', he is in grave danger of joining that group of planners who know less and less about more and more. In seeking to identify the precise role and function of the various disciplines contributing to the organisation and management of the built environment probably the most difficult of all to define is the town planner. He is increasingly required to discover a wider variety of solutions to an expanding number of problems. There is clearly, therefore, a place for other specialist professions injecting their knowledge and expertise as and when appropriate. General categories of contribution are distinguished by McLoughlin[1] who groups them into 'activity contributors' such as demographers, economists, and persons with a knowledge of specialist activities such as extractive industries, recreation, and tourism; 'space contributors' such as architects, landscape architects, engineers, land surveyors, valuers, agriculturalists, geographers and geologists; 'communications contributors' such as transport engineers, specialists in air traffic, telecommunications and public transport. Also 'channel contributors' which includes engineers of many kinds as well as architects; and finally other contributors providing a general service such as sociologists, political scientists, systems analysts, mathematicians, computer programmers and management consultants. In this way urban and regional planning can be seen to embrace almost anyone with the slightest interest in the human environment who wants to take part.

Those who are widely accepted as playing a leading role and generally merit professional recognition, in addition to the membership of the Royal Town Planning Institute, are surveyors, architects, landscape architects, economists, engineers, and sociologists.

The surveyor

The general practice surveyor concerned with estate management and valuation has his origins in the measurement of land; this was extended first to the value of buildings, then to their cost, and more recently to the effects upon urban development of various activities. The introduction of comprehensive land use planning in 1947 placed heavy demands upon the existing professions, particularly the surveying profession, who bore the brunt of the responsibilities conferred by the Act of examining their local authority area, analysing the results, and preparing the development plans. To this day many senior town planners are also chartered surveyors, there is a close relationship and a natural progression between their respective disciplines. With a knowledge of construction techniques, economics, law, town planning and valuation, the surveyor is made well aware of the physical, administrative, legal, and financial constraints that beset the management and condition of the built environment. Within the sphere of town and country planning he currently performs the following functions:

1. He acts as an adviser and advocate for persons affected by planning decisions and proposals.
2. He works as a member of planning teams not only in a general capacity as a surveyor/planner but also frequently as a specialist quantity surveyor, valuer, or building surveyor.
3. In the field of land economy he plays a prominent part, possessing an ability to comprehend market forces, measure, predict, and control their effect.
4. The 1968 Town and Country Planning Act places great emphasis upon the survey and analysis of the economic characteristics of an area, a subject the surveyor is singularly equipped to supervise.
5. Traditionally the task of conducting shopping surveys, the calculation of retail catchment areas, and the assessment of shopping-floorspace requirements, has fallen to the chartered surveyor. To a lesser extent the same is true of office and industrial development, for with his understanding of the property market and his appreciation of planning criteria he is in an excellent position to undertake these tasks.
6. The techniques of measurement and evaluation employed in professional surveying practice provide one of the few absolute measures of performance available to town planning, that of return upon investment. Although not always appropriate, particularly where there are a large number of intangibles, most schemes possess substantial elements that can be costed and compared. This facility can, however, be a drawback and many valuers acting as members of a planning team adopt an over-cautious approach, for whereas the planner is permitted to generalise, and the architect portray his designs in outline, a valuer's figures often appear too specific and rigid. This can be overcome by the use of certain operational research techniques such as sensitivity analysis and probability distribution.
7. The surveyor in town planning must increasingly be prepared and practised in the use of a whole range of comparatively new techniques including Cost Benefit Analysis, Critical

Path Analysis, Gravity Models, Linear Programming, Discounted Cash Flow, and be conversant with the capabilities of a computer.

8. Town planning as a profession appears blissfully unaware of the nature and importance of land tenure as a determining factor in the urban environment. This view is eloquently put by Switzer: 'Without ownership of rights in land, a system of tenure—no physical development can take place. Tenure is the bridge from intention, resources and technical skill to realisation. Knowledge of tenure and the ability to understand its legal, financial and social implications is fundamental to effective and efficient land use, and I regard it as being the surveyor's special and basic contribution.'[2]

9. With an ever-increasing proportion of investment in connection with the built environment being undertaken by public agencies it is vital to the planning of the nation's resources to be able to forecast, guide and regulate prospective development on a national and regional as well as local basis. Again the surveyor has a considerable contribution to make.

10. Specific topics within the overall planning process where the surveyor's expertise is much in demand include central area redevelopment, cost benefit analysis, rehabilitation projects and conservation schemes.

The landscape architect

This discipline has experienced the fluctuations of professional favour over the last 100 years or so. Before the middle of the last century landscape architects such as Repton and Loudon were accorded a status closely akin to that of the architect. The advent of the landscape gardener, however, relegated him to the lowly position of an 'external decorator'. Since the First World War and the establishment of the Institute of Landscape Architects in 1929 and particularly over the last ten years he is now accepted as a specialist in the planning team in his own right whose term of reference is 'the whole of the outdoor environment in both town and countryside' and whose attention is directed to a wide

16

range of diverse problems from 'the small scale where we include pavings, fencing, the detailing and planting of open spaces in towns and around buildings . . . At the other extreme are the problems of conservation and management of coast and countryside, and in between comes the full range of design and layout tasks for recreation, industry, town development and the like'.[3] These all-embracing skills concern town and country planning in the following areas:

1. The landscape architect prepares, as a preliminary to any project of development, a plan of the site examining the contours, geology, soil conditions, availability of water, local microclimate, existing vegetation, and general surroundings, all of which might influence the scale and design of the scheme.

2. Having appraised the nature of the site he is further occupied with the task of relating this to the designated function. In doing so he must consider the possible movements of vehicles, pedestrians, and utilities, the proposed density of development and any potential hazards, all the time searching for ways in which he can facilitate development, promote safety and enhance the environmental quality.

3. The landscape architect by propitious planting can alleviate the incursion and imposition of noise, fumes and unsightly appearance.

4. He is responsible for the provision, selection, and location of outdoor furniture and fittings such as seats, benches, plant holders, street lamps, litterbins, and signposts.

5. The singular expertise of the landscape architect makes an invaluable contribution to the design and implementation of urban renewal projects. The choice of simple yet attractive materials, the tasteful refurbishing of the fabric of the dwellings, the pleasant and effective closure of streets, the clever use of space and proportion, the skilful planting of trees and bushes and the consideration of cost, management and maintenance, are part and parcel of the art of landscape architecture.

6. Although the value of landscape can, in all probability, be evaluated both economically and socially it has yet to be done. Techniques for conveying the feel or aesthetic quality

of a place have, however, been developed using a sort of 'bird's-eye' plan of a space, and plotting with symbols what can be seen from various points. This technique is called ISOVIST and has been used by the Central Electricity Generating Board in the siting of power stations. Another similar approach was employed in the planning of the Durham sections of the national motorway network where visual corridor maps were drawn up defining those areas most visible. This was conducted in varying weather conditions and a general limit of three miles on either side was established within which blemishes were selected for special treatment. In the same context Gordon Cullen has devised a Landscape Notation System for Alcan in analysing and describing landscape. Likewise Kevin Lynch in the United States was more interested in people's reactions to their surroundings, and got them to describe routes they followed naming landmarks and preparing maps showing what individuals thought about their city.

The economist

With both economics and town planning pursuing the same study of the allocation of resources there is inevitably an affinity between them. Economics, however, places greater emphasis upon the maximisation of efficiency and production, whereas town planning seeks to maximise the welfare of the community. The economist, with his tools of analysis, knowledge of markets, and understanding of location can assist the process of town planning in the following areas:

1. In that town and country planning is largely the physical expression at a regional or local scale of national economic planning the economist has a significant part to play in the translation of national policy into a local context.
2. The 1971 Act charges local planning authorities with the responsibility in preparing their development plan of paying regard to 'the economic planning and development of the region as a whole'. The economist in the planning team must, therefore, be prepared to examine the repercussions of individual local policies upon surrounding areas.

3. Regional planning provides the level at which economic planning predominates, perhaps to the exclusion of other social and physical aspects. The planning techniques employed in regional survey and analysis are mainly those of the economist namely input–output analysis, economic base, and the technique for area planning.

4. At the stage in the planning process where alternative plans are compared and contrasted, the evaluation stage, the economist again comes into his own. Cost benefit analysis, the planning balance sheet, cost effectiveness, and threshold analysis are approaches derived from economics.

5. The construction and use of mathematical models and their application at all levels of the planning process has advanced enormously over recent years. Many of these are either essentially economic models or require a substantial amount of economic data.

6. In relation to the specific topics of industrial location and employment the economist is required to provide a broad indication of policy, need, distribution, and degree so that the other members of the planning team can decide more precisely the type of manufacture, the amount of floorspace, the design, the exact siting, and the supply of ancillary services, utilities and residential accommodation.

7. The introduction of the economic method of allocating resources among competing uses, and the regulation of demand and supply, via the mechanism of marginal cost pricing into certain problem areas of planning, have received considerable support of late, particularly in respect of transportation and recreation planning.

The sociologist

The application of social aims and objectives to the philosophy and design of urban form has a long and distinguished tradition. Underlying religious, moral and political themes in the creation of communities can be traced as far back as Aristotle, Plato, and Socrates, through Aquinas, More and Savonarola, to Owen, Buckingham and Salt. With a few notable exceptions such as

Howard, Corbusier and Lloyd Wright, the role and practice of social planning was virtually eclipsed by early Public Health, Housing, and Town Planning Acts which tended to equate social concern with physical condition. Recently, however, the theoretical division between the character of the built environment and the nature of the human environment has been broken down, and the inextricable relationship between social planning and physical planning has at last been recognised. The contribution of the sociologist is increasingly welcomed in the planning process. Sociology is a behavioural as opposed to physical science, but social behaviour and attitudes frequently determine the use of land. Planning can therefore be seen as a form of urban ecology engaged in the study of the interrelationship of living things and their environment, with sociology an integral discipline. Social analysis assists the planning team in the following ways:

1. The sociologist is concerned with achieving and maintaining equality of opportunity. Cherry describes this aspect as 'developing the full potential of all communities by a process of maximisation of opportunity and a widening of choice'.[4] This often involves the protection of minority interests such as the poor, the underprivileged and the immigrant.

2. He assesses the provision and performance of social services and facilities from the public's point of view and integrates their organisation, management and location within the local authority development plan.

3. He identifies the desires, demands, priorities and problems of individuals or groups within the community in an attempt to establish the goals and objectives which will guide the formulation of a planning policy. In doing so he must balance the need for the efficient organisation of society with the preservation of individual freedom, thus providing 'planning with a human face'.

4. The sociologist is called upon to describe the intricate pattern of social relations and the way of life of the inhabitants of areas likely to be affected by planning activity. This may range all the way from describing the social patterns in local 'neighbourhood' groups.[5] This will include the examination of such problems as those caused by colour, class and creed, the disturbance of family ties, the journey to

work, high-rise living, and migration to new estates and new towns.

5. As a preliminary step in the preparation of any plan it is therefore necessary to conduct a social survey identifying the values and attitudes held by various sections of the community. The sociologist is equipped to prepare, implement and analyse such a survey.

6. Certain social processes, or forces, influence the nature of the urban environment, causing crisis areas and community breakdown. Chapin isolates and defines three such major social processes that affect land use and command the attention of the sociologist and planner alike; he calls them 'dominance', 'gradient' and 'segregation'.[6] Dominance is the control of one area over another, gradient is the degree of dominance, and segregation is the related process of clustering. Thus, the central business district is one centre of dominance possessing a certain gradient or influence over surrounding residential areas which could result in the segregation of lower-paid service workers dwellings and urban decay.

7. With the growing awareness of the need for public participation within the process of planning both urban and rural areas, the sociologist's task of ascertaining community desires takes on a more important role; that of acting as advocate on behalf of the inhabitants of an area.

8. The upsurge of demand for greater recreation facilities due to increased leisure time, higher standards of living and greater mobility places a further duty on the sociologist, ensuring that the development plan reflects individual preference in this respect.

9. It is also his responsibility, with others, to make forecasts and predictions regarding the future state of society given existing demographic, social, and economic trends.

10. Finally, it lies with the sociologist to comprehend the purpose and performance of the planning system. Increasingly sociological analysis is being focused on the process of planning itself, not just on the effect of the physical environment upon human behaviour.

21

The architect

Traditionally the architect has always been associated with the design, development and ordering of towns. Alongside surveying the contribution made by the architectural profession to the organisation, management and practice of town planning has been considerable. His role in the planning team can be summarised as follows:

1. He provides a three-dimensional perspective to two-dimensional plans.
2. There exists a strong similarity between the process of designing for the space and movement within and about dwellings and the process of planning the distribution of land uses and the communication between them.
3. The architect frequently finds himself responsible for the preparation of detailed planning schemes, and the production of planning briefs specifying permitted forms of development, their limitations and restrictions as to size, height, density, construction, materials, access and parking. In other words he is called upon to assist in compiling a detailed framework for commercial proposals within the context of the development plan in order to stimulate private investment.
4. As the finished product or end result of the majority of planning proposals takes the form of a building, it is inevitable that the profession exclusively concerned with the built form should be represented and consulted at every stage throughout the process of determining the context within which building should take place.
5. In recent years great emphasis has been placed upon the role and function of the 'urban designer' who falls neatly between the respective professions of architect and town planner and is likely to be drawn from both. His attention is directed not only towards the impact of individual buildings but also the physical repercussions of groups of buildings, the space around them, the movement between them, and the forces that direct the planning and development processes—a hybrid animal indeed!
6. The architect is also involved in the preparation of detailed

planning schemes such as town centre redevelopment, and the construction and organisation of major building complexes, such as hospitals and universities.

7. The expertise of the architectural profession is particularly valuable at the local scale. All too frequently, however, the practice of development control is carried out as a matter of routine, and rather uninspired, administrative procedure. The greater participation of architects at this stage might provide a more imaginative implementation of the development plan proposals and a more respectful recognition of planning in general.

8. The future of the profession within the planning process has been described, perhaps rather generously, by the Royal Institute of British Architects' own steering committee on the architect in planning reporting in 1965 in the following manner: 'Architects have a contribution to make at all levels of planning. In national planning they have a consultative role; at regional level they should be members of the planning team; at local level, however, where town design and redevelopment should form a large sector of the work, the design skills of the architect must play a decisive part.'

The need to plan—references

1 Keeble, L., Principles and Practice of Town and Country Planning, *Estates Gazette* (1969).
2 Thomas Sharp.
3 McLoughlin, J. B., *Urban and Regional Planning: A Systems Approach*, Allen and Unwin (1969).
4 T.P.I. Discussion Note: The Changing Shape of the Planning Process, *T.P.I.* (1971).
5 Cherry, G., *Town Planning in its Social Context*, Leonard Hill (1970).
6 See page 77.
7 See page 100.
8 T.P.I. *op. cit.*

Recommended further reading

Amos, J. F., 'The Development of the Planning Process', *Town Planning Institute Journal*, **57**, 7, 1971.

Benevolo, L., *The Origins of Modern Town Planning*, Routledge and Kegan Paul (1967).

Broady, M., *Planning for People*, The Bedford Square Press (1968).

Levin, P., 'Towards Decision Making Rules for Urban Planners', *B.R.S.* (1968).

The professions in planning—references

1 McLoughlin, J. B., *Urban and Regional Planning. A Systems Approach*, Allen and Unwin (1969).
2 Switzer, J. F. Q., 'The Surveyor in Society', *Chartered Surveyor*, August (1969).
3 Weddle, A. E., *Technique of Landscape Architecture*, Heinemann (1967).
4 Cherry, G., *Town Planning in its Social Context*, Leonard Hill (1970).
5 Western, J., 'The role of the sociologist in town planning', *Royal Town Planning Institute Journal*, May, 1972.
6 Chapin, F. S., *Urban Land Use Planning*, University of Illinois (1965).

2 The emergence of modern town planning

From earliest times man has striven to attain a perfect physical environment. The Egyptians expressed themselves monumentally but statically, the Greeks created a more varied and dynamic urban style which the Romans standardised in their functional manner, the Middle Ages achieved that unlikely state of harmonious cacophony, the Renaissance contributed unsurpassed beauty and magnificence, the Baroque, 'a planned achievement' as opposed to the ideal plan and the Age of Enlightenment a conscience as well as a concept.

England has been particulary fortunate in its urban heritage. The Romans were well versed in the layout, organisation and management of towns, every general being said to carry an 'army issue town planning scheme in his knapsack'.[1] The Normans were experienced town builders. The Middle Ages were free from the internal strife that ravaged continental settlements, whilst the seventeenth and eighteenth centuries were rich with fine examples of urban development, notably the work of Inigo Jones, Christopher Wren, John Nash, Robert and James Adam, John Wood, Dobson, Grainger and James Craig.

The nineteenth-century philanthropists

The nineteenth century witnessed the climax of the industrial revolution, and the worst of its anomalies. The process of urbanisation had become a stampede, the uncontrollable influx of the rural poor flooding into towns in search of employment reached alarming proportions. Between 1821 and 1851 over 4 million people moved to the towns, a problem that would severely tax the abilities of present-day town planners. The resultant conditions were almost indescribable, verminous, filthy, insanitary, disease-ridden back-to-back hovels, squalidly assembled in overcrowded uniform ranks.

It is little wonder that at a time which echoed the militancy of the Paris Commune and when the clamour of revolution rang throughout Europe, a fear regarding the collective power of the poor, and a concern over the creation of a nation divided, should reverberate through the establishment. It is reflected in the writings of Disraeli, Marx, Chadwick and Chalmers who advocated the splitting up of poor communities, and Canon Barnett who urged Oxford undergraduates to live as 'settlers' in the East End of London thus setting the scene for Lady Henrietta's Toynbee Hall.

This despoliation of the town and exploitation of the industrial labour force did not go entirely unheeded. The century was distinguished by a number of Utopian Socialists, a term coined by Karl Marx to describe a group of social thinkers whose attitude was unscientific and idealistic and who hoped to improve working-class conditions by individual benevolence, philanthropy, and enterprise. These reformers concentrated on the development of separate new communities outside urban areas, and there emerged a succession of plans based on a variety of politicial, social, and philosophical ideas.

First, and perhaps foremost, amongst these philanthropists was Robert Owen (1771–1858) who proposed the creation of agricultural villages of between 800 and 1200 persons catering for all the social, educational and employment needs of the community.[2] His plans, submitted to the parliamentary committee looking at the problems of the working classes in 1817, and to the County of Lanark in 1820, envisaged these 1000-strong communities having residence near their place of employment, communal living for the older children, central heating, private lodgings only for families with children under three years old, being agriculturally based but including some industry on the outskirts. Owen himself set the example by establishing an industrial complex at New Lanark, which provided excellent working and living conditions, cheap but unsubsidised shops, and an adult education centre. It is worth noting that he also increased output and made substantial profits.

Owen's influence is clearly detectable in the writings of James Silk Buckingham (1786–1855). His ideas on co-operation and association are set out in his book *National Evils and Practical Remedies* published in 1849. He proposed the development of a specially planned, socially integrated community, which he called Victoria, in deference to the Queen. It was to be built in open country, a mile square, with a population of 10 000 housed in numerous buildings arranged on a quadrangular basis, larger in

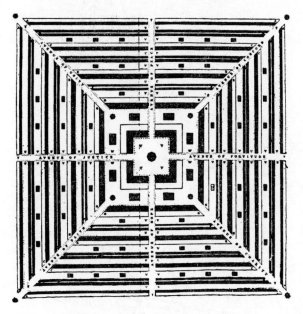

Fig. 1   Victoria

the centre and gradually becoming smaller towards the outskirts, surrounded by 10 000 acres of agricultural land, and owned and managed by a public company with the inhabitants as shareholders. Whereas Owen practised a form of paternalistic communism, Buckingham preached integration and temperance. His plans contained strong moral and religious overtones, for in Victoria there was to be no tobacco, no alcohol and no weapons

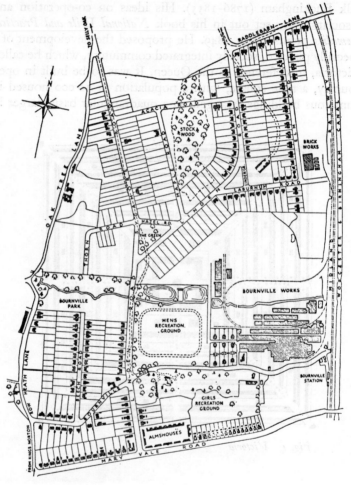

Fig. 2 Bourneville in 1898

SOURCE: R. Bell and C. Bell, *City Fathers*

of war. His schemes were never carried out owing to a lack of financial support.

The concept of attempting to improve the working-class environment continued to flourish throughout the nineteenth century. In 1853 Sir Titus Salt moved his factory and workers away from the appallingly grimy and congested conditions of Bradford to a green field site outside the town where he constructed what was considered to be a model industrial community, Saltaire, on an admittedly dense, uninspired, monotonous gridiron pattern but with easy access to the open country.

A quarter of a century later, in 1879, George Cadbury, faced with the need to provide new premises to allow for expansion, built the more suburban town of Bourneville outside Birmingham which was open to all workers irrespective of their place of employment. Shortly afterwards, in 1888, William Lever, a soap manufacturer, constructed Port Sunlight as a model village for his employees just three miles south of Birkenhead. It consisted of most pleasant cottages with small back gardens, open front gardens and allotments in the centre of housing blocks. In essence it portrayed the same brand of paternalism as existed in Saltaire and New Lanark, and reaped the same commercial rewards.

Public health legislation

As a method of administering the nation's resources in a local context with a measure of equity for all classes, town and country planning as we know it today has its roots in the public health and housing legislation of the late nineteenth century. By the 1840's urban conditions were so appalling, politicians so alarmed by continental upheavals, and the climate of opinion so favourable, that a series of legislative measures were enacted to combat the growth of disease and squalor caused by the lack of adequate sanitation and standard of accommodation. The Public Health Act of 1848 was passed at a time when an epidemic of cholera had killed 54 000 people in England and it founded a General Board of Health which exercised functions similar to those of the Poor Law Commissioners. Through unpopularity it was abolished in 1858. The 1848 Act was followed by the Housing Acts of Shaftesbury (1851,) Torrens (1868), and Cross (1875), which were consolidated in the major Public Health Act of 1875. This Act introduced a set of codes or standards in respect of the level, width and construction of new streets; the structure of houses, their walls, foundations, roofs, and chimneys; the layout of buildings and external space requirements, and their sanitary facilities; as well as providing powers for closing down dwellings thought to be unfit for human habitation. To implement these regulations the country was divided into urban and rural sanitary districts, themselves responsible to the Local Government Board established in 1871. Much of the credit for these advances lies with Sir Edwin Chadwick the politician, and Sir John Simon the administrator. Although conditions in towns were undoubtedly improved, a wider range of facilities provided, and a great awareness of the need and requirements of the working class induced, the primary concern had been with hygiene and sanitation, as opposed to equity and increased opportunity.

The Garden City movement

Towards the end of the nineteenth century the various philanthropic concepts were drawn together and embodied in one plan by Ebenezer Howard (1850–1928). In his book, *A Peaceful Path to Social Reform*, published in 1898, he set out his plan for a satellite town called a Garden City which he portrayed on a grand scale. It would comprise 6000 acres, 32 000 inhabitants, a central area of 1000 acres, individual plots 20 feet by 130 feet, with a gross density of 30 persons per acre. There would be six boulevards each 120 feet wide extending radially from the centre; these would assist in forming six wards which would provide the basis of local government and community services. The 'city' would be self-sufficient in terms of employment, possessing its own industry, commerce, shops, and agricultural production. Howard envisaged a whole molecular infrastructure of garden cities clustering around a central city of about 50 000 population. His philosophy was almost certainly influenced by the writings of William Morris, particularly in respect of the necessary

30

reorganisation of society along collective socialist lines and a basic distrust of the existing city. Physically he appears to have incorporated several of the ideas of Robert Pemberton who designed, in 1854, a settlement in New Zealand which he called Happy Colony.

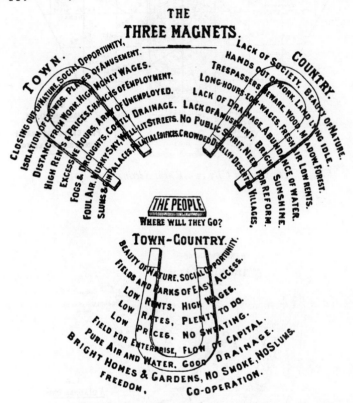

Fig. 3 Howard's Three Magnets—demonstrating the respective advantages and disadvantages of both town and country and the amelioration of the drawbacks in the Garden City ideal

A great deal of criticism has been levelled at Howard's plans as being unrealistic in their adherence to geometric proportion, but he presented his design of concentric circles of varying land use as a universal rather than as a particular model, the actual plan being drawn once the site had been selected.

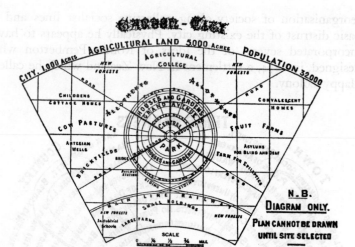

Fig. 4   *The Garden City in a Rural Setting*

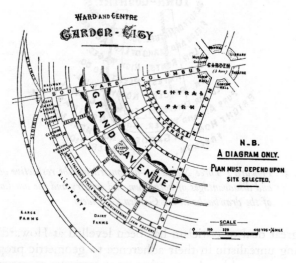

Fig. 5   *Section showing a Ward and the Centre of the Garden City*

In 1899 Howard formed the Garden City Association, the forerunner of the Town and Country Planning Association, with the intention of putting his theories into practice. A company

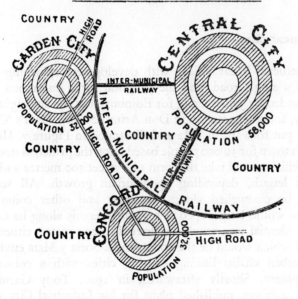

Fig. 6   City Growth

SOURCE: Ebenezer Howard, *Garden Cities of Tomorrow*

called the Garden City Pioneer Company was registered in 1902 with the express purpose of finding a site. After a brief survey one was found at Letchworth in Hertfordshire and, in 1903, the First Garden City Limited was in business. Letchworth was designed by the architects Raymond Unwin and Barry Parker in 1904. Due to financial constraints its development was slow, but it was entirely privately sponsored. Unwin and Parker also drew up the plans for Hampstead Garden Suburb, the concept of Dame Henrietta Barnett, in 1907. After the First World War, Howard and his associates attempted to consolidate the garden city movement at a time of post-war construction, and in 1919 Welwyn Garden City was begun. Welwyn attempted for the first time to secure a 'social balance' by a skilful integration of varying socio-economic groups, but like its precursor Letchworth its growth was hampered by financial constringency.

The linear city

The medieval linear village with development spawning either side of a single road, and the proposal for a linear new town propounded by James Craig for Edinburgh in the late eighteenth century, found expression in Don Arturo Soria y Mata's 'Ciudad Lineal' put forward in 1882 and illustrated in Figure 7. He suggested a town for 30 000 people based upon the principal transport route which would take the form of a street 500 metres wide and infinite length, depending upon urban growth. All services would be channelled along the street and other community facilities would be grouped at regular intervals along its course. The residential area would be limited to 200 metres either side, beyond which would lie the countryside. Soria y Mata envisaged these urban chains linking existing cities with a cobweb of development. Shortly afterwards, in 1901, Tony Garnier, a French architect, published plans for his Industrial City which possessed a definite centre but with a lineal structure and placing great emphasis upon zoning and the separation of various urban functions.

In 1933 Le Corbusier, the great Swiss architect, planner and visionary, author of *Urbanisme* (1923), *Towards a New Architecture* (1925) and many other notable works, designer of Unité d'Habitation (1945) an 18-storey tower block box of homes, and Chandigarh, the new capital of the Punjab, proposed cities 'La Ville Radieuse' and 'City of Tomorrow', based on a linear system, seeking to ease congestion by the use of skyscrapers and elevated roads. In his City of Tomorrow, designed for 3 million

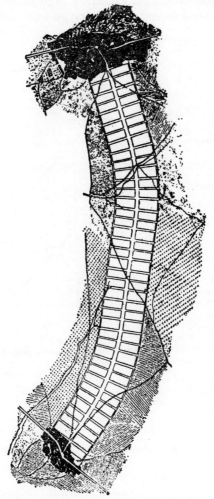

Fig. 7   Don Arturo Soria y Mata's proposed lineal city

people, there would be subways for servicing, a co-ordinated transport system, high-rise business and entertainment centre

surrounded by 5–7-storey residential blocks, and then detached
dormitory garden city suburbs. In Ville Radieuse, planned for
1½ million, there would be extremely high densities with skyscrapers on the periphery of the city as well as in the centre.

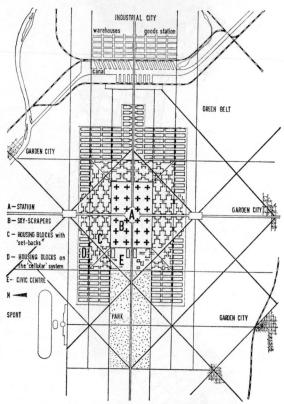

Fig. 8   An outline of Le Corbusier's master plan for Chandigarh

Le Corbusier also planned Chandigarh in the early fifties along a
lineal approach.

In the footsteps of Soria y Mata and Le Corbusier, the Modern
Architectural Research, or 'Mars', Group worked out a development plan for London. Although prepared in 1937 it was not
published until 1941. It applied the linear concept to the complete

36

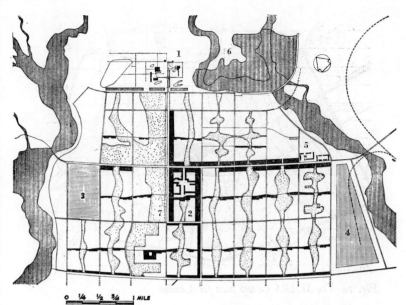

Fig. 9   Key 1. *Capital complex*   *5. Grain and timber markets*
          2. City centre   *6. Lake*
          3. University   *7. Town park*
          4. Industrial area

More detailed plan for the northern sector of Chandigarh

SOURCE: Frederick Gibberd, *Town Design*

redevelopment of the metropolis in the form of a herringbone
layout with the backbone providing access to the administrative
and commercial centres, and fourteen districts of 600 000 persons
each set at right angles to it. A main arterial and orbital railway
were included in the plan, as well as a hierarchy for social
organisation based upon a unit of 1000 persons, six units forming
a neighbourhood, about six neighbourhoods to a borough, and
approximately twelve boroughs to a district. This original and
far-seeing master plan was far too revolutionary and has sadly
lapsed into this historical perspective.

The most recent developments adopting a lineal approach have
been the plans for Cumbernauld prepared in 1958 by Hugh
Wilson and the scheme for Hook New Town published in 1961
by the London County Council. The advocates of the linear
plan list its advantages as:

37

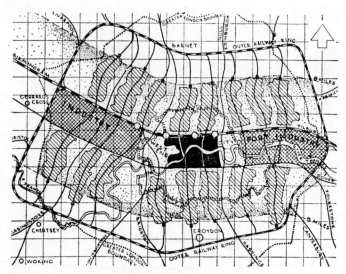

Fig. 10 The MARS Group plan for London

a a simple economical form of traffic segregation
b a pattern of movement and location comprehensible to the average citizen
c the town centre grows in proportion to the demands of residential and industrial expansion
d subsequent possibility of expansion to absorb a larger population.[3]

Its critics are more numerous and its defects more apparent:
a accessibility to central areas is impaired
b separation of arterial and local traffic is exceptionally difficult to achieve
c services have to be provided over a longer distance and are therefore more expensive.

The neighbourhood unit

The social upheaval of the nineteenth century, the physical repercussions upon urban form and the reaction of reformers all contributed to the concept and creation of model communities to accommodate the working class. Some by dispersal to satellite towns and others by the establishment of urban villages. A common theme runs through all attempts to formulate standards for residential area layout and town design, that is the search for the ideal size of population which relates to both the provision of services and the retention of identity. Robert Owen considered 800 to 1200 persons to be the appropriate size, James Silk Buckingham thought 10 000; in France, Fourier designed 'Phalansteries' for about 1800 inhabitants and Ebenezer Howard divided his garden cities into wards of around 5000 aiming to provide social services, integration of classes, and a sense of community.

In America, two architects, Henry Wright and Clarence Stein, having toured and studied the work of the English Garden City movement, developed the idea of a neighbourhood unit even further. They set up the City Housing Corporation in 1924 to build an American Garden City. Their first attempt was at Sunnyside, New York, which owing to local regulations was constructed on a 'gridiron' pattern, with large lawn-covered courts leading off the streets. Probably its most notable inhabitant was Lewis Mumford who lived there for eleven years and described it as being 'framed to the human scale'. Clarence Stein was particularly impressed with Raymond Unwin and Barry Parker's low-density *cul-de-sac* layout, and in 1928 he prepared the plan for the ill-fated town of Radburn. The projected population was to be 25 000, divided into three neighbourhoods of around 8000 each, the size required to support an elementary school. Its prime objective was to take the Garden City concept and adapt it to the requirements of the motor age, segregating the pedestrian from the vehicle by means of footpaths, under-passes and bridges, providing rear access for cars and grouping residential 'superblocks' around a backbone of continuous parkland. Wright and Stein considered their design to be universally applicable, but their experiment was criticised on the grounds that having developed so close to existing built-up areas they had in effect extended suburbia, exacerbated commuting problems, neglected to provide local employment opportunities, ignored the entertainment requirements of young people and, by the nature of the house type, displayed a bias towards white-

39

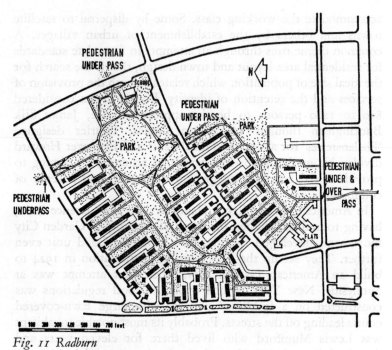

Fig. 11 Radburn

SOURCE: J. Tetlow and A. Goss, *Homes, Towns and Traffic*

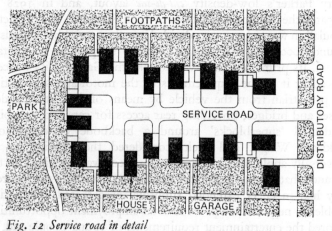

Fig. 12 Service road in detail

SOURCE: J. Tetlow and A. Goss, *Homes, Towns and Traffic*

collar workers and white Anglo-Saxon Protestants, thereby causing local dissention. The City Housing Corporation was hit by the Depression and forced into liquidation in 1933, Radburn itself remaining uncompleted.

Many of the ideas incorporated in the plan for Radburn were originally put forward in 1910 by Clarence Perry in his publication *The Wider Use of the School Plant*. It was he who first coined the term 'neighbourhood unit', which he explains in some detail in Volume VII of the *Regional Survey of New York and its Environs*. Perry was not an architect but a social worker and is more closely associated with the Greenbelt Towns developed in the thirties than with the actual construction of Radburn. In proposing what he described as 'a scheme of arrangement for the family life community' he saw the neighbourhood unit as ensuring that all residents were 'within convenient access to an elementary school, adequate common playspaces, and retail shopping facilities. Furthermore, their districts will enjoy a distinctive character because of qualities pertaining to its terrain and structure, not least of which will be a reduced risk from vehicular accidents.'[1]

Perry laid down six principles upon which the design of neighbourhoods should be based:

1. The size should be related to the catchment area of an elementary school
2. The residential area should be bounded on all sides by arterial streets, there should be no through traffic
3. There should be ample provision of small parks and play areas
4. There should be a central point to the neighbourhood containing the school and other services
5. District shops should be located on the periphery, thus serving approximately four neighbourhoods
6. There should be a hierarchy of streets facilitating access but discouraging through traffic.

These precepts were taken up by Wesley Dougill in his writings about the use of school buildings as the foundation for neighbourhood planning,[2] and in his examination of Wythenshawe, near Manchester, as an example of neighbourhood units in practice.[3, 4] Along the same lines was the notion of 'precinct' planning put forward during the Second World War by the Assistant Commissioner of the Metropolitan Police, Sir Alker Tripp. He too stressed the need for a hierarchy of arterial, sub-arterial and local roads. The sub-arterial roads would bound and create residential, commercial or industrial areas which would be known as 'precincts'. His work was significant because it recognised the separate functions that are provided by different roads, and was the forerunner of Professor Colin Buchanan's noted work, *Traffic in Towns*.[5]

At about the same time the National Council of Social Service produced a report that looked at the social needs of residential areas. It stated that in existing residential development the journey from home to work was too long and there was inadequate provision of community facilities. It suggested that a greater degree of social balance should be achieved in future urban development, and that community facilities should be located at the centre of a neighbourhood area, no further than 10 to 15 minutes' walk away from the population of 7000 to 10 000. Methods of obtaining social balance were considered by the Dudley Report a year later, in 1944, which also criticised the existing density zoning as being too inflexible as well as noting that there was insufficient variety of dwelling types. It too favoured a population of approximately 10 000 for each neighbourhood, which should be no more than 10 minutes' walk away from the community centre. The area of the neighbourhood would be 168 to 482 acres depending upon the topography and appropriate density, and to link residential blocks a continuous park, footpath and playground network was suggested. Once again the primary school was advocated as being the focal point of the neighbourhood, but unlike Perry the report suggests that the shops would also be similarly situated. The report's findings were generally accepted by the Ministry, apart from the fact that they thought the size of the population should be 5000.

New Towns

Drawing upon the experience of the Garden City movement, and prompted by the Town and Country Planning Association, the

42

government started to display interest in the notion of new towns during the 1930's. Following in the footsteps of Howard and other nineteenth century reformers the idea had gained momentum with the report of the Committee on Unhealthy Areas,[1] the Committee on Garden Cities and Satellite Towns,[2] and, most important of all, the Barlow Report,[3] which analysed the factors affecting the distribution of the industrial population with particular reference to the disadvantages of allowing further concentration of industry and suggested possible remedies. It hinted at dispersion and suggested the formation of a research body to consider solutions, while a minority report fervently advocated the establishment of satellite towns and garden cities. No action was taken until after the Second World War when Lewis (later Lord) Silkin, was appointed Minister of Town and Country Planning. He was a firm believer in the New Town philosophy and in 1945 the New Towns Committee under Lord Reith was set up to consider 'the promotion of New Towns in furtherence of a policy of planned decentralisation for congested urban areas'. Its recommendations were embodied in the New Towns Act of 1946. It placed great weight upon attaining a satisfactory social balance of self-contained communities, probably as a reaction to the drab, monotonous, one-class, pre-war LCC estates such as Becontree and Dagenham. The time was ripe for a positive policy in this direction, there still existed a strong control over the economy from the war, there was a Labour government willing to exercise it, London had suffered terrible destruction and required redevelopment, and Abercrombie's plan for London propounded the dispersal of 1·25 million persons, 0·5 million to be re-located in New Towns whose sites were suggested. Since the 1946 New Towns Act some 28 New Towns have been designated including three, Northampton, Peterborough and Warrington, that strictly rank as town expansion schemes.

Between 1947 and 1950 the first phase had been designated, fourteen in all, eight in the London ring, Basildon, Bracknell, Crawley, Harlow, Hatfield, Hemel Hempstead, Stevenage and Welwyn Garden City; two in the North East, Peterlee and Newton Aycliffe; two in Scotland, Glenrothes and East Kilbride; and one, Cwmbran, in Wales. These are sometimes described as

Fig. 13 British New Towns

Glenrothes
Cumbernauld
Livingston
East Kilbride
Irvine

Washington
Peterlee
Aycliffe

Central Lancs
Skelmersdale
Warrington
Runcorn

Telford
Newtown
Corby
Peterborough
Redditch
Northampton
Milton Keynes
Stevenage
Cwmbran
Welwyn
Hatfield
Hemel Hempstead
Harlow
Basildon
Bracknell
Crawley

the Mark I or first-generation New Towns. Unlike their Garden City predecessors they aim to achieve a 'social balance' in both the individual neighbourhood units and the community as a whole. For example, Crawley strived to reflect the class characteristics and social balance that existed throughout the country. Thus, when there was found to be 20% 'middle class' nationally, they planned for the integration of 20% 'middle class' in the neighbourhood units as well as in the town at large. In practice this is difficult to achieve because people tend to segregate themselves at the local level.[4] The very concept of neighbourhood units was held in great esteem. In Stevenage, for instance, the original town

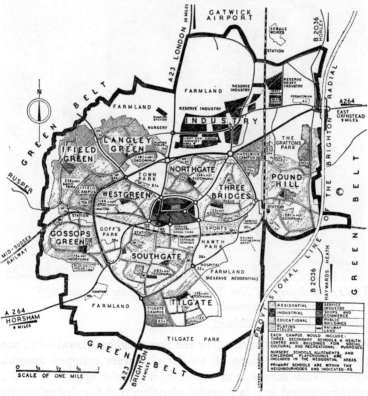

Fig. 14 The original plan for Crawley New Town showing the physical separation and separate identity of neighbourhoods

45

KEY:
1. Central area
   Housing
2. 100 p.p.a.
3. 70 p.p.a.
4. 40 p.p.a.
5. Special housing
6. Industry
7. Secondary
   schools
8. Primary
   schools
9. Open space
10. Woodland
11. Lakes
12. Cemetery
13. Heliport
14. Hospital

N

0   1   2   3 miles

Fig. 15 Hook proposed New Town demonstrating the integrated, high density lineal approach

SOURCE: Frederick Gibberd, *Town Design*

centre formed the nucleus for the first neighbourhood of 10 000 persons and five more of similar size were grouped around. From social survey and research it would appear that the neighbourhood unit is a useful planning tool for designing the provision of community facilities but inhabitants tend to associate themselves with very much smaller residential areas such as

46

streets, blocks, or wards. It has been suggested that the concept of neighbourhoods as envisaged in the development plan had little significance in Stevenage.[5] Even when the neighbourhoods did seem to work, at least from a functional point of view, it was found that they did so to the exclusion of the town centre. In Harlow and Basildon people seemed either reluctant or unable to travel from one neighbourhood to another, which weakened the various community organisations and led to individuals possessing a very small circle of friends. This, in part, is said to account for that mysterious but malignant ailment, the 'New Town blues'. There was a temporary halt in new town construction between 1951 and 1961, largely as the result of a change of government. The 1952 Town Development Act directed attention instead towards the expansion of existing towns, providing financial support and encouraging local authorities to agree amongst themselves regarding the planning and management of overspill schemes. Most of these were on the lines of the Garden Cities but lacking in adequate social facilities. In this period only one New Town was designated, Cumbernauld in 1956, commonly referred to as Mark II. It represented the movement away from seeking social balance by complete integration and its community structure was far less physically determined than the first generation of New Towns. There was less adherence to the formal idea of an architecturally designed neighbourhood unit and less physical division of the town. By allowing for a higher density, more concentrated population grouped around a hill-top town centre and almost total pedestrian-vehicle segregation, and ensuring that everyone was within walking distance of everyone else, it was hoped that social intercourse would be facilitated. In similar vein the London County Council put forward proposals for a new town in the South East called Hook. Although it was never built, the plans, often referred to as the 'Hook Book', envisaged a strong dominant town centre, high densities, and great accessibility to community facilities.

The 1959 New Towns Act gave fresh impetus to designation and development, enacted in the light of the apparently successful economic performance of the immediate post-war towns. The New Towns of the early sixties, however, were largely unconnected with London, concentrating instead on Birmingham, Merseyside,

47

the North East, and Scotland. They were, in order of designation, Skelmersdale, Livingston, Telford, Redditch, Runcorn, Washing-

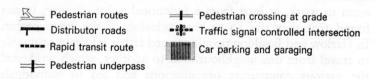

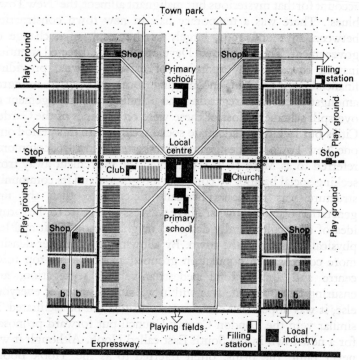

Fig. 16 Diagram of the community structure at Runcorn comprising 8000 people divided into four neighbourhoods of 2000 persons each

SOURCE: Runcorn Development Corporation

ton, and Irvine. Shortly afterwards the designation of Northampton, Peterborough and Warrington took place where development under New Town Act powers is to occur on a partnership

48

basis between the development corporations and the existing local authorities. In all these later Mark II New Towns increased mobility and planned accessibility have tended to invalidate even further the idea of a fixed residential neighbourhood size. Moreover, the notion of separating various functions such as employment, shopping, education, recreation and residence has also been questioned and in Washington, for example, where a basic 'village' unit of about 4500 persons can still be discerned, shops, primary school, pub, and employment are provided in the local village centre. The unit is thus a convenient size for all daily needs and contained to the extent where the residents will have a sense of belonging. The planner now aims to introduce greater flexibility into his schemes by designing for the 'group', which is a very small social unit of up to 50 families, then for the 'place' which is the successor to the neighbourhood unit but still gives a sense of identity, being up to 500 families strong, then to the 'village', which consists of several places, and finally to the town itself.

The original New Town concept of a population size between 20 000 and 60 000 has been found to be too small to stimulate the necessary economic growth and balance of employment. The ultimate size of most towns has therefore been increased, and the most recent designations have been in respect of 'New Cities'. These are Milton Keynes in Buckinghamshire with a planned size of 250 000 and the Central Lancashire New Town in the Preston-Leyland-Chorley area, expected to grow to 500 000. Other New Town innovations are the 'in-town' development by GLC at Thamesmead intended to accommodate 60 000 Londoners of various socio-economic groups, and the more limited satellite towns of Newcastle, Cramlington and North Killingworth.

Considering that the early New Towns were designed in the absence of any previous theoretical study or practical research it is perhaps surprising the degree of success they have obtained and the relative insignificance of the mistakes they have incurred.[6] Although they have frequently been criticised for the parsimonious approach they were obliged to pursue in respect of providing those civic facilities that would have fulfilled their original objectives community interest and social life in the New Towns is beginning to flourish. Perhaps the most notable achievement of New Town development has been the way in which it has attempted to reconcile the seemingly endless conflict of the pedestrian and the motor car. Furthermore, the realisation is beginning to dawn

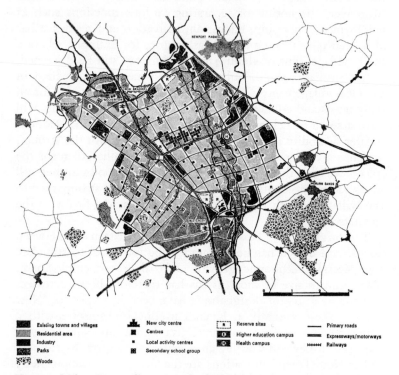

Existing towns and villages	New city centre	Reserve sites	Primary roads
Residential area	Centres	Higher education campus	Expressways/motorways
Industry	Local activity centres	Health campus	Railways
Parks	Secondary school group		
Woods			

Fig. 17 Milton Keynes illustrating the dispersed low density chequerboard design

that a new community of such significant magnitude requires to be related to nearby towns and cities, and in 1973 greater efforts are being made to study regional and sub-regional conditions before the location, size, and function of the New Town is determined.

Undoubtedly a large number of people have discovered a fresh and more acceptable way of life since transferring from the congested 'twilight' areas of the cities. It is unwise however to exaggerate the impact of New Town development. Up to

1968, after 20 years of New Town policy, their total population had only grown to 554000, representing approximately 1% of the population of the country, and currently stands at rather less than 1·4%. Although certain development of peripheral areas and expansion of existing towns proves comparatively inexpensive by ensuring the full economic use of existing services and facilities, it has recently been suggested that owing to higher direct costs of improvement, costs associated with greater distance, inflexible public utility and transportation systems, together with increasing obsolescence in the conurbations, New Town construction presents a cheap and viable alternative. Nevertheless, even under such circumstances, total cost per capita has appeared to rise with growth, and in any event cost minimisation only makes sense if profitability is fixed. In attempting to steer growth away from existing congested urban areas the New Towns, particularly those around London, did manage to attract industry to their new estates. The accompanying workers, however, were all too often the key, skilled, relatively well-paid employees whose numbers were scarcely significant as a remedial measure to counteract congestion in the cities, and whose predominance militated against the establishment of a socially integrated community in the receiving New Towns.

The creation of a well-integrated socially balanced community has traditionally been a prime objective in the establishment of new towns. They have, however, been found to attract people by their apparent characteristic of 'social exclusion', whereby the very poor are offered little encouragement to move. Studies have shown that in British New Towns higher income groups tend to leave and a distinctive segregation between neighbourhoods within a town occurs. Housing difficulties are presented because the 'filtering' process, whereby low-income groups are accommodated in stock made cheap by age, conversion or division, does not exist in new towns. Either substantial housing subsidies are required or these low-income groups are excluded altogether. The Burns Report describes the New Towns as catering for the 'middle man', discouraging the poor and immobile and failing to attract the executive. In the same context the New Towns have traditionally sought to achieve 'self-containment'. During their first ten years the early New Towns possessed a relatively self-contained structure but despite an overall balance between jobs provided and works employed there has been an increasing amount of work travel between each town and the older established towns around. The Jobs Ratio, that is the number of jobs supplied per 100 employed residents, has increased. Within the 8 London New Towns the ratio went up from 98·6 between 1951 and 1961 to 132·8 between 1961 and 1966. Throughout the country the Mark I New Towns remain comparatively balanced communities, however, possessing an overall average job ratio of 102·8. Again, in the London New Towns the number of inhabitants who work elsewhere has fallen slightly between 1951–61 and 1961–66 from 29% to 27% and the employment expansion in the early sixties following the experience of the initial decade of development tends to suggest that New Towns have job deficiencies in their early stages but once the basic social and industrial structure has been established employment growth gains in momentum and proceeds to outrun the growth of population. This in turn increases the number of people who travel in every day and thus creates a wider, more dependent hinterland. A recent survey by Ogilvy, reported in the *Town Planning Review*, 1971, put the actual increase in numbers travelling in at over 60% and those travelling out at approximately 17%. This cross-movement has reduced the self-sufficiency of New Towns, although at Welwyn Garden City, which it can be argued is at a more advanced stage of development than the others, the trend has stabilised.

The objects of self-containment, integration, and balance may result in certain economies but may also give rise to a lower level of productivity, a risk of instability, a curtailment of adaptability, and the problem that periods of decline can have more serious repercussions on smaller urban areas than larger ones. A closed labour market is also very difficult to maintain, witness the fact that for every ten workers who find employment within the early British New Towns another seven commute out every day. Conversely in the more recent Scottish New Towns another trait has developed, large numbers of workers are preferring to return to the old cities to live and travelling out to the industrial new town estates every day to work.

The investment in New Town development is also favoured as a method of stimulating investment and growth in the economy at times of decline by promoting demand. However, the time lags between the recognition of economic problems and the implementation of growth policies is often too long to allow such New Town investment to be used as a counter-cyclical device. Furthermore, any such effective economic measures require the ability to be used in the opposite way—to slow down development at times of new town development with its 'front-heavy investment' followed by the slowing down of growth could be disasterous to private enterprise critical cash flow problems. The notion that New Towns could provide a kind of domestic *détente*, intercepting migrants from rural areas, thereby giving a breathing space to the cities has never been an important factor in this country and has virtually disappeared since rural migration has fallen to a mere trickle and plays a decreasing role in metropolitan growth. Perhaps one of the most forgotten aspects in favour of a New Town development policy is that it permits and facilitates the public ownership of land, thus allowing the community to automatically recapture the 'unearned increment'.

Another theoretically attractive claim for adopting the New Town approach is the proposition that it acts as a kind of urban planning laboratory. Because of the control over development, timing, programming, magnitude, and location, the stimulation and planning of construction, layout and investment policy can be made on a more rational basis. The infra-structure can be provided more effectively and efficiently and the resultant performance more accurately assessed. An interesting example of just such experimentation can be seen at Le Voudreuil, one of the 8 French New Towns attempting to deflect commercial growth away from existing urban areas. Situated near Rouen it is one of the smallest, with a planned population of 140 000, but is being designed from its earliest stages to control air, water, noise, and visual pollution, thus providing a test bed for innovation.

Whatever the future of New Towns in this country, and assuredly they will continue to play an important part in urban and regional planning, albeit with a changing form and capacity, one final problem remains. The great weight attached to public participation in recent years presents particular difficulties, for in New

Town development detailed and comparatively long-term plans have to be prepared before any population exists, thereby precluding consultation. Nevertheless, despite this and other apparent drawbacks this bold and inventive policy seems certain to form part of the pattern of development not only in this country but throughout Europe and the rest of the world.

Private enterprise in New Town development

At various times it has been suggested that private enterprise should play a greater role in new town development. After all, Letchworth and Welwyn Garden Cities were established on private finance. The United States has experienced a number of such ventures ranging from the commercially motivated 'company towns' like Pullman, to the more Utopian greenbelt towns that were constructed during the depression of the thirties on Garden City principles and let at low rents. The accent appears to have been on the provision of accommodation to the detriment of social amenities and community services as at Radburn and Sunnyside. The worst example of this manifestion is Levittown on Long Island, New York, where 50 000 people live in identical homes and scant regard has been paid to local employment, the town becoming a glorified 'commuterville'. The most recent developments at Columbia and Reston appear to be rectifying these deficiencies.

Apart from Howard's exploits there have few such attempts in this country. One that never got off the ground was British Petroleum's proposal in 1955 to construct a new town of 25 000 population called All Hallows on the Isle of Grain in Kent principally for the employees of their oil refinery. They were refused planning permission by the Minister on the ground that the scheme appropriated too much agricultural land. One of the most recent attempts was that at New Ash Green, again in Kent, where Span developers undertook to build a small self-contained community of about 7000 persons in co-operation with the Greater London Council as an alternative to urban sprawl. The GLC withdrew their support after construction had started, and Span were financially unable to continue. Bovis, another large developer and builder, have taken over responsibility but on a very different and more conservative basis.

Naturally a great deal of private investment of a commercial industrial and residential nature goes into existing government-sponsored New Towns and the general policy is to induce more. There is, indeed, a speculative swing towards a more total commitment by developers in the construction of new communities probably on a comparatively small scale and in conjunction with local authorities.

The administration of New Towns

Once a New Town has been designated by means of draft order and any consequent local public inquiry has been held, a Development Corporation is established to take overall responsibility for the management of the town and the implementation of the plan. Although their powers are fairly comprehensive the local authorities and statutory undertakers are still liable for administering such services as health, education, sewage disposal, gas, water, and electricity. Where necessary the Development Corporation can assist either technically or financially. As one might expect, the relationship between them is not always harmonious. The Corporations are wholly financed by the Exchequer who, with other central government departments, must approve all expenditure and be assured that a reasonable return can be expected. Thus, on the principle of 'he who pays the piper calls the tune', New Town policy is directly controlled by Whitehall. Once the development of a particular New Town nears completion its assets, liabilities, and responsibility of management are transferred to the New Towns Commission, an *ad hoc* public body set up for the purpose. The Commission will then set up a Local Executive in the town to fulfil its administrative duties; this has normally comprised the old Corporation's staff.

A Balanced Industrial Structure

The severe unemployment that spread throughout the country between the two world wars caused the government to give serious attention to the role and location of industry. The effects of the depression hit some regions harder than others, and a direct link between unemployment and industrial structure was discerned. A scheme to re-train redundant labour from declining industries was introduced in 1928, and following a number of studies into the problem four Special Areas, in South Wales, the North East of England, West Cumberland and Clydeside, where unemployment was particularly acute, were designated under the Special Areas Act 1934. Commissioners were appointed under the Act to assist in improving the prevailing social and economic conditions. It was not until 1936 and the setting up of the Special Areas Reconstruction Association, however, that financial assistance was made available to prospective firms considering development in the Special Areas. Even then it was limited to small businesses, until the Special Areas Act 1937 extended it to larger concerns as well as introducing a system of tax incentives on a regional basis. It also attempted to encourage the unemployed from 'depressed' areas to retain and move to other parts of the country. This policy was largely ineffective because of the high level of unemployment throughout the nation.

A major landmark, in terms of town and country planning as well as industrial location, was reached in 1940 with the publication of the Report of the Royal Commission on the Distribution of Industrial Population under the chairmanship of Sir Montague Barlow. The Commission had been charged with inquiring 'into the causes which have influenced the present distribution of industrial population' and to 'consider what economic or strategical disadvantages arise from the concentration of industries' and then 'report what remedial measures, if any, should be taken in the national interest'.[1] The Commission proposed the creation of a central agency to oversee the redevelopment of congested areas and assist in the decentralisation of industry and population. It recommended that dispersion should be directed to Garden Cities and Satellite towns which would be equipped with trading estates. Because the outbreak of the Second World War mopped up surplus labour for military service and wartime munition production, no immediate action was taken. The stage was set, however, for comprehensive planning at national, regional, and local levels, and it is only recently that the policies advocated by the Barlow Report have been questioned.

The 1944 White Paper on Employment Policy, and the subsequent Distribution of Industry Act 1945, again focused attention on the need to achieve balanced industrial development in Special Areas and a degree of control over industrial location was exercised by means of Building Licences and the designation of 'Development' Areas which were approximately the same as the Special Areas. At the same time the Board of Trade were empowered to establish industrial trading estates and to build factories on them in order to attract firms to the areas of concern.

The Town and Country Planning Act 1947, besides reforming the entire system of planning, introduced the Industrial Development Certificate for premises over 5000 square feet as a successor to building licence control in directing the location of industrial development. It also extended Development Area status to North East Lancashire, Merseyside and parts of the Highlands. Between 1947 and the Local Employment Act of 1960 few measures in respect of industrial structure were enacted. Because of a general 'upswing' in the economy the post-war situation to 1960 was comparatively healthy, and Development Areas received over 50% of new industrial building.

Since 1960 a wider and more sophisticated range of controls and inducements has been introduced and this is reflected in the current situation.

Present policy

Two broad categories of measures aimed at obtaining a balanced industrial structure and alleviating unemployment exist today. First, the negative controls preventing expansion in locations deemed unsuitable, such as planning permission itself and I.D.C. requirements. Second, positive inducement to industry to locate where development is required, such as grants, tax concessions and subsidised sites. The areas of concern are classified generally as Scheduled Areas and comprise Special Development Areas, Development Areas, and Intermediate Areas.

Special Development Areas were designated in 1967 and consist mainly of the coalmining parts of South Wales, Northumberland,

Durham, Cumberland and Ayrshire. Development Areas are the declining regions first identified in 1945, replaced by Development Districts in 1960 and selected on a basis as having an employment level above 4·5%, and in turn superseded in 1966 by Development Areas under the Industrial Development Act. They are not now selected on such strict unemployment criteria and the larger area covered allows industrialists a greater freedom to choose their own location. Almost the whole of Scotland, Wales, large parts of the North of England and sections of Cornwall and Devon are included in this category. The Intermediate Areas were introduced in 1969 following the report and recommendations of the Hunt Committee. They are sometimes described as the 'Grey areas' and represent areas of slow natural growth as opposed to actual decline.

Since the Budget announced in the House of Commons by the Chancellor of the Exchequer on the 22nd March, 1972, assistance to firms locating themselves in Scheduled Areas is as follows:

1. Building grants
2. Development grants—which vary from one category to another
3. Labour subsidies—the regional employment premiums receivable in Development Areas ends in September 1974
4. Relaxation from Industrial Development Certificate control—they are not required at all in Development Areas, and only for proposals over 15 000 square feet throughout the rest of the country, apart from the South East where the limit is 10 000 square feet
5. Industrial training grants
6. Loans—at modest rates of interest
7. Removal grants
8. Rent-free periods
9. Preferential treatment in the placing of government contracts.

Nearly £300 million per annum is being invested by central government to encourage industry to locate in Scheduled Areas and an admitted improvement in the regional disparity of unemployment can be distinguished. There is still a need, however, to integrate national, regional and local planning more effectively, possibly by means of more powerful regional development agencies. These could co-ordinate the efforts of individual

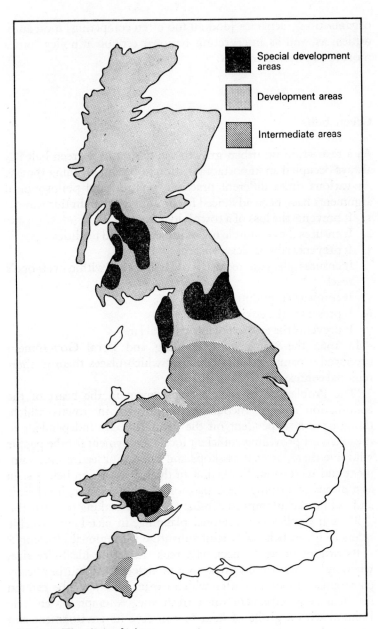

Fig. 18 The Assisted Areas

organisations, separate [and all too often competing] local authorities, as well as interpreting national economic policy into a more local physical context.

Green belts

As a restriction on urban growth the notion of a green belt has always occupied an important position in British planning theory. At various times different practical, political and philosophical arguments have been advanced for limiting growth in this way:

1. It prevents the loss of a town's identity
2. It ensures the economic use of urban land and facilities
3. It prevents ribbon development
4. It ensures adequate recreational facilities are within everyone's reach
5. It combats air pollution
6. It preserves the environment
7. It prevents the erosion of agricultural land

In 1962 the Ministry of Housing and Local Government produced a pamphlet on *Green Belts* which places them in their regional context.[1]

'The Problem is to reduce employment in the heart of the conurbation and to encourage its growth in towns which, though partly dependent on the great city, are independent to the extent of providing sufficient local employment for the people who live there, as well as shops and opportunities for entertainment and recreation. Looked at in this way, a green belt is seen as a means of shaping the expansion of a city on a regional scale and not just an attempt to combat the forces making for growth.'

Thus it implies city regional planning, in fact Lewis Keeble refers to green belts as 'a faint substitute for regional planning'.[2]

Its origins lie as far back as Greek theory on ideal city size, whereby a town would grow to a predetermined and physically constrained dimension after which expansion should be catered for in a new settlement on a fresh site. Attempts to encircle London with a girdle of land to conserve its environment and prevent its further growth also have a long history. In the

60

reign of Elizabeth I a proclamation was delivered in 1580 prohibiting the erection of any dwelling within three miles of the City boundary declaring that 'a city of great multitudes needs restrictions to prevent crowded housing and great poverty'.[3] Elizabethan policy failed, and it was not until the advent of the nineteenth century reformers that the concept of a green belt was revived. In nearly all of the periods Utopians envisaged new towns of a chosen size set in the countryside surrounded by protected open space. A green belt policy was implicit in the writings of Ebenezer Howard and in 1919 the Garden Cities and Town and Country Planning Association openly advocated the imposition of rural belts around urban areas. In 1901 Lord Meath, inspired by Chicago's 'green girdle', suggested a similar scheme for London consisting of a chain of parkways set five to nine miles out from the city centre connecting existing open spaces. Shortly afterwards in 1910 G. L. Pepler proposed a London Ringway 326 feet wide, ten miles out, and in 1914 the London Society produced a plan for the capital which included a circular structure of open spaces even closer in. Further consideration was given to the idea during the 1920's and 1930's, most notable of which was the Greater London Regional Planning Committee who retained Raymond Unwin as consultant. He put forward two alternatives. First, that a flexible barrier approach should be adopted which could retreat through time with growth, with certain special areas being preserved. Second, which he did not recommend, was the establishment of a fixed permanent open space in which no development should take place. Despite Unwin's reservations it was this latter suggestion which survived to Sir Patrick Abercrombie's Greater London Plan and was the forerunner of our present metropolitan green belt.

During the thirties both the Middlesex and London County Councils bought land for the provision of regional open space and in 1947 they obtained the power to designate land for such purposes without having to purchase it. Towards the end of the Second World War in 1944 Abercrombie produced his Greater London Plan in which, reinforced by the findings of the Barlow Commission relating to the control of growth, he proposed the application of four rings of population growth to limit development. The inner two referred to residential density but the third ring defined a green belt within which no new settlement would occur and where expansion of existing communities would be very restricted. Despite the continued growth of London the green belt has largely survived intact, although a bit 'dog-eared' at the edges.

The respective county plans prepared under the 1947 Town and Country Planning Act proposed a green belt slightly smaller than that contained in the Greater London Plan. Their submissions were greatly influenced by central government, and in 1955 Duncan Sandys, then Minister of Housing and Local Government, in Circular 42/55 extended the principle of green belts to provincial centres for the following reasons:[4]

a to check the further growth of large built-up areas

b to prevent neighbouring towns from merging into one another

c to preserve the special character of a town such as Oxford, Cambridge, York or Norwich.

Local planning authorities seized the opportunity with relish and, as shown in Figure 17, within four years approximately 6% of the country's land surface was covered by green belt proposals. At the time of writing there is still only one statutory green belt, that encircling London, although many others, some charted over ten years ago, still await approval.

In attaining their original objective, confining urban sprawl, they have proved comparatively successful. They have also provided a pleasant environment for the post-war development of many New Towns and it can be said that they focus attention on the need to examine future town expansion even more closely. On the other side of the coin they have been criticised as contributing towards the spiralling increases in urban land prices, and by concentrating development in existing centres they have added to the problem of congestion. Moreover, their very presence does not actually ensure or facilitate public access to, or the recreational use of, the land so restricted. It can also be seen that many areas designated or proposed as green belt are anything but attractive; they include spoil heaps, tips, and neglected or derelict land. It might be far better to conserve land possessing great amenity or outstanding natural beauty which truly warrants selective attention. The value of landscape or recreational

Fig. 19 Green Belts in England and Wales as at 1 May 1962

potential should be the criteria. This could provide a series of green wedges protruding into developed areas which allows for the release of land for housing and associated functions whilst preserving a number of 'green lungs' permitting the city to breathe. This would also have the effect of reducing the present tendency of development to 'spark the gap' across the green belts and create even worse problems to effective village planning. Certainly green belt policy is destined to come under severe pressure in the coming years, and an alternative strategy that is less arbitrary and more flexible is clearly called for.

Regional planning

The nature and role of regional planning springs from the criticism that central government policy is often too remote and local government administration too parochial. The need emerges for an intermediary at the regional scale to provide a meeting place for national economic planning and more local physical land use planning. The overall expression of a national plan should not be exclusively concerned with merely securing, for example, a 5% economic growth, but should also seek to provide an appropriate framework for the planning of such elements as country parks, motorways, water catchment and mineral resources. Although as yet there is no common approach or accepted procedure, it is the regional scale that best lends itself to initially translating economic policy into physical form.

The concept of regional planning is thus largely based upon national economic planning and the need to translate this into a physical context that both defines the problem and facilitates the implementation of solutions. The overall management of a country's resources by central government involves a certain degree of interference with market forces to ensure that no one part of the nation, or sector of the community, benefits unduly at the cost of another. It also implies, however, a distribution or redistribution of assets in such a way as to benefit the whole and every sector of the community. At its outset, therefore, any attempt at a rational approach towards comprehensive regional planning is beset by divisions in interest and attitude.

Two principal aspects of regional planning can thus be identified, economic and physical. It is with the latter, the physical aspect, that this section is concerned, although it cannot be emphasised enough that its nature is largely determined by the former with its roots firmly planted in location theory and the philosophy of the hierarchy of settlements.

The puzzle of defining a region for planning purposes has caused much research, debate and controversy. A region is capable of meaning all things to all men and no special classification to assist in definition exists. The following categories of regional scales amply portray the problem:

Physical—a regional identity can be discerned by a particular topography, such as the Lake District; or a form of agriculture, such as vineyards, hopfields and sheep farming; or a distinctive landscape, like the Devonshire lanes or Cotswold cottages; or by an area of water catchment.

Economic—a region might relate to a certain economic sphere of influence like a market town, shopping centre, or focus of employment whose tentacles of commuting delimit the boundaries. Similarly it might be identified by a common economic problem such as unemployment in coalmining.

Ethnic—probably one of the most obvious influences of regional identity is a common heritage, tradition, accent or language. People are often only too anxious to attach labels such as North Walean, Lancastrian or Man of Kent to themselves.

Administrative—a more recent development is the selection of a region for the purposes of administration or management. This can relate to local government, as with metropolitan administration by the Greater London Council, or to statutory undertakers like the various Regional Electricity, Gas or Water Boards.

Regional scientists have traditionally classified these aspects under three differently styled, but similarly conceived, headings. First, the *homogeneous* region that relates to a natural, and often static, combination of physical, social, ethnic or other characteristics. Second, the *nodal* or *polar* region which is based upon more dynamic and economic activities grouped around a central place. And third, the *programming* or *policy-orientated* region, almost identical to the previously described administrative region. Usually it is a form of pragmatic compromise that actually determines the nature of a region, with a large degree of overlap between the respective categories.

Perhaps the first attempt at land use planning on the regional scale was Sir Patrick Abercrombie's London Plan in 1944. London's influence has since been more widely discerned, and the strategic plan for the South East published in 1967 looks at the physical problems of accommodating a projected population increase while at the same time checking excessive growth. Another instance of regional planning in this country is the *South Hampshire Study* which investigated the future requirements of the Southampton-Portsmouth Region. This, however, is closer to the scale that is more commonly described as Sub-Regional, which is employed in the implementation of strategic planning when all elements of the planning process are to be considered, and there is a need to transcend existing local authority boundaries. It is represented by the *Teesside Study* undertaken by private consultants and published in 1969, the *North Gloucestershire Sub-Regional Study* initiated in 1966 and published in 1970, and the *Coventry, Solihull, Warwickshire Sub-Regional Planning Study* which also reported in 1970.

Early attempts to control the use of land in this country were almost exclusively local in application. The first Town Planning Act in 1909 did not so much as hint at the fact that demand for land should be reconciled on a basis less parochial than the existing local authority boundaries, let alone on a regional scale. It was not until the 1920's and 1930's with the southward drift of labour, the disparity of earnings, rising unemployment in the North, combined with steady and occasionally spectacular growth in the South, that any great concern was displayed regarding the imbalance of regional resources. In a period of what we consider to be serious unemployment, it is worth remembering that the number of unemployed in Jarrow in 1934 was almost 70%. The first legislative attempt to combat the worst excesses of the Depression was the Special Areas Act of 1934 which defined certain areas, including South Wales, the North East, Glasgow and the areas around Barrow-in-Furness, as warranting special financial assistance to stimulate industrial growth and thus employment. Although some potential demand was deflected, the 'boom' continued unabated in the South East.

In consequence the government set up a Royal Commission to report on the distribution of the industrial population, the Barlow Report, which was published in 1940. This set a pattern for future regional planning policies by calling for a balanced distribution and appropriate diversification of industry and employment throughout the various areas of Great Britain. With the onset of the Second World War little was done immediately but the report remained as a blueprint for future action. Despite the Minister being charged with 'securing consistency and continuity in the framing and execution of a national policy with respect to the use and development of land throughout England and Wales' in 1943 there was little conscious endeavour towards an integrated regional policy implicit in the 1947 Town and Country Planning Act. the 'never had it so good' reflationary period during the 1950's delayed the need for concerted government action. The reappearance of unemployment in the less favoured regions combined with the increasing obsolescence of development plans in the early 1960's focused attention on the problem of regional imbalance. As a result a series of regional studies were instituted. They were conducted jointly by the Ministry and the constituent local authorities, and were first directed at the South East, the North West and the West Midlands. *The South East Study* was produced in 1964 and demonstrated an unprecedented scale of physical planning, with proposals for whole new cities in the Solent, Milton Keynes and Newbury areas, together with new town development and expansion af existing towns like Peterborough, Ipswich, and Swindon, all intended to act as counter-magnets to the insuperable growth of London.

Nevertheless, *The South East Study* was still severely criticised for undertaking its investigation, and putting forward its recommendations, in isolation, not placing enough weight upon the need and condition of other regions. The pressure for consistency in physical planning at the regional level and continuity with national economic policy, encouraged the Labour Government in 1965 to transfer the responsibility for its direction to the ill-fated Department of Economic Affairs. At the same time ten Regional Economic Planning Councils were set up, eight in England and one each in Scotland and Wales. The

Councils comprise of individual members of the public selected by the Minister and drawn from such fields as industry, politics, and the universities. They act in a purely advisory capacity, having no executive power to implement their proposals. They are supported by Regional Planning Boards which are staffed by civil servants representing the various ministries concerned with regional matters.

The creation of this regional planning machinery was intended to provide a framework for the execution of national policy and thus set broad objectives for each particular region and to generate a climate within which these objectives could be achieved. Owing to the lack of administrative authority disenchantment has spread among members of the various Councils who have felt a certain impotency and frustration at being relegated to what has been described as merely the role of regional stocktakers. Not only have the Councils as a whole been left in a vacuum, but they have also acted in isolation, one region often competing with another for industrial favours and growth.

Whilst they have not always dovetailed together in the manner expected, it should, in all fairness, be said that they have provided a more comprehensive and flexible machinery for the operation of physical planning and the allocation of national resources between regions. The keynote of their policy, in the form of a plan, will therefore be primarily concerned with broad strategies regarding future commercial expansion, general accessibility, urban growth, and perhaps large-scale recreation facilities. The plan should not be fixed and rigid but aim to stimulate the adoption of its strategic proposals at the local scale. Because regional planning should express national policy it is greatly affected by the various tools of economic planning such as Industrial Development Certificates, tax concessions, investment incentives, loans, grants, and so on. Perhaps too much emphasis is placed upon industrial employment and more consideration should be given to other aspects such as planned decline, leisure facilities, agricultural production, and service industry.

One further feature of regional planning merits attention and that is the development of the theory of 'Growth Points' or 'Growth Poles' which aims at focusing economic activity on particular points within a region. These need not necessarily be

68

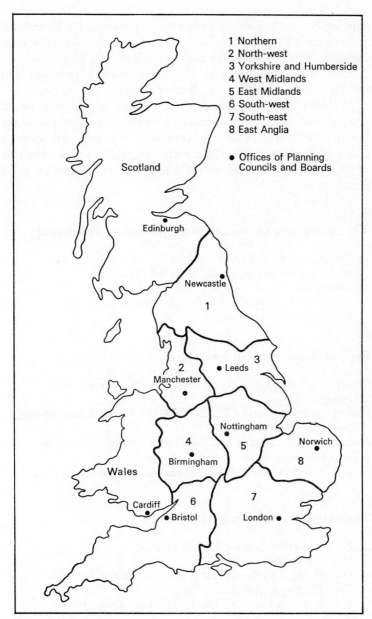

1 Northern
2 North-west
3 Yorkshire and Humberside
4 West Midlands
5 East Midlands
6 South-west
7 South-east
8 East Anglia

● Offices of Planning
Councils and Boards

Scotland

Edinburgh

Newcastle

1

Wales

2
Manchester

Leeds
3

Nottingham

4
Birmingham

5

Norwich

8

Cardiff

6

Bristol

7

London

Fig. 20 The Planning Regions

existing centres but would have a latent potential for exceptional growth that can be stimulated by the introduction of certain industry, or services, or by the up-grading of a particular road system. This would release the latent growth potential and produce beneficial multiplier effects throughout the region.

A clearer and more consistant hierarchy of planning might emerge with the implementation of Parliament's proposals for the reorganisation of local government, for there still exists a major dichotomy in what Westminster considers to be the role of regional planning, and what the regions themselves view as its function.

The emergence of modern town planning—references

1 Bell, C. and R. Bell., *City Fathers: The early history of town planning in Britain*, Barrie and Rockcliff (1969).
2 Owen, R., *A New View of Society* (1813).
3 Hillman, M., *Towards a Linear New Town. Essays in Local Government Enterprise*, Merlin (1965).

Further recommended reading

Cherry, G., *Town Planning in its Social Context*, Leonard Hill (1970).
Keeble, L., Principles and Practice of Town and Country Planning, *Estates Gazette* (1969).
Morris, A. E. R., History of Urban Form, *Official Architect and Planner* series of articles (1971).
Tetlow, J. and Goss, A., *Homes, Towns and Traffic*, Faber (1968).

The neighbourhood unit—references

1 Perry, C., *Housing for the Machine Age*.
2 Dougill, W., *Educational Buildings*.
3 Dougill, W., 'Wythenshawe: A modern Satellite Town', *Town Planning Review*, June (1935).
4 Tetlow, J. and Goss, A., *Homes, Towns and Traffic*, Faber (1968).
5 *Traffic in Towns*, HMSO (1965).

Further recommended reading

Ashworth, W., *The Genesis of Modern British Town Planning*,
Routledge (1954).
Geddes, P., *Cities in Evolution*, Benn (1968).
Mumford, L., *The City in History*, Penguin (1966).
Rosenau, H., *The Ideal City* (1959).

New Towns—references

1 *Report of the Unhealthy Areas Committee*, HMSO (1900).
2 *Report of the Departmental Committee on Garden Cities and
  Satellite Towns*, HMSO (1935).
3 *Report of the Royal Commission on the Geographical Distribution of
  the Industrial Population*, HMSO (1940).
4 Willmott, P., *East Kilbride and Stevenage: Some Sociological
  Characteristics*.
5 Willmott, P., 'Housing Density and Town Design in a New
  Town: Stevenage', *Town Planning Review*, **34.**
6 Tetlow, J. and A. Goss., *Homes, Towns and Traffic*, Faber
  (1968).

Further recommended reading

Archer, R. W., 'Prospects for Private Enterprise New Towns',
Official Architect and Planner, July (1971).
Duff, A. C., *Britain's New Towns*, Pall Mall Press (1961).
Osborn, F. J. and Whittick. A., *The New Towns*, Leonard Hill
(1969).

A balanced industrial structure—references

1 *Report of the Royal Commission on the Distribution of Industrial
  Population*, Cmnd 6153, HMSO (1940).

Further recommended reading

Burns, W., 'National and Regional Planning Policies', *Royal Town
Planning Institute Journal*, September, 1971.
Hall, P., *Theory and Practice of Regional Planning*, Pemberton (1971).
McCrone, G., *Regional Policy in Britain*, Allen and Unwin (1969).
Self, P., 'Regional Planning in Britain', *Urban Studies*, **1**, 1.

Green belts—references

1 Ministry of Housing and Local Government, *Green Belts*, HMSO (1962).
2 Keeble, L., Principles and Practice of Town and Country Planning, *Estates Gazette* (1969).
3 Mandelker, D. R., *Green Belts and Urban Growth*, University of Wisconsin (1962).
4 *Ibid.*

Further recommended reading

Burke, G. L., *Green Heart Metropolis*, Macmillan (1966).
Thomas, D., *London's Green Belt*, Faber (1960).

Regional planning

Recommended reading

Boudeville, J. R., 'Problems of Regional Economic Planning', *Town and Country Planning 1963*, **31.**
Hall, P., *Theory and Practice of Regional Planning*, Pemberton (1970).
Lichfield, N., 'Scope of the Regional Plan', *Regional Studies*, **1**, 1967.
McCrone, G., *Regional Policy in Britain*, Allen and Unwin (1969).
Minshull, R., *Regional Geography: Theory and Practice*, Hutchinson (1968).
Robertson, D., *The Relationship between Physical and Economic Planning*, Town and Country Planning Summer School (1965).

3 The foundations of town planning legislation

The foundations of modern town planning legislation were laid in the Public Health and Housing Acts of the nineteenth century which set out to ameliorate the 'monster clots of humanity' where 'the working man is pacing the low, dim, swampy habitation good enough for the creation of wealth'.[1] Stimulated by Ebenezer Howard's example, and spurred on by the pressure of influential bodies advocating the adoption in this country of the powers available to municipal authorities in Germany to plan the extensions of towns in advance and control the subsequent development,[2] the government introduced the Housing, Town Planning, etc. Bill in 1909.

The Housing, Town Planning, etc. Act 1909

This Act enabled local authorities to prepare schemes fore-casting, guiding, and controlling future development. It did not relate to land already developed or unlikely to be developed. Local authorities proposing such a scheme had first to obtain permission from the Local Government Board, and, in certain circumstances, from Parliament. Due to the voluntary nature and limited scope of the Act, the onerous compensation provisions,[3] the slump in estate development, and the First World War, only

73

three schemes were in fact undertaken in the ten years between 1909 and 1919.

The Housing, Town Planning, etc. Act 1919

This Act removed the necessity of obtaining the consent of the Local Government Board before preparing a scheme. It also enabled two or more authorities to prepare joint schemes for planning purposes, thus providing the first glimmerings of regional planning. It did, however, make the preparation of schemes for all land in the course of development, or likely to be used for building purposes, obligatory upon all boroughs and urban districts with a population of over 20 000. The Act also introduced the idea of 'interim development' whereby the Minister was empowered to permit development to proceed while the scheme was being prepared even though it might not eventually conform to the policy. In practice an interim development order was issued by the relevant local authority, which if not obtained could seriously jeopardise a developer's right to compensation if subsequent action was taken to implement the scheme.

The Town Planning Act 1925

For the first time town planning was separated from housing and although no new provisions were enacted all existing legislation was consolidated in this one measure.

The Local Government Act 1929

This Act introduced county councils into the hierarchy of planning authorities. They were given wide ranging highway responsibilities, as well as being empowered to act in place of a county district council which had neglected to prepare a planning scheme when required to do so. They were also entitled to be represented on joint committees, the formation of which the

74

Minister could direct together with the proportion of each constituent authorities representation. Any urban or rural district council was entitled under the Act to voluntarily relinquish its planning powers to the county council.

The Town and Country Planning Act 1932

All existing legislation relating to town planning was repealed and a new code, including the reference for the first time to country planning, was enacted. Many important changes were made, the most notable of which were:

1. it extended the power to make schemes to land already built upon or never likely to be built upon. This advance heralded the onset of comprehensive planning
2. it extended the provisions in respect of Interim Development Control
3. the necessity of obtaining the Minister's consent for a planning scheme was reimposed. It also had to be laid before Parliament for 21 days following the Minister's consent
4. the imposition of a fixed date upon local authorities by which schemes had to be prepared was repealed
5. some degree of flexibility to allow for the modification and amendment of schemes was introduced
6. increased power was given to local authorities to secure the retention of amenities, including the protection of trees and woodland, and the control over hoardings and advertisements

The Minister of Town and Country Planning Act 1943

The responsibility for planning had rested with the Minister of Health until 1942 when it was transferred to the Minister of Works and Planning. In 1943 these powers and duties were assigned to a separate Minister who was charged with 'securing consistency and continuity in the framing and execution of a national policy with respect to the use and development of land throughout England and Wales'.

The Town and Country Planning (Interim Development) Act 1943

Although the changes made by this Act were few, they were none the less important. The principal measure brought all land throughout England and Wales for which no planning scheme had been made under Interim Development Control, therefore any person wishing to undertake development had first to obtain permission, otherwise the development could be removed without payment of compensation if it did not accord with any subsequent scheme.

The Town and Country Planning Act 1944

This Act, which was hailed as introducing an element of 'positive planning' for the first time, authorised local authorities to acquire land which had suffered extensive war damage, sometimes called 'blitzed' land, or which suffered from bad layout or obsolete development, sometimes described as 'blighted' land. Procedures for compulsory purchase were expedited, the powers of acquisition, management, and disposal widened, and the basis of compensation adjusted to the 1939 value.

The Town and Country Planning Act 1947

This Act provided a landmark in the history of town planning legislation. It repealed all other enactments and inaugurated comprehensive planning. Its main provisions can be grouped under two headings, financial and physical planning. The financial provisions are dealt with elsewhere.[4]

In respect of the administration of physical planning in England and Wales, the responsibility was vested in county councils and county borough councils, taking the place of the 1400 previous local authorities. These new authorities were required to prepare and submit a 'development plan' for their area to the Minister within three years from 1 July 1948. These plans indicated how they proposed that the land in their area should be used. They were intended to be subject to revision every five years. Having drawn up the development plan no owner of land, with certain exceptions, was allowed to 'develop' his land without first obtaining planning permission from the local planning authority. Appeal against a local planning authority's decision lay to the Minister. Wide powers to control development and enforce their decisions were granted to the new authorities. It is impossible to exaggerate the importance of the 1947 Act for it provided the most comprehensive and radical framework for the control of land use in the world. The development plan and development control systems it established operated without any significant change for over twenty years, and during that time this machinery for the administration of planning and the implementation of policy has, despite its shortcomings, been the envy of the world.[5]

The present position

No sooner had the Town and Country Planning Act 1962 been passed consolidating existing legislation than pressure was exerted to review the planning system and consider possible change. Criticism was levelled at the prevailing procedure on the following grounds. It was said to be based upon development plans that were too certain, fixed and rigid, which inexorably led to a stultification of the planning system and an inordinate number of appeals. They were said to reflect local land use rather than integrated planning policy. The entire process had become overloaded, cumbersome, and slow, there being in the region of 400 000 applications for planning permission each year, of which over 12 000 went to appeal. Delay, then as now, brought planning into disrepute. Whilst the notion of development control was considered essential to effective land use planning, the plan upon which it operated appeared to stress the negative aspects of control as opposed to providing a positive stimulus to the creation of a good environment. The administration was over-centralised, general principles of a strategic nature were concealed amongst a host of detail; consequently the Minister required on average about three years to consider the submission of a development plan, by which time it might well have become

77

out-of-date. There was said to be little or no co-ordination between contiguous authorities which seriously detracted from the practice of effective regional planning. Further, it was stated that there had been inadequate participation by the public in the planning process, and insufficient regard paid to their interest.[1]

All these defects, and more, were described in the report by the Minister's Planning Advisory Group which was set up in 1964 to review the future of development plans. Published in 1965 the report made a number of proposals which were introduced in the 1968 Town and Country Planning Act, and now appear re-enacted in the 1971 Town and Country Planning Act.

Town and Country Planning Act 1968

This measure introduced a development plan system possessing a new form, content and procedure. It created a two-tier hierarchy of plans, aimed at providing a broader and more flexible range of plans at a strategic level, and yet a more certain, pertinent, and detailed picture at the local scale. These provisions are now included in the 1971 Town and Country Planning Act. As and when the Secretary of State for the Environment is satisfied that a local planning authority is of the appropriate area, and suitably staffed, they will be required to adopt the new procedures. This will entail the preparation of a *structure plan* and subsequent *local plans* for its area. Together these will form the Development Plan.

The structure plan

This is basically a written statement accompanied by any necessary supporting diagrammatic illustrations and is designed to introduce a large measure of flexibility into the system. The structure plan is intended to translate national and regional, economic and social policies into a local context, and in doing so provide a framework for the implementation of local plans. Whilst establishing the general aims and proposals for the area it should also contain the overall development control policy

78

which can then be applied in particular circumstances at the more detailed and specific local plan stage. Whereas the 1962 style development plan had, to a large extent, failed in integrating the various land use systems and the agencies responsible for them, the structure plan will provide a basis for co-ordinating decisions between the various local authority departments and committees, as well as between the planning authority itself and the various constituent authorities and statutory undertakers who possess an interest in different aspects of the plan. Moreover, the planning of these various systems will often entail a certain degree of overlap between neighbouring authorities. Co-operation and co-ordination between them in terms of aims, policy, standards and survey material is therefore imperative.

One aspect where the structure plan is intended to improve on the past performance of the 'old style' development plans is in respect of those areas that have a high priority for comprehensive and intensive treatment. Because of their magnitude, the cost involved, and a lack of urgency the old Comprehensive Development Areas conceived in the 1947 Act and perpetuated in the 1962 Act were all too often abortive or still-born. In an attempt to remedy this situation the new procedure allows for the indication of Action Areas which must be included in the structure plan. Another element that has been much neglected is the role that can be played by forces other than the local authority, and it is important that the structure plan should have regard to the degree and proportion of public and private investment implicit in the respective planning policy and the contribution that various external agencies can play in its implementation.

Structure plans are not geared to a specific date, for different elements in the plan will require different time scales. Rather it will draw attention to those aspects that demand treatment in the short run, such as action area programmes and new housing development. It will outline the various stages at which particular policies will be put into practice. The projected population in 1981 and 1991 will be indicated so as to establish a basis upon which the housing, employment, communication and public facility needs can be judged. Some objectives of the plan will not be related to any precise date but will denote the long-term strategy for the area. Unlike the quinquennial reviews of the old style 1947 and 1962 Act development plans, structure plans will be subject to continual review depending upon the changing needs and conditions of the community.

Format

Naturally the exact nature of the structure plan will largely be determined by the individual characteristics of the area concerned. There will, however, be certain features in common between all plans. They will all relate to national and regional policy as well as taking into account the strategies of neighbouring authorities. They should also contain:

a. a descriptive analysis of the social, economic and physical characteristics of the area

b. a critical appraisal of the success or failure of existing policies and a summary of any commitments that might affect future policy

c. a county structure plan should define the authority's position in respect of adjoining areas and identify any mutual sub-regional spheres of influence. It should also examine the main planning issues in the countryside, such as journey to work, employment, population growth or decline, agriculture, forestry and conservation

d. an urban structure plan should also examine the links it has with surrounding authorities and assess the nature of its hinterland. It will describe the principal functions of the town, whether they be industrial, commercial, marketing, or associated with tourism. It will examine the pattern, distribution and nature of activities throughout the town and identify any problems that arise therefrom such as obsolescence, traffic congestion, lack of open space and outdated layout

e. from this appraisal the authority should state its aims in terms of the area's efficiency and environment. This will provide a broad indication of what the plan is seeking to achieve

f. the crucial stage of the structure plan is the formulation of the strategy which co-ordinates the aims of the plan and sets out the way in which it is hoped they will be accomplished. The plan will normally explain how the strategy was selected from the various alternatives that presented themselves, and illustrate the more detailed proposals and policies for particular areas and specific subjects.

The following subjects or elements would be appropriate for individual attention within the structure plan.[2]

Population	Shopping
Employment	Education
Resources	Social and community services
Housing	Recreation and leisure
Industry	Conservation
Commerce	Utility services
Transportation	Minerals

Local plans

There are three different types of local plans.

1. *District Plans*—intended for the comprehensive planning of large areas.

2. *Action Area Plans*—for comprehensive planning of those areas indicated in the structure plan for improvement, development, or redevelopment, starting within the next ten years.

3. *Subject Plans*—which deal with particular aspects within the structure plan.

All of them consist of a map together with other diagrams, illustrations and a written statement. Although a local planning authority may undertake the preparation of local plans, and embark upon the various steps involved in public participation, they cannot become statutorily enforceable until the structure plan has been approved.

The overall purpose of local plans is to make the new system of development plans more adaptable to changing circumstances, being more detailed and more certain in character whilst at the same time being more flexible in application. The very nature of local plans is expected to vary according to prevailing circumstances in different areas. There is, therefore, a wide range of possible local plans with no standard form of presentation or procedure for implementation. There is no specific scale set down for them, apart from a minimum scale of 1:25 000 for rural areas,

81

1:10 000 for villages and towns in counties, 1:10 000, but more usually 1:2500, for district plans of large towns, and 1:1250 for central area plans. Because they are likely to get out of date quicker than structure plans, and great weight is attached to their currency, they do not require the Secretary of State's approval, and the responsibility for their review, alteration, repeal, and replacement lies with the local planning authority. In exceptional circumstances the Secretary of State may direct that the plan shall not have any effect unless it has his approval.

There are four major functions common to most local plans:
1. they apply the strategy of structure plans
2. they provide a detailed basis for development control
3. they provide a basis for co-ordinating development
4. they bring local and detailed planning issues before the public.

Not only must the local plan relate to the structure plan, indicating the method whereby overall objectives are translated into more specific policies and proposals for the area they cover, but it must also be consistent with other local plans. This presumes that full consultation between the local planning authority and the constituent local authorities, together with the appropriate measures to ensure full citizen participation, take place.

Where the involvement and co-operation of private development agencies is required the local planning authority may prepare what is described as a 'planning brief'. This will show such things as the general layout circulation, access, and design standards and controls. The developer will thus have a more certain idea of the potential of any particular site and the constraints that might be placed upon him. It is hoped that this certainty will expedite the development process and stimulate a greater degree of enterprise by the elimination of risk and the losses occasioned by delay in negotiation over planning permission.

Action area plans

These plans are intended to guide the comprehensive planning of areas suitable for treatment within ten years, and as such are the leading instrument for short-term change. If the preparation of an action area plan is thought apposite for a particular area it must initially be indicated in the structure plan. Once this is done the plan must then be prepared as soon as is practicable.

The essence of these plans is their urgency, for they are intended to replace the Comprehensive Development Area plans initiated by the 1947 Town and Country Planning Act which tended to reflect the optimism of local planning authorities ideals, rather than the pragmatism of their abilities. The action area is, therefore, more tightly drawn and concerned with intensive investment and innovation. It may relate to a whole range of proposed development, city centre, district centre, old and new residential areas, industrial, civic, commercial, shopping, or recreation uses. Further, they may be concerned with the reclamation of derelict land, conservation areas, or country parks.

The action proposed need not relate exclusively to that taken by public agencies but might include private development or perhaps a combination of both.

Subject plans

Where matters require a detailed development policy, but which are not suitable for inclusion in the comprehensive district plan, a subject plan may be prepared. This will generally relate to issues that cover a wide area, such as the reclamation of derelict land in a number of places within a county, the visual treatment of a motorway corridor, or a policy towards footpaths throughout a local authority area.

The foundations of town planning legislation—references

1 Jones, E., *Notes to the People* (1851).
2 Horsfall, T. C., *The Example of Germany*, Manchester, U.P. (1904).
3 See page 258.
4 See page 257.
5 For a fuller account see Cullingworth, J. B., *Town and Country Planning in England and Wales*, Allen and Unwin (1970).

The present position—references

1 Ministry of Housing and Local Government, *White Paper on Town and Country Planning*, HMSO (1967).
2 Ministry of Housing and Local Government, *Development Plans: A Manual on Form and Content*, HMSO (1970).

4 The organisation and administration of town planning

Central government

The need for a common policy, philosophy, and framework regarding the management of national environmental strategy, local government, and regional planning, combined with the desperate urgency to combat pollution, congestion, urban decay, and a housing shortage, spurred the government in October 1970 into taking a bold and novel step. What were previously the separate and relatively autonomous Ministries of Housing and Local Government, Public Building and Works, and Transport, only loosely grouped under Anthony Crosland, were combined together as the Department of the Environment and their legislative, financial, and administrative powers concentrated under one person, the Secretary of State for the Environment. Three ministers are directly responsible to him whose areas are described respectively as Housing and Construction, Local Government and Development, and Transport Industries. Although a great deal of similarity exists between these new ministries and those previous, it has become clear that there has in fact been a significant re-apportionment of their exact terms of reference and day-to-day responsibilities.

The rationale of this reorganisation is set out in the White

Paper Cmnd 4506 on the Machinery of Government as follows: the aim is to

a. improve the quality of policy formulation and decision taking in government by providing ministers, collectively in Cabinet and individually within their Departments, with well-defined options to the contribution they can make to meeting national needs
b. match the field of responsibility of Departments to coherent fields of policy and administration
c. ensure that the government machine responds to new policies and programmes as these emerge.

This remodelling is in line with current trends in management techniques and decision making and was not only applied to those ministries relating to the environment but formed part of a complete re-ordering of central government responsibilities. The Board of Trade, a large portion of the Ministry of Technology and part of the Department of Employment and Productivity were incorporated as the Department of Trade and Industry. To formulate and examine national strategy and determine priorities a new 'central policy review staff' was set up in the Cabinet Office under Lord Rothschild.

To assist in its unification, support its common purpose and ensure a greater degree of flexibility, the Department of the Environment (DOE) moved its headquarters to a single building in Marsham Street off Horseferry Road. It is, perhaps, ironical that a department pledged to secure and improve our environmental heritage is itself housed in such a monstrous monolith. The very size of the Department must itself present problems, the sheer logistics involved in running an establishment of over 70 000 staff must be enormous.

The functions of the department

The Secretary of State is still charged with the duty of 'securing consistency and continuity in the framing of a national policy with respect to the use and development of land throughout England and Wales' as set down in Section 1 of the Ministry of Town and Country Act 1943. He thus preserves the ultimate authority for all policy relating to the control of land use, and is the chief executive for the organisation and management of planning in this country.

It is difficult to summarise the Secretary's, and therefore the Department's, wide powers of policy formulation and instigation, but in general terms he holds all the statutory powers previously held by the three separate ministries. His prime interest will be with matters of a strategic nature regarding overall policy and programming, and in particular co-ordinating the fight against environmental pollution. The Minister of Housing and Construction has responsibility for all aspects of the housing programme, and also for relations with the building and civil engineering industry, building research and development, and government accommodation. The Minister for Transport Industries looks after Ports, general policy on nationalised transport industries, freight, international aspects of inland transport, road and vehicle safety and licensing, sport and recreation, and the Channel Tunnel. The Minister for Local Government and Development is responsible for transport planning and road passenger transport, regional and land use planning, local government and its reorganisation, water, sewerage and refuse disposal, and the countryside and conservation.[1] A press release issued shortly after the establishment of the Department indicated that the major priorities were the reform of housing finance, local government, planning and a drive to make the polluter pay for his pollution. Many countries abroad are expressing a similar concern in respect of the environment. France have appointed a minister who is charged with pleading its cause against all other departments who threaten it. The President of the United States is informed on these aspects by high ranking and influential advisers. Nowhere, however, are such a wide array of powers as exist within the DOE available to one minister.

Control of land use

The Minister, now the Secretary of State, has always held the responsibility of approving the individual development plans

87

submitted by local planning authorities. It is in this way that he has nationally secured consistency and continuity of land use throughout the country. Under the 1971 Town and Country Planning Act, those authorities which are operating under Part I of the Act whereby the development plan will be split into two parts, the structure plan and the local plans, will still be required to submit the structure plan for the Secretary of State's approval. Any persons wishing to object to the plan may do so to the Secretary of State within the prescribed period. He must consider their objections and may decide to hold a local public inquiry or afford the objectors a private hearing. He may then approve the structure plan with or without modifications, and in so doing will aim to fit the various pieces of particular local authorities policy into the jigsaw of a regional and national plan. If a local planning authority fails to prepare or review a structure plan the Secretary of State is equipped with default powers whereby he may appoint another body to undertake the task at the expense of the authority in default.

The control exercised by central government over local authorities is often of a more flexible and advisory nature. It takes the form of memoranda, Design and Planning Bulletins, circulars, directives and notes. Between them these furnish a broad framework of policy which guides and controls the use and development of land. Obviously each particular area has its own problems and requires special attention, but once again to secure consistency and continuity the Secretary of State will lay down certain guidelines or principles which provide a common approach. The Development Control Policy Notes, for example, attempt to ensure that an informed and equitable judgement is made in respect of applications for planning permission over a range of possible land uses.[2]

The Secretary of State also possesses extensive powers for introducing delegated legislation. The General Development Orders enable him to remove a substantial amount of trivial matters from the normal planning procedures by automatically conferring planning permission upon them. The Town and Country Planning General Development Order 1963, as amended by that of 1969, authorises the carrying out of twenty-three classes of specified development which are referred to under the

88

general heading of 'permitted development'. The Use Classes Order 1963 specifies nineteen categories of use which assist both applicants and authorities in deciding whether or not a change of use is 'material' and thus constitutes an act of development requiring planning permission. It states that if a change of use takes place from one use to another within the same use class it is not 'material' and therefore does not require planning permission; it goes no further. Other Orders relate to the control of advertisements, caravans, offices, factories, trees, inquiries and a host of other topics too long to list.

Another function connected with central government control of planning is where the Secretary of State acts in a quasi-judicial capacity in the hearing and determining of appeals. A person aggrieved by a planning decision may appeal to the Secretary of State, who is positioned at the apex of the planning pyramid. It can be argued that because of this position he is in conflict with one of the principal rules of natural justice that 'no man shall be a judge in his own cause'. It is perhaps fortunate that the Inspectorate, who actually sit in judgement at local public inquiries or receive the written representation, and either decide or make recommendations to the Secretary of State in respect of the appeal, is staffed by persons of such high professional repute and unquestioned integrity. A system in which the administrative and legislative powers are separated by the establishment of special courts, similar to the *droit administratif* under the Conseil d'Etat as exists in France, has much in theory to recommend it, but would be plagued with practical problems.

In the normal course of events applications for planning permission will be dealt with by the local planning authorities. The Secretary of State may consider, however, that certain issues are of such outstanding importance that he would prefer to decide upon them himself at first instance. Such applications are then said to be 'called in'. This procedure is likely to be applied to development of a particularly controversial nature, such as the proposal to site a hotel in a particularly prominent position on the Avon Gorge, or where the Department has not prepared a broad policy towards a land use with singular characteristics but wishes to maintain balance and control, such as is currently the case with out-of-town shopping centres.

One of the more contentious problems that confronts the Department of the Environment is the issue of regional planning. It has proved difficult to administer in the past and will probably continue to do so in the future. Because it is so inextricably bound in with economic policy it was envisaged in the sixties that the responsibility should lie with one of the ministries concerned with economic affairs. The Ministry of Housing and Local Government would merely attempt to translate the economic objectives into a physical plan. For a number of reasons this did not prove satisfactory and now the DOE will have leading responsibility for regional policy. There will, however, remain a large element of inter-departmental liaison and control, for industrial development is still very much the preserve of the Department of Trade and Industry. Moreover, Scotland, Wales and Northern Ireland retain a large measure of independence regarding regional development.

Local government

While the ultimate responsibility for the organisation and management of planning rests with central government, who direct and administer the relevant legislation, it is the local planning authorities who implement the statutory provisions 'on the ground'.

The present system

This task is currently undertaken in England and Wales by local authorities who are either county boroughs or administrative counties. The county boroughs are 'all-purpose authorities' and under an obligation to discharge all the local authority functions within their area. There are 83 of them and they represent most of the major towns and cities in the country, the largest of them being Birmingham with a population well in excess of one million. The 58 administrative counties are themselves sub-divided into municipal or non-county boroughs, urban districts, and rural districts. Rural districts are further split into parishes. The local authority functions are apportioned between the county and

90

the various constituent county districts. The degree of apportionment or delegation largely depends upon the size of the county district.

London, having singular metropolitan problems, possesses an exceptional administrative structure. Planning powers are shared between the Greater London Council, who prepare the overall structure plan, and the 32 Greater London Boroughs plus the City of London, who also prepare structure plans on the lines of the Greater London Development Plan as well as preparing the local plans. The GLC may not prepare local plans other than action area plans indicated in the structure plan. They are, however, responsible for the strategic planning of an administrative area of over six hundred square miles and eight million persons.

Local government reform

Existing local authority areas were conceived out of nineteenth-century expedience, principally to implement the succession of public health acts that emerged at that time. Industrial and commercial growth has outmoded the old boundaries and the organisation of local authorities has been subject to prolonged and intensive scrutiny over the last twenty-five years. A Local Authority Boundary Commission was established in 1945, followed by the Local Government Commission in 1958, both of which spent a great deal of time and effort examining the demarcation of various areas, responsibilities. Although a few readjustments were made it was not until the reports in 1967 of the Committee on the Management of Local Government and the Committee on the Staffing of Local Government were received that a concerted and comprehensive attempt was made to rectify the deficiencies caused by a fragmented, out-dated, poorly staffed, badly structured, ill-based and all too often hostile system of local government. A Royal Commission on Local Government in England was set up under the chairmanship of Lord Redcliffe-Maud which reported in June 1969. The members of the Commission were singularly united in their criticism of the existing structure its very boundaries were anachronistic. It did not accord with the changing social and

91

economic patterns of an urbanised community, the proper planning of land use and development was not feasible with so great a piecemeal dissemination of authority and delegation of power, particularly as between county boroughs, counties, and districts, and finally many local authorities were too small and lacking in both funds and expertise to carry out their work competently, which in turn led to excessive interference from central government.

In considering the alternative methods of securing reform certain elements of general agreement can be discerned. First, there are special areas that require individual treatment, often described, perhaps erroneously, as 'metropolitan areas', such as Merseyside, the West Midlands, West Yorkshire, Greater Manchester, and Tyneside. Second, all new authorities must be larger in terms of population and resources than the majority of existing councils. Third, there should be a body of some kind which acts as a regional intermediary between the new authorities and central government. Fourth, there is a need to ensure that adequate public participation takes place at the 'grass roots' level and that authorities are founded for this purpose.

The exact nature of the reorganisation has been more controversial. The majority of the Royal Commission, and the then Labour Government, favoured a system of 'unitary authorities' based upon city regions where single function areas would be distinguished, small enough to administer the personal services and large enough to undertake strategic planning. One dissenting member of the Commission, Mr. Derek Senior, and the Conservative Government elected in 1970 and responsible for local government reform, come down on the side of a two-tier system. In advocating this approach Senior contends that whereas a top level authority of substantial size and area is required for strategic planning a second local level authority is more appropriate for administering personal services.

Local government Bill

At the time of writing it is proposed that from 31 March 1974 onwards there will be six different types of local authority. In the metropolitan areas there will be metropolitan county councils,

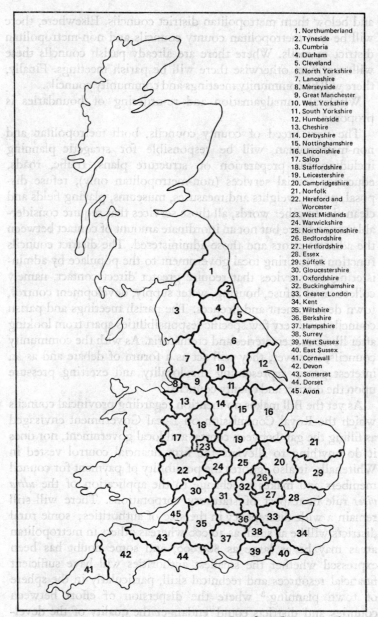

1. Northumberland
2. Tyneside
3. Cumbria
4. Durham
5. Cleveland
6. North Yorkshire
7. Lancashire
8. Merseyside
9. Great Manchester
10. West Yorkshire
11. South Yorkshire
12. Humberside
13. Cheshire
14. Derbyshire
15. Nottinghamshire
16. Lincolnshire
17. Salop
18. Staffordshire
19. Leicestershire
20. Cambridgeshire
21. Norfolk
22. Hereford and Worcester
23. West Midlands
24. Warwickshire
25. Northamptonshire
26. Bedfordshire
27. Hertfordshire
28. Essex
29. Suffolk
30. Gloucestershire
31. Oxfordshire
32. Buckinghamshire
33. Greater London
34. Kent
35. Wiltshire
36. Berkshire
37. Hampshire
38. Surrey
39. West Sussex
40. East Sussex
41. Cornwall
42. Devon
43. Somerset
44. Dorset
45. Avon

Fig. 21 Proposals by the Local Government Boundary Commission for new districts in non-metropolitan counties in England

93

and below them metropolitan district councils. Elsewhere, there will be non-metropolitan county councils and non-metropolitan district councils. Where there are already parish councils these will continue, otherwise there will be parish meetings. Finally, there will be community meetings and community councils.

Wholesale amalgamation and re-ordering of boundaries is proposed.

The new breed of county councils, both metropolitan and non-metropolitan, will be responsible for stragetic planning including the preparation of structure plans, traffic, roads, education, social services (non-metropolitan only), refuse disposal, police, weights and measures, museums, playing fields and clean air. In other words, all those services that require considerable expenditure but not an inordinate amount of contact between the administrators and those administered. The district councils function is to bring local government to the populace by administering the services that require greater direct contact, namely collection of refuse, housing, water supply, development control, town development and licences. The parish meetings and parish councils have very few specific responsibilities apart from looking after libraries, cemeteries and crematoria. As with the community councils, however, they will act as a forum of debate and as an interest group representing the locality and exerting pressure upon the district and county councils.

As yet the Bill makes no mention regarding provincial councils which the Royal Commission on Local Government envisaged as filling the gap between central and local government, nor does it do anything to alleviate the firm financial control vested in Whitehall; it also ignores the possibility of payment for council members and makes no change to the application of the *ultra vires* rule in respect of statutory corporations. There will still remain a wide discrepancy in the size of authorities; some rural districts will be as small as 30 000 whereas others in metropolitan areas may be as large as 800 000, and some doubt has been expressed whether the smallest authorities will have sufficient financial resources and technical skill, particularly in the sphere of town planning,[3] where the dispersion of effort between counties and districts could 'endanger the quality of the developing environment'.[4]

Departmental organisation in town planning

With the present structure of town planning in England and Wales, and the variety of local authorities in that exist in terms of area, population, characteristics, and problems, there is also a great disparity in the way individual town planning departments are administered. In many authorities planning does not even warrant a separate department but is a section of the engineers', surveyors', or architects' department. This is particularly true, as Cullingworth explains,[5] in county boroughs where the responsibility for town and country planning has evolved over a comparatively long period of time, whereas in county authorities planning did not become a general duty until 1947 and therefore separate departments tended to be set up with the advent of a comprehensive approach.

It is difficult to generalise when attempting to describe the establishment structure of planning departments, because each authority will try to group its staff in the most efficient manner depending upon the work at hand. It can be said, however, that the most common division separates the functions of Development Plan and Development Control, with larger boroughs and counties increasingly opting for a Research Section as well. The Development Plan section will be responsible for the formulation of policy, and the preparation of respective plans. It may be further sub-divided with regard to research, central areas, urban design, conservation, or implementation. The Development Control section is normally responsible for the detailed examination of all proposals and the consideration of applications for planning permission. In many authorities there will be separate development control officers for different parts of the borough or county. This section is also playing an increasing role in the implementation of planning proposals, the preparation of local plans, and the monitoring of plan performance.

Corporate planning

With the increasing complexity of urban, rural, and environmental problems the machinery of local government is under

95

increasing pressure to provide more and better services. Sophisticated techniques and professional expertise are required to provide viable solutions. There is often conflict between persons, agencies and departments in the allocation of resources to competing projects and policies. A growing relationship and inter-dependence throughout the whole gamut of local government services and facilities is seen to exist. The distribution of land between rival uses is not sufficient as a planning policy; there are social, aesthetic, administrative, economic and budgetary considerations to be taken into account. Thus there emerges the exigency to provide a new and more appropriate management system to meet these demands. A system that manages the affairs of a local authority as a whole. The case for overall local authority policy planning is put far more cogently and succinctly by Professor J. D. Stewart in his paper to the Town and Country Summer School 1969:

'Local authority policy planning sets objectives for the authority in relation to the needs both of its area and of the individuals, families and organisations within that area. Local authority policy planning determines the strategies to be followed in pursuing these objectives. Local authority policy planning is concerned not with physical development alone, but also with social change: it is concerned not with capital expenditure alone, but also with revenue expenditure. It is planning not only land use, but also financial resources and manpower. It is planning the activities of the authority in relation to the needs and the problems it faces.'

For far too long local government has been undertaken by what is little more than a collection of semi-autonomous departments, reinforced by the custom-drawn boundaries of professional institutions, and providing essentially separate services. Reports over the last decade, such as the Buchanan Report on Traffic in Towns, the Plowden Report on Education, and the Seebohm Report on Social Services, have all pointed towards the need for integrated policy making and a unified management structure. The most popular description for this new approach to the management of local government is 'corporate planning'. It involves bringing together the right expertise at the right time for the right problem, and thus implies a greater 'articulation'

96

between professions as well as recognising all the relevant constraints, be they financial, administrative, physical or political.

Corporate planning has already been adopted in a number of local authorities, one of the earliest being Coventry who set out the main aims of their Corporate Management System as follows:

'*a*. to develop a management system that will assist the elected members to make policy decisions and to ensure the effective implementation of these decisions

b. to consider the resources, needs and problems of the authority as a totality with a view to formulating objectives and coherent plans to achieve those objectives

c. to break down barriers between committees and between departments by focusing attention on what the City Council seeks to achieve rather than by considering the development of individual services

d. to identify and evaluate alternative ways of meeting objectives with a view to making the optimum use of resources

e. to co-ordinate all the various plans of the authority, including the structure plan, and to ensure that these are integrated with a total management plan

f. to foster a corporate approach and spirit amongst elected members and officers to make the greatest use of their talents

g. thereby to ensure a planned and balanced development of the facilities available in the City to provide for its future prosperity and the well-being of the citizens.'

To put this policy into practice Coventry identified nine broad areas of concern, known as programme areas, such as education, housing, transportation, and established interdisciplinary teams of officers to staff them. Therefore, the programme area team concerned with the provision of housing, for example, has representatives from the City Engineer's, Estates, Treasurer's, Town Clerk's, Housing, Architecture and Planning, Public Health, Social Services and Education Departments. In this way the provision of housing does not become an end in itself but is seen in the context of the overall policy for the City.

Another common aspect of corporate planning is the appointment of a Chief Executive Officer, sometimes called a Town Manager, who can co-ordinate the general management of departments. He in turn would be responsible to a small policy committee of the council who would direct broad strategy, identify major objectives, and ensure a satisfactory balance of priorities, and allocate resources accordingly.

Planning programming budgeting systems (P.P.B.S.)

One way in which corporate planning can be applied is by the introduction of the management technique P.P.B.S. which concerns itself with the detailed running of the authority and the most efficient way of implementing and servicing the Corporate Plan. This method was first propounded in the United States by the Rand Corporation and subsequently adopted by the Pentagon to direct American defence policy and later by Mayor Lindsey in New York. It was introduced into this country in the mid-nineteen sixties and is now practised in a number of local authorities. P.P.B.S. attempts to bring budgetary policy and planning policy together in the decision-making process. It further aims to reconcile short-term financing with long-term physical planning. Moreover, it postulates that the name of a department and the number of staff employed within it are often irrelevant to the job in hand, hence the establishment of programme areas. Most important of all it sifts and examines decisions at first instance thereby forestalling the undertaking of abortive work and centralising the decision making.

The organisation and administration of town planning—references

1 White, B., *Sourcebook of Planning Information*, Bingley (1971).
2 Ministry of Housing and Local Government *Development Control Policy Notes*, HMSO (1969).
3 Amos, F. J. C., *Royal Town Planning Institute Journal*, February, 1972.
4 Memorandum on the Local Government Bill, *Royal Town Planning Institute Journal*, April, 1972.
5 Cullingworth, J. B., *Town and Country Planning in England and Wales*, Allen and Unwin (1969).

Further recommended reading

Brown, R. G. S., *The Administrative Process in Britain*, Methuen (1970).

Cripps, E., 'A Management System for Planning', *Town Planning Institute Journal*, May, 1969.

Knowles, R. S. B., *Modern Management in Local Government*, Butterworth (1970).

Stewart, J., *Local Authority Decision Making*, Charles Knight (1971).

Stewart, J., 'The Administrative Structure of Planning', *Town Planning Institute Journal*, 55, 7, 1969.

Stewart, J. and Eddison, T., 'Structure Planning and Corporate Planning', *Royal Town Planning Institute Journal*, 57, 8, 1971.

5   The planning process

The planner has been defined as 'an artist of rationality with reference to human activity'[1] which implies that the path he pursues and the manner in which he pursues it is reasoned and logical. This in turn suggests a hypothesis, argument, or scheme which is formulated, tested and proved; thus following a chain of reasoning, or, put another way, a process. The process of planning the human environment requires the ability to analyse and comprehend the existing situation in the context of its social, economic and political, as well as its physical, circumstance; forecast any likely changes that are apparent from prevailing trends; understand the extent to which these changes will affect other aspects of the environment; judge their desirability; decide upon the best strategy and tactics to guide and control change; and assess the performance of the chosen strategy and tactics. The old 1947 Town and Country Planning Act style of approach was based on the simple adage of 'survey, analysis, plan', thus giving a process with both beginning and end, but which resulted in a static, inflexible 'once and for all time' master plan drawn up in the light of circumstances subsisting at one particular moment and designed for selected dates in the future. Although five-yearly reviews were allowed for, rather optimistically as it happened, it was a process incapable of adjustment to changing events. It could only be amended in fits and starts.

Because of its intricate nature, and the delicate balance that exists between the various related component parts, the process of planning should be continuative, it should not present a final definite panacea. It should be able to foresee, guide, and influence change, taking a long-term perspective of short-term occurrences. It should be sufficiently adaptable to permit review, modification and revision. Planning is concerned about the future, but, as Sir Winston Churchill said, 'It is always wise to look ahead, but difficult to look farther than you can see.' The aim, therefore, should not be to specify in great detail the nature, size, and condition of things to come, but rather to establish a procedure or framework that facilitates the manipulation of events in the desired direction. To achieve this it is always necessary to clarify at first instance the principal aims of the plan; in other words, specify what are the desired social, economic, political and physical directions. This will not only provide standards by which the performance of the plan can be judged, but also supply a method for selecting from alternative plans in the first place.

Due to the need for continuity, adaptability, and revision, all geared towards the task of producing the best planning decision all the time, a procedure somewhat vulgarly called 'optimisation', urban and regional planning has been described as a cyclic process.[2] This can be demonstrated by setting out an example of the interrelated steps involved, one amongst many for there exist various opinions regarding the exact nature of the process and number of steps.

Step 1: the first step is to appraise or survey the area, agencies, organisations, individuals, and activities 'at play', and identify the way in which planning might function in the redress of any imbalance or anomaly that is present in the locality.

Step 2: probably one of the most important, and previously one of the most neglected, aspects of the process is the formulation of broad community 'goals'. Although they tend to be rather nebulous, often being framed as vague generalisations, they do have the effect of setting the stage. In essence they reflect the overall demands and desires of the community at large, testing the political temperature, and expressing the criteria by which the plan might be ultimately assessed. In practice, for example, they are couched in the following terms: 'to provide a better standard of housing throughout the local authority area' or 'to ensure that adequate open space is available within reasonable walking distance of all residential areas'. From these broad strategies a host of tactical decisions can subsequently be made.

Step 3: involves the identification of 'objectives', that is the more precise ways in which the goals might be achieved. In attaining the goal of a better standard of housing it might involve a policy of rehabilitating existing accommodation or undertaking wide-scale redevelopment, or perhaps a combination of both. This might be tackled by public or private sector development, or again by way of a joint venture. These, then, are the objectives. The drawing up of both goals and objectives will require extensive consultation and public participation to ensure that all community views and values are fully considered. Moreover, wherever possible they should be ranked according to the priorities placed upon them by the society that produced them. In this way the provision of more schools might gain precedence over the installation of a new sewerage system, or the case for a swimming bath might be advanced ahead of that for a car park.

Step 4: the possible alternative means of achieving these goals and objectives should be examined and compiled. There might be only one possible 'course of action', alternatively there might be many, but in virtually all cases they will be girdled around by various constraints, financial, legal, social, or political. The development in question might be too expensive, the policy might contravene the law of land, the majority party on the council might not favour the release of land for private specu-lation, or the residents might not favour the construction of a ring road. All the thousands of component parts that constitute solutions to each objective, which in turn seek to fulfil a particular goal, must be analysed and tested; in this way a range of potential policies are formulated.

Step 5: all the complete courses of action are compared and measured. This 'evaluation' stage is roughly akin to a sifting procedure. Some strategies will be immediately eliminated being obviously unacceptable for one reason or another, the others might require the use of detailed and sophisticated techniques of selection to choose between them. This could include cost benefit analysis, rigorous financial appraisal, or the construction of a goal achievement matrix.[3] This last approach is a reminder that the evaluation should test and assess the performance of each respective policy against the goals and objectives already established.

Step 6: the chosen plan should be put into practice or 'implemented'. This entails, on the one hand, positive action on behalf of the planning authority, not only in respect of public development but also in the stimulation of desired private sector enterprise. On the other, it requires a large amount of control and regulation over development of a more negative or restrictive nature.

Step 7: once the plan is operational there is a continuous need to scrutinise the way in which it is working. This 'monitoring' stage reviews the performance of the policy regarding its effectiveness and efficiency. Where it has strayed from its course or where changing circumstances have overtaken it, adjustment might have to be made. The original plan might indicate, for example, that over the first five years an increase in the population of 10 000 is programmed. From this projected expansion any number of detailed planning decisions and other repercussions might have evolved, the provision of additional shops, schools, houses, hospital beds, jobs and so forth. If after the first two years growth falls far short of expectations steps can be taken to rectify the situation if careful and continuous monitoring has been carried out. Additional planning permission for residential development or incentives to attract industry might provide the answer. Conversely, there could be a change of political power, either nationally or locally, and the very goals and objectives upon which the plan was devised might be questioned. These ever-changing factors thus produce an endless re-cycling of the process.

The planning process can thus be summarised as a perpetual series of steps as follows:

1. Preliminary Study
2. Formulation of Goals
3. Identification of Objectives
4. Preparation of Alternative Strategies
5. Evaluation

103

6. Implementation

7. Monitoring and Review

This description is by no means exhaustive or authoritative but it does serve to illustrate the departure from traditional land use planning. It should, however, be emphasised that no matter how sophisticated the process, and there is no merit in complexity, any plan or policy will only be as good as the data available and the people who prepare it.

Planning and systems theory

Any community consists of a wide variety of geographic, social, political, economic and cultural patterns which both act and interact to form the nature and condition of society. The relationship between these various patterns is constantly changing, giving rise to new and different conditions, some beneficial to the community, some deleterious. It is the planner's function to comprehend this tangled web of relationships, and where necessary to guide, control and change their composition. To achieve this, planning is concerned with prediction, not only of population size and land use in isolation, but also of human and other activities as well. It has been said that planners are now the prisoners of the discovery that in the city everything affects everything else.

Town and country planning, as we know it, is increasingly being subjected to a 'systems' approach. The term 'system' is defined in the *Oxford English Dictionary* as 'A complex whole, a set of connected things or parts, a department of knowledge or belief considered as a whole, a method or organization.' Town planning is certainly complex, comprising many separate but related elements such as transportation, employment, housing, recreation, and education, which being impossible to treat individually, have created an area of concern or department of knowledge that is viewed as a whole, both governmentally and professionally. The human environment itself can be seen as a system[1] within which a wide range of human activities take place, work, leisure, shopping, and development, for example.

These activities are connected by channels of communication, such as rivers, roads, footpaths, pipelines and cables. These activities and their respective connections occur within 'space', not just on land, but between areas of land and also through time. The human environment is thus concerned with change, therefore the planning of it must be dynamic, not static, and it is a systems approach which helps to analyse dynamic conditions. Seen in this way the system is not actually the real world but merely a way of looking at it, supplying a greater insight into the forces and agencies that dictate its condition, providing a surer, more consistent, and more sophisticated way of tackling problems. The advocates of the systems view would maintain that the approach represents a movement away from the entrenched 'physical determinism' so long associated with the planning profession, prepossessed as it was with standards of design and movement, neglecting the social decision-making aspects of the planning process, and being relegated to a position of 'land use accountancy'. The purpose of planning should be the attainment of a satisfactory state, health, prosperity, and general well-being of the community which is not always related to, or in accord with, what is often considered to be the most propitious spatial and physical organisation of urban areas. A greater understanding of social circumstances as well as physical condition is called for. Again it is considered that the systems view can account for this.

The origins of the systems approach can be found in the natural sciences, a General Systems Theory being developed by von Bertallanffy, a biologist who besides proposing a systematic analysis of the interrelated parts of a problem also postulated that a set of rules or laws could be distinguished which applied to any system or problem.[2] The control or regulation of the system through the relationship and communication between its various constituent parts was first described in physiology and has since been developed as the study of 'cybernetics'. Together general theory and cybernetic study form the systems approach, the one providing comprehension, the other permitting application. More recently the approach has been put into practice and further extended in the field of business management, equipped as it is with mathematical tools of expression and analysis. There exists, in fact, a very close relationship between cybernetics, operations research, modelling, and systems analysis, for each discipline or technique gives a closer, more detailed, yet comprehensive appraisal of the results of a particular course of action. The application of this approach in the context of managing urban and rural resources inevitably differs, because planning, possessing so many imponderables, containing so many different elements each with their own criteria, lacks a universal measure of performance. It also requires vast amounts of accurate information that are rarely available, although the growth of a systems approach has been greatly aided by the increasing introduction of computers in planning studies.

In formulating policy in this direction the planner takes the city as an entity and examines the system that dictates its nature and form, a considerable task in itself as the very definition of what actually constitutes the system is arguable and arbitrary. Although he can rarely intervene directly, he attempts to establish a framework or set of procedures that regulate the activities 'at play'. In other words, he acts in a management capacity, planning, organising, controlling, communicating and continually analysing the system. The management of the human and built environment that both concerns the social and physical sciences and depends upon decisions taken by elected representatives is, however, probably the most Herculean task of all. Moreover, planning is directed towards the future but again lacks sufficient techniques with which to assess future performance.

The city, town or other urban environment has this dynamic nature of varying components which requires an understanding of the guidance and control of change in terms of a system. Systems analysis can operate with changing circumstances in the relevant quantities, rates, and quality concerned. In this way the development plan for an area can be made pertinent at all times, not just now, or at some remote date in the future. An entertaining example of the relationship of the structure of towns and the effect on human behaviour is to be found in the field of science fiction. Isaac Asimov's *Foundation* trilogy provides a superb account of systems and probability analyses and their application in a planning process.

Planning and decision theory

Allied with the emergence of the idea of a systems approach towards town planning there has occurred an examination of the way in which plans and policies are decided, and an investigation regarding the extent to which these decisions are rational. A rational decision being one where all the various alternative courses of action are considered, the consequences resulting from them are identified and compared, and the preferred alternatives selected in the light of the most valued ends. In addition, the various courses of action that present themselves should reflect the overall aims for the community. Too often in the past the profession has overlooked the need to begin planning exercises by defining the goals and objectives, assuming that they are known, agreed, and understood. In a dynamic situation such as the planning process the forces of rapid change are continually creating fresh problems and fluctuating circumstances. If a local planning authority can establish clearly stated and agreed objectives, the possible solutions are more readily discovered, for the definition of objectives almost invariably leads to the recognition of methods and measures of attainment and the methods themselves usually suggest alternative procedures for approaching the solution to the problem. Much inefficient and complacent town planning has occurred because there has been so little recognition of the nature of today that to envisage the shape of tomorrow has been impossible. It has been said that it is often more important to state the right problem than to solve it.

The process of reaching the best decision is known as 'optimisation', but it must be remembered that the planning process takes place within a value-laden political context. The conflict between planning and politics is a critical one and can often result in the selection and adoption of plans that are not optimal. Planning, by its very nature and terms of reference, is concerned with the future, politics is all too often influenced by the present. The planner himself should seek to attain an unprejudiced attitude within the procedure of decision making, his task is principally restricted to producing technically feasible plans and submitting them for political consideration and decision. Greater accent has also been placed upon the mechanism of political decision making in recent years, and particularly upon the social implications that flow from it. It is possible to improve decision making in all fields by improving both the professional and political understanding and approach to the decision process, and also by improving the techniques for selecting specific decisions.

This development of techniques within the sphere of decision theory has continued to receive a growing emphasis. There has been an increasing reliance upon a mathematical approach incorporating the use of gaming, simulation, modelling, and a host of other operational research techniques. Their application has grown to such an extent that there is a danger of them being regarded as a panacea for all problem solving and a prime determinant in the actual making of decisions. It is essential that policies should be chosen as the result of responsible thought processes and reasoning, and that such logical analyses should not be replaced by any therapeutic rag-bag of operational techniques.[1] Scientific method cannot guarantee a satisfactory solution or assure the planner of a correct decision. It can only assist him in working towards decisions which are reasoned and appear sensible depending upon the amount of information available in the first place. A good decision is a matter of thought but a good outcome is a matter of luck, and the best that any planner can hope for are decisions that appear to be satisfactory when viewed in retrospect.

Because planning is a continuing process, and therefore almost wholly future-orientated, an essential requirement in making the necessary and best decisions is the ability to forecast. In essence, forecasting is estimating, which involves understanding a process well enough to be able to describe its important relationships and to gauge the values of its variables. It is neither guesswork nor the slavish application of over-simple rules.[2] As conditions change and circumstances vary each new decision requires fresh evaluation. The constituent variables that comprise the plan, which might be population, employment, and communications for example, will require repeated analysis to check their performance and identify any departures from the original strategy. It cannot be emphasised enough that because reality is immensely complicated town planning is not a 'once and for all time', but a recurrent decision-making process requiring constant review and revision.

The planning process—references

1 Seeley, J., 'What is planning? Definition and strategy', *Journal of the American Institute of Planners*, May, 1964.
2 McLoughlin, J. B., *Urban and Regional Planning: A Systems Approach*, Faber and Faber (1969).

Further recommended reading

Chadwick, G., *A Systems View of Planning*, Pergamon (1972).

Planning and systems theory—references

1 McLoughlin, J. B., *Urban and Regional Planning: A Systems Approach*, Faber (1969).
2 McDougall, G., 'A Critique of the Systems View of Planning', *Oxford Working Papers in Planning Education and Research*, 9 (1971).

Further recommended reading

Chadwick, G. F., *A Systems View of Planning*, Pergamon (1971).

Planning and decision theory—references

1 Yewdall, G., *Management Decision Making*, Pan (1969).
2 Couts, D., 'What is forecasting?', *Management Decision Making*, (ed.) Yewdall, G., Pan (1969).

Further recommended reading

Beer, S., *Management Science; The business use of Operational Research*, Aldus (1967).
Levin, P., *Towards Decision-making Rules for Urban Planners*, B.R.S. (1968).
Lindblom, C. and Braybrook D., *Strategy, for Decision Policy: Evaluation as a Social Process*, Free Press of Glencoe (1965).
Science Journal, Special Issue on Forecasting the Future, **3**, 10, 1967.

PART TWO

Survey Preparation and Techniques of Analysis

6 Survey preparation and techniques of analysis

Introduction

In order to understand the society within which planning is to operate, to identify its problems and needs, to have a more complete comprehension of its varying and interacting elements and their effects upon each other, to formulate policies, to choose between them, to measure them in practice and to adjust them when necessary, the town planner must be suitably equipped with a variety of tools and techniques. Planning must be based upon knowledge, knowledge depends upon information and information depends upon survey.

Because of the all-embracing nature of town planning and its comprehensive terms of reference, a wide and yet detailed survey of the many components that together form the built environment is required. In addition, the information yielded by such survey must be subjected to analysis to permit a full understanding of the conditions and relationships that exist between these various components. To this end, a range and variety of techniques that facilitate analysis, expedite comprehension and assist in forecasting are demanded. What then must the planner survey and appraise?

1. *Physical characteristics:* the nature, scale and form of the environment are the canvas upon which the plan is painted. A knowledge and record of the topography, geology, climate,

minerals, areas of special interest, location of rich agricultural land and the sources of pollution are prime requirements of the land use planner. With this information he is able to construct both land use maps and 'sieve' maps which between them will indicate the extent of existing development and the potential direction of future development. It is important that these land use maps are kept up-to-date, the record of change greatly helps in understanding the nature of urban growth and the pattern of settlements.

2. *Utilities:* one aspect that is often neglected and much maligned, lacking as it does the charismatic appeal of so many other more topical elements of town planning, is the 'digestive process' of urban areas. A map of existing sewerage, water, gas, refuse, and electricity facilities should be maintained together with a note of their age, condition, and capacity. It is surprising what influence the availability of utilities has in shaping planning policy and determining the scale of development.

3. *Population:* an appreciation of the size, density, character- istics and distribution of the population is nearly always the starting point in the preparation of all plans and policies. Without an idea of the existing and likely future needs of the community in terms of family size, age and structure, the planner is deprived of any premise.

4. *Employment:* the study of population leads naturally on to the need for jobs, demand for labour, and the consequent level of unemployment in a local, regional and national context. These must be fully appraised before the town planner can tackle the seemingly never-ending problem of attaining a true balance and stability within his area of concern. He must be able to forecast decline as well as growth, in order to achieve an optimum distribution of land between competing uses. He must also identify the different demands of basic employment and service employment.

5. *Housing:* from the location of employment springs the need for accommodation. The planner is occupied with the task of ascertaining the size, condition, age, tenure, distribution, density, rate of growth and occupancy rates of the existing stock of housing. From this he can again plot future need and determine

policy in respect of rehabilitation, redevelopment and overspill schemes.

6. *Shopping:* to ensure the most appropriate location for retail facilities the planner is obliged to assess the needs and potential of his local authority area. This entails establishing the regional hierarchy of centres, gauging any deficiencies in the existing pattern and catering for future proposals. It also involves an understanding of shopping habits and trends which might suggest a change in the hierarchy or a shift in emphasis.

7. *Education:* although often separately dealt with in local authority management, the provision and location of educational facilities is largely dependent upon population survey, and an analysis of the trends, changes, and implications in their social context.

8. *Leisure and recreation:* with the growth in available leisure hours and the upsurge in demand for recreation, this area has rapidly become accepted as a major part of the planning process. There exist many challenges in planning future facilities more carefully, making fuller use of existing facilities, preparing a more flexible approach towards the multi-use of school playing fields, initiating increased professional training for recreational management, propagating greater liaison between local authorities and ensuring fuller integration of research into recreation. Before this can be done a deeper knowledge of the forces that dictate demand and determine supply is required. This involves, yet again, the carrying out of extensive survey work and the creation of suitable techniques of analysis.

9. *Movement:* one of the principal factors contributing to the size and nature of urban development is accessibility, which in turn depends upon the degree of, and propensity for, movement. This includes the movement of both people and goods, and has given rise to an entirely new discipline, with its own language, which concerns itself with such tasks as origin and destination, pedestrian and desire line surveys. These in turn are employed in land use transportation studies in the assignment of traffic to networks, and in the testing of routes, capacities, and standards.

10. *Management:* with the growing awareness of the need for better organisation and administration, both in planning and in local government, there has recently been an explosion in the

development and application of management techniques. Corporate planning, planning programming budgeting, linear programming, criticial path analysis and network analysis have all been attempted in different forms and in varying circumstances.

11. *Evaluation:* although it is rather unusual to single out one stage of the planning process and afford it separate attention, it is from this critical area of selection that several important techniques have emerged and been subsequently refined.

In the preparation of any survey or the construction of any technique it is essential to recognise that they themselves require planning. The cost must be estimated, the number of staff involved calculated, and the overall approach decided. Any bias or prejudice which can often creep in either surrepitiously or sub-consciously must be avoided, for there is often a tendency in survey work and analysis to seek out desired information which substantiates preconceived plans.

Sources of information

With the introduction and application of increasingly sophisticated techniques in all fields of study, the researcher, and eventually the decision maker, is becoming ever conscious of the need for accurate, reliable, and up-to-date information. Ideally the data required should be obtained first hand by way of surveys designed specifically for the particular problem at the precise time. Due to the ever present constraints of time and money this of course is not always possible. The researcher, and certainly the student concerned with thesis or project work, is frequently forced to resort to existing sources, often poorly referenced, inadequately compiled, and rarely collated.

The vast majority of published information and statistics result from government inquiry, of which there is certainly no shortage. The cynic, indeed, might suggest that too much data can be every bit as misleading as too little. Owing to the sheer volume of official documentation there has been no publication post-war of the *Guide to Official Statistics* but Her Majesty's Stationery Office produces a series of *Guides to Official Sources* which relate to particular areas of study such as population, agricultural production, or unemployment. Each year HMSO also issue *Government Publications* which lists and outlines every publication for which the government has been responsible over the past twelve months. In an attempt to introduce some order into the situation the Central Office of Information acts as the government's medium for the dissemination of facts and figures, especially in respect of the national press.

Each separate Department and Ministry is itself responsible for the production and propagation of a plethora of facts, figures and fancies. The Central Statistical Office issues, for example, an *Annual Abstract of Regional Statistics*, a *Monthly Digest of Statistics, and Economic Trends*, as well as providing useful classifications for industrial and employment appraisal. The Registrar General, of course, compiles the decennial *Census of Population* which is becoming, controversially, more inquisitive on each occasion. He is also responsible for the more specific *Quarterly Returns* which detail certain aspects of population and housing more closely. A regional breakdown of housing statistics is provided in the two quarterly publications *Housing Statistics* and *Local Housing Statistics*. One further example of central government sources of information is given by the Department for Trade and Industry who, among their many studies, produce a journal, a *Census of Distribution* and a *Census of Production* which between them greatly facilitate the examination of industrial and employment trends and problems.

Of paramount importance to the individual researcher is the intelligent use of library resources. It is here that he can inspect and review previous discussion relating to his particular field of study, examine the current situation, and formulate his own approach. In order to do this with any degree of success he must first be informed in respect of the system of classification employed. If a comprehensive analysis is called for then the British Museum receives a copy of all works published in this country, and the Bodleian Library in Oxford is almost as thorough. It must be remembered that most library catalogues do not reference periodical articles, and it is from this source that the most relevant information is often gleaned. Although most journals and periodicals prepare their own cumulative indexes it does not permit a wide-ranging investigation of all published

117

material on a particular subject. It is for this reason that the Library Association produces an annual *Subject Index to Periodicals* and individual libraries in educational establishments sometimes attempt to compile their own Periodical Index. A number of other comprehensive bibliographies have been drawn up but almost as soon as they are published they are out-of-date.

On a narrower front it is an infinitely more manageable task to undertake a bibliography directed at a particular field of study or professional activity. To this end a variety of indexes, abstracts, reviews, and encyclopaedias have evolved. The production of 'packaged information' is swiftly emerging as a major industry in its own right. The Department of the Environment produces an *Index to Periodical Articles*, originally for internal distribution but now readily available and much sought after. Professional Institutions, such as the R.I.C.S. Technical Information Service with its *Monthly and Weekly Briefing* and the RIBA with its *Annual Review of Periodical Articles* provide valuable information services for their members. The *British Humanities Index*, the *Building Science Abstracts*, the *Sociological Abstracts* and a host of other similar compilations scan and reference a wide array of sources and topics. Many practitioners in various disciplines would be foundering without their respective *Encyclopaedias* on Housing, Planning, Taxation and Compulsory Purchase Law. There exist a multitude of other sources such as newspapers, like the *Times Index*; research, like the Royal Town Planning Institute *Register of Planning Research*; specific topics, like the *Economist Reports on the Regions 1965 to 1968* and the *Association of Planning Librarians Bibliographies*; they are, however, too numerous even to list, let alone describe. One largely untapped source that is worthy of mention is the growing collection of unpublished dissertations and theses that rest in college and university libraries throughout the country, the result of an army of researchers, innumerable man-hours, and no small anguish. Of inestimable worth in the sphere of planning is Brenda White's recent publication *Source Book of Planning Information*, a veritable cornucopia for the lonely researcher.

There are several problems associated with the 'information market'. Firstly, data often exist but are difficult to obtain or abstract. It might not fall within the scope of the more popular referencing or cataloguing systems, or it might be camouflaged by an erroneous title or classification. Secondly, although the information exists it might be of a confidential nature. There are many who can picture the Inland Revenue casting a covetous eye at the census returns, or who are familar with the diffidence of government departments and private sector concerns alike in the release of information. Thirdly, information is often related to inconvenient or inappropriate areas. This has always been particularly true with housing, population, and employment statistics which have been based upon the custom-drawn boundaries of local government areas. This situation is likely to improve with the 'gridding' of the country for statistical purposes. Fourthly, it is sometimes the case that information relates to the wrong periods of time, is grouped inconveniently, or is slow in being published. Again the most notable example of this occurrence refers to census materials which is geared to its decennial cycle and takes as long as five years for all the collected information to be produced. Sample surveys during the intervening years and the application of computers will perhaps alleviate these problems. Finally, as has been previously intimated, information about information is not always available. A great deal of relevant unpublished material might lie gathering dust on the more remote library shelves for lack of adequate recognition and classification. It is worthy of note that the University of Essex has compiled a most valuable *Catalogue of Surveys*.

The great demand for facts and figures over recent years has given rise to an unparalleled growth in the establishment of 'data banks'. As with many techniques whereby the means so often appear to justify the end, these 'banks' have, of themselves, caused a vast information explosion. It is difficult to determine exactly how many exist, or where they are, or even what they refer to, for currently they are specialised and might be concerned with credit worthiness, criminal records, car ownership, as well as professional matters such as cost control, applications for planning permission and other related matters. They are largely computer aided, their aim being to preserve past records, collate current information as well as promoting and facilitating interest in survey methods. They should act as a locus for national and international co-operation in research work, thus preventing any waste of energy whilst hopefully improving standards.

A final word of caution is perhaps appropriate, for no matter how diligent the compiler, no set of statistics, no source of information, and certainly no computer print-out, should ever be treated as 'perfect'. Comprehension, manipulation, and interpretation of data are every bit as important as collection.

7 Population

Demography, or population studies, represents the starting point for planning at all scales, providing guidelines for deciding total land requirements, and a basis for allocating land between various competing uses. Most planning surveys and techniques require a substantial input of population information, and the nature of a community's population make-up and distribution dictates the policy for most urban needs including housing, shopping, employment, education, and health services. A town planner's term of reference is principally directed towards people and their needs. He must therefore study the existing population structure, examine any inherent changes that are occurring, and equip himself to make future predictions.

1. The existing population

A knowledge of the present is necessary in order to plan the future. The following aspects of population must therefore be studied.

Size—If a particular local authority area is to be appraised the first prerequisite is to establish the current total population. This may appear to be a relatively simple task, but in practice it is complicated by several problems. At any point in time a resident indigenous population will be supplemented by visitors whose stay will be of varying duration. The inclusion of tourists, temporary visitors, and such things as army camps can distort the picture and hamper long-term planning.

Characteristics—besides the overall total, it is essential to know the breakdown of the population in terms of age, sex and socio-economic group. In this way the specific needs of a community can be judged, and the provision of facilities can be linked with the respective demands. It is also possible to make a comparison between the local authority and regional, national and even international characteristics. This will indicate, for example, whether or not the authority suffers a particular problem in respect of an abnormally high incidence of low income group workers, old age pensioners or children of school age necessitating special attention or preferential treatment.

Distribution—having established the size and characteristic of the population it is common practice to examine the distribution of all identified groups. This will assist, for instance, in the formulation of redevelopment programmes, but most especially in the more detailed land use location decisions. Where best to place new schools, libraries, health centres and offices, for example.

The calculation of the size of the existing population is obtained from the Registrar General's Census of the Population, undertaken every ten years in this country with a 10% sample in the fifth intervening year. He also issues annual estimates and quarterly returns to facilitate planning policy. Owing to the obvious delay inherent in producing full and detailed census statistics, an approximation of current population figures is often required; this can be achieved by 'censal ratio' methods whereby the last census is brought up-to-date by means of simple apportionment based upon previous statistics. Thus, if over the first ten of the last fifteen years the growth rate for a particular area had been 2% per annum this is still assumed to be constant and a population of 100 000 at the last census five years previous is taken to be 110 410 now. Change in population takes place because of 'natural' change, the difference between births and deaths, and 'migration', the difference between emigration and immigration from and to a particular area. Birth and death rates in measuring existing population are comparatively easy to assess, altering little over short periods of time. Migration is very much more complex to judge. The electoral role provides what is probably the most reliable source of information in this respect, although rating lists are sent by the Inland Revenue to the Registrar General giving some indication of new building and demolition. Lists of patients on doctors' panels can be of further assistance in tracing internal migration, that is migration within the country, and there exists a National Health Service register which correlates them for the United Kingdom. They are not, however, particularly accurate for planning purposes as the process itself takes time, and many people either delay registration immediately or do not register at all. In the United States they employ a technique in gauging migration which relates to the change in numbers of children enrolling at elementary schools, which is found to be in sufficiently reliable proportion to the overall population to give a rough indication. In some countries, such as Sweden, Holland and Japan, the situation is eased by obligatory notification of change of address which provides a virtually continuous census.

Some local planning authorities and regional boards have mounted sample surveys of their own, particularly in respect of detailed information regarding social conditions. This can be a most expensive operation, and the data, which are still generally on a sample basis, are not a substantial improvement on other 'desk' techniques for mere numerical population purposes. It does, however, supply a useful check and can be of inestimable worth in uncovering information not included in the official census.

2. The trends in existing population

Before being able to predict future population changes it is necessary to examine existing trends and consider their future relevance.

Size—it is important to know if there are any symptoms of change in the factors that govern population size, whether or not numbers are declining, stable or increasing. What are the respective birth, death, marriage and fertility rates, what is the level of migration, and what are the determining factors?

Characteristics—any population analysis should ascertain certain characteristic trends. Planning policy will be affected by a tendency towards an ageing population, more women with an inclination to work, increasing levels of literacy, higher educational standards, earlier marriage, rising levels of household formation and a host of other factors.

Distribution—the town planner should be informed about alterations in the distribution of identified groups. The continual urban process whereby a particular class or community 'invades' successive areas, placing social and economic pressures upon the town, requires investigation and monitoring. In this way policies can be drawn up to facilitate or rectify certain situations and circumstances depending upon the desired aims of the community.

3. The future population

By its very nature planning is future-orientated and in order to assess probable needs in terms of schools, houses, shops, offices, factories, and the like, over forthcoming periods of time it is necessary to make predictions regarding the future population. Since the provision, location, and nature of facilities depend upon the size, character and distribution of population, demographic expertise is critical to town and country planning.

Forecasting the level and nature of future population is a speculative enterprise. At their simplest, projections can be merely a continuation of the recent past into the future by extending a straight line graph or adopting a formula which assumes that current trends will persist unchanged. The procedure is made more complex by introducing such factors as varying birth, death, sex, marriage, fertility and migration rates.

Birth and death rates are fairly simple to project, and as there is rarely more than a 5% variance from year to year the short-term significance to an individual local planning authority is slight. The long-term total national population creates harder problems, for birth rate itself is dependent upon fertility and marriage rates. Fertility rates play a large part in determining the birth rate

124

and have been steadily increasing, particularly in the younger age groups, since the war. The tendency towards younger marriage is likely to have a substantial effect on population growth, especially when fertility rates are higher at this age. It is difficult to forecast whether this trait of younger marriages and more children at an early age will eventually lead to larger families or is purely a matter of couples bringing their family forward.

Death rates have been continually falling throughout the world, particularly the decrease in infant mortality, which has dropped from 30 per thousand to around 6 per thousand in this country alone over the last fifty years. Barring the outbreak of epidemics, or the onset of cataclysmic holocausts, it is likely that the downward trend in death rates will continue, but will become progressively smaller both overall and through the age range.

One popular technique for forecasting population is the Cohort Survival Method which adjusts census figures forward by age and sex groups, year by year, to the date of the forecast, making separate adjustments for changes in birth, death, fertility, and migration rates. In essence what it does is to trace a particular age group, for example 0–4 years, through their estimated life cycle making deductions for projected deaths based upon life tables, and amendments for net migration. The next 0–4 age group is calculated by reference to the fertility rate of the number of 'survivors' remaining in preceeding groups or cohorts. Special adjustments are made to allow for local trends, foreseen unique occurrences, and the death rate of migrants. Separate calculations are undertaken for male and female, high and low assessments being made for both.

In all population forecasts the most difficult factor to allow for is internal migration, relying as it does upon economic circumstance and social preference. Three principal characteristics can, however, be discerned. There continues to be a slight drift away from the northern parts of the country, rural depopulation persists unabated, and the most recent development is a movement away from the congested centres of large towns. Inter-regional migration has become a major planning problem and some success in arresting the drain of manpower from the North has been achieved. The seemingly inexorable growth of the South East has also been dampened down, switching instead to East Anglia and the South West.

If internal migration presents problems in assessment, then external migration is next to impossible. To a large extent it is subject to the vagaries of political change. In 1957, for example, 72 000 persons on balance left the country, whereas four years later, in 1961, there was a net influx, immigration over emigration, of 170 000 which dropped within a further two years to an intake of 10 000. Migration figures, both internal and external, illustrate the inherent difficulties of applying quantitative analysis to subjective variables. Even then, crude numerical forecasts are insufficient when a detailed breakdown of social characteristics is required, and it is part and parcel of the planning process to possess the ability to prediding both social and economic changes. Even changes in the age or sex structure of the population, which are the easiest to forecast, could be upset by medical advance; it might soon be possible to choose the sex of offspring, for example.

In recent years a great deal of research has been invested in setting up more sophisticated techniques to cope with population projection and forecasting. Mathematical models, such as EMCON, which was used in Ipswich and Sheffield, and the model developed jointly by the London School of Economics and the Greater London Council for use in predicting long-term metropolitan growth, have been introduced to assist the town planner in formulating policy.

Population policy

There is rarely any attempt at directly guiding the overall level of population, for government intervention in ordering such things as the birth rate is not thought to be a proper field for public action. This view is reinforced by the singular lack of success on the part of past population projections, all sixteen forecasts prepared by the 1949 Royal Commission have fallen well below actual current levels. Influence, except for such incentives as family allowance, is normally exercised as an element in other planning policies such as housing, employment and communi-

126

cations. One recent development in the United States that might be suitably applied in this country, however, is an analysis of daytime population distribution as well as night-time or residential distribution. This information would greatly assist in establishing strategies to combat urban congestion and institute more advanced locational criteria. At the present time consideration of this aspect has been restricted to the current population but could be usefully extended to future appraisal.

Hazardous, complex and occasionally inaccurate as population studies are, it scarcely requires reiterating that without adequate data regarding the size, nature and distribution of population most other surveys would be rendered abortive and the whole spectrum of planning policy would be put in question.

Population—recommended reading

Cox, P., *Demography*, Cambridge U.P. (1970).
Cullingworth, J. B. and Orr, S. C. (eds.), *Regional and Urban Studies*, Allen and Unwin (1969).
Jackson, J. N., *Surveys for Town and Country Planning*, Hutchinson (1963).
Kelsall, R. K., *Population*, Longmans (1967).
Stone, P. A., *Urban Development in Britain: Population Trends and Housing*, Cambridge U.P. (1970).

8　Employment

The level of employment is commonly used as a measure for assessing both economic performance and social condition. Because of this it has important political connotations and thus merits considerable attention throughout the planning process. The nature of employment opportunity, and the magnitude of potential growth or decline, dictates, to a large extent, the future size of population for a particular area, and is therefore essential information in calculating community requirements in terms of housing, shopping, and other facilities. It is further necessary in estimating the actual space needs of industry and commerce themselves. In any study of employment three fundamental aspects can be readily identified, the worker, the employer, and the area.

The worker

The town planner aims to match the need for employment with the availability of jobs, but in order to do this he must be able to predict change, and then be in a position to guide and control development. Certain elements warrant analysis in any employment study and can be said to constitute a rough procedure.

1. Definition of study area—although this is often determined by local authority boundaries it is important to realise that any

particular labour market can vary in size according to prevailing economic circumstances. In times of recession, or localised high unemployment, workers may well be prepared to travel exceptionally long distances to obtain employment. Distance is therefore critical, but so too are time and money. Cheap or subsidised fares could entice labour from an unusually wide area.

2. Activity rates—these indicate the total quantity of labour that is likely to be available at any particular time, and rely heavily upon an exhaustive study of population structure. The first step is to ascertain the total size of the population of working age. Next, because activity rates are sex, age and income specific, the overall working population should be sub-divided into groups reflecting these characteristics. The activity rate itself is used to measure the total number of employed persons per hundred of the population, and is therefore expressed as a percentage. The average for an entire population of an area, for example, varies between 44% and 50%. When split into male and female workers on a basis of age and marital status, however, differing pictures emerge. Male activity rates, consistently above 90% until retirement age, reach their highest level between the ages of 30 and 55 and then decline gradually for ten years with a significant drop to below 40% after the age of 65 and around 10% after 70. Unmarried females attain their highest activity rate of about 90% between the age of 25 and 30, after which there is a gradual decline until 60 years of age when the rate rapidly falls off to around 5% after 65. Married females, on the other hand, reach their highest level of just over 40% between 35 and 50 and fall away to around 8% after the age of 60. Whilst the make-up of the population and subsequent analysis of activity rates can thus be seen to exert considerable influence in assessing the supply of labour, other factors that determine the actual amount of time expended are the number of hours worked, and the amount of annual holidays, which vary from industry to industry and are subject to change through time. Forecasting future levels of the availability of labour will have to take account of changes in the age of marriage, school leaving, and retirement, as well as changes in working hours, longevity, and annual holidays. The same

problems of prediction will exist in the study of employment as those discussed in population projection.

3. Earning capacity will play a prominent part in deciding the actual activity rates, particularly those of female labour. No definitive rules can be laid down, however, because in some areas, where incomes are low and the risk of unemployment high, overall activity rates will be higher because families will be striving to secure an acceptable or adequate amount sufficient for their needs. In other areas, where incomes are higher and their incidence more secure, activity rates will also be higher because the more attractive terms will induce more women out to work. When appraising income opportunities and employment potential it is customary to review existing rates of unemployment which provide a crude indicator of untapped supply. Unemployment figures do, however, possess certain inherent drawbacks; some people, for one reason or another, are unemployable and others want to work but do not register. Other problems in measuring the supply of labour are encountered where an imbalance in the local structure of employment arises. This might occur where, for example, there are not sufficient jobs for women, or where few opportunities exist for better educated school leavers, or more commonly where there is one firm or one industry dominance, subject to severe economic fluctuations, in a certain locality.

4. Social attitudes can have a considerable effect upon the level of employment and the supply of labour. This factor is again particularly noticeable in respect of female workers. In the North East of England, where there is a long tradition of women going out to work, there are very high female activity rates, whereas in South Wales, where circumstances differ, they are extremely low. This naturally reflects the long-term lack of opportunity; nevertheless, social attitudes do vary from area to area. One aspect of this, of increasing importance, is the relationship between workplace and home. In the South East, for instance, the journey to work is significantly longer than elsewhere in the country, giving a greater mobility of labour. In traditional mining areas, however, great premium is placed upon proximity to work.

5. Labour reserves—as has been stated the lack of opportunity can seriously lower activity rates, resulting in a pool of wasteful unemployed labour. L. C. Hunter pinpoints the problem with great clarity,[1] 'In an economy like ours, beset by labour shortages, it must be an aim of planned development that potential labour supplies are fully utilised. If labour reserves can be brought into action by providing more job openings, as we can reasonably assume, the future provision of jobs should be adequate not just to employ imported additions to the area labour force but also to take up the slack in the existing market situation.' The difficulty lies in distinguishing those areas where this problem occurs. This might be indicated by a high rate of unemployment or low activity rates, but without having regard to more detailed information relating to changes occurring within an industry and the gradual transition of workers from one job to another, or the influx of immigrant labour to areas of great potential opportunity, the picture can be misleading.

The employer

In general the entrepreneur is concerned with obtaining optimum access to raw materials, the market for his services or product, labour, utilities, communications and complementary services. The planner concentrates upon achieving a balanced industrial structure, alleviating urban congestion, and maximising the allocation of land between competing uses. Naturally there is bound to be the occasional conflict of interest between them, but once again the town planner must comprehend the forces that dictate change in the demand for employment in order to formulate his policy satisfactorily in respect of the other components of urban structure with which it is associated.

1. Industrial Structure—a knowledge and understanding of the current situation might highlight trends of production and employment that greatly influence the future pattern of development. It is necessary to examine the nature and scale of existing firms to detect signs of growth, decline, or change. A relatively simple indicator is the 'location quotient' which compares the number of workers in a particular local industry with the national

average for the same industry. When figures for a number of years are available, signs of growth or decline, either locally or nationally, might emerge, thus providing some basis for analysis. If, for example, the local employment quotient is above one, with the national average setting the unitary base, it is likely that the employer will be seeking, by whatever means, to reduce his payroll unless exceptional circumstances prevail, bringing about a reduction in the area's total level of employment. A forewarning of this will enable steps to be taken regarding the provision of alternative jobs.

Similarly employment might be based upon a declining industry such as shipbuilding, and the necessary action to stimulate a fresh demand for labour must be put in hand. This might take the form of retraining schemes, or preferential treatment such as cheap accommodation being afforded to prospective new employers. Areas that are themselves declining can often be discerned by examining the proportion of the working population that falls within a particular age range. In such an area there is often a significantly lower percentage of men falling within the 15 to 40 age range than exists nationally, in contrast to expanding areas where the opposite is the case.

Certain concerns possess specialised labour requirements or land needs, such as the pottery industry or glassblowing in the first instance, and the woollen industry and mineral extraction in the latter. Another aspect of location that affects the viability of production, and thus the demand for labour, is the importance of 'linkages'. Many industries require to be in close physical proximity to certain subsidiary companies or complementary services, others act as positive generators of supplementary services and undertakings. Yet again it is encumbent upon the town planner to chart the relationships that exist between the diffuse factors that determine industrial growth and employment. J. N. Jackson suggests one way in which this can be achieved.[2] 'One method might be for industrialists to rate pre-determined industrial factors as an important advantage, or of little importance, or as a disadvantage of their existing location . . . Replies can be tabulated by locality or by industry, and for the factors separately or in combination. In addition an 'advantage ratio' can be computed. This is simply the number of forms indicating that the factor is an advantage divided by the number that indicated it to be a disadvantage.'

Technological change—perhaps the most difficult element determining the demand for labour to predict. More often than not such advances initially reduce the number of jobs directly available. In the long run, however, where the result is increased productivity, greater investment leading to an enhanced demand for workers might ensue. In addition the industry benefiting from innovation and displaying a healthy and efficient economic performance often acts as a stimulus for growth in other directions, with unrelated firms being attracted to the area by the sweet smell of success. The advent of the cybernetic revolution has lent an air of uncertainty to forecasting the future nature of employment. In Japan the competition for space, coupled with appalling commuting problems, has led to a radical change in office management whereby the employee remains at home to work, his only contact with colleagues and superiors being by way of two-way closed-circuit television installed in his own house. Although not directly applicable to the whole range of employment opportunities, particularly industrial, it illustrates the devastating effect of technology upon locational decisions.

To assist in the procedure of forecasting demand, existing patterns of employment can be projected forward at prevailing average growth rates, in a roughly similar way to population forecasts. This kind of estimate tends to be rather crude and inaccurate unless certain trend factors regarding employment rates in particular industries and the growth or decline of these concerns are included. Information regarding future patterns can be abstracted from such sources as the ill-fated National Plan, published in 1965, which detailed projected growth, industry by industry, on a national basis; this can then be translated into a more appropriate context depending upon actual local circumstances. Growth rates are, however, somewhat problematic and a degree of uncertainty is bound to creep in.

The area

Having established the probable levels of demand for, and supply of, labour, the town planner must plot the course of action for his

133

particular local authority area. He must decide to what extent development can be left to private sector forces, exactly how much direct intervention is required, and of what kind. As labour markets are unlikely to coincide with local authority boundaries, liaison with neighbouring authorities is essential, for the repercussions of growth or decline are likely to spread out far beyond the area of immediate administrative concern. A need, therefore, emerges to define importing and exporting areas of workers in order to paint a more complete picture of the labour market. The nature of employment opportunity and the degree of industrial development exert a considerable influence upon the physical form and character of urban areas. Residential, retail, commercial and service distributions are derived from industrial location factors. Transportation both determines, and is likewise determined by, potential growth. Although the distribution of industry on a national basis is presently the prerogative of central government, its precise siting and detailed layout is the responsibilty of the relevant local planning authority. Regard on their part must therefore be paid to accessibility, the provision of services and utilities, the disposal of refuse and industrial effluent, visual intrusion, noise, fumes, vibration, the prevailing wind, air currents, and other similar factors. They should decide whether or not local industry and community needs would be best served by the establishment of a trading estate. Despite the fact that such estates take time to 'mature' because many entrepreneurs take up options in advance, they retain certain distinct advantages. A wide variety of undertaking can be catered for, thus providing a stable employment base; moreover, a range of sports, medical, canteen, rail, and parking facilities can be provided communally. These estates, and for that matter any form of industrial development, can be expediently employed as a 'buffer' between motorways and other urban land uses, which is especially tempting if access to the motorway is furnished.

Sources of information

The principal sources of information are supplied by central government. A census of production is conducted every five years and the findings are published in the *Annual Abstract of Statistics* and the *Board of Trade Journal*. A similar census of distribution is carried out for wholesale and retail activities. Current statistics on manpower, unemployment, retraining schemes, wages, costs, and industrial structure in general are issued in the *Department of Employment Gazette* which is published monthly. This is now supplemented by the annual *Year Book of Labour Statistics*. The various nationalised industries also produce annual reports that provide employment data. One of the most useful aids to industrial employment surveys is the Standard Industrial Classification compiled by the Central Statistical Office and last revised in 1968. This lays down convenient groupings of commercial and industrial enterprises. In the same vein is the Registrar General's publication which sets out a classification of occupations which can be used in handling information derived from the census of production.

Forecasting techniques

In the overall assessment of the various constituent components that affect and determine employment several techniques are available to assist in prediction and planning. They are all at an early stage of development, and owing to the large number of components involved, their variable nature, and the long time scale, wide margins of error can often appear. Because of these inherent difficulties the techniques employed must be sufficiently flexible to adjust to changing circumstances. J. T. Hughes places great emphasis upon this aspect:[3] 'Planners of all levels must be prepared to review the broad strategy and details of their proposals to take account of new trends. That is why it is important not to aim at a grand once-and-for-all-time projection but to set up machinery and techniques which will provide a continual revision of estimates in the light of new developments.'

    1. Economic base is a technique applied in regional planning and represents a slightly more sophisticated approach towards employment projection than that provided by the Location Co-efficient, which merely compares the proportion of an industry's labour force within one area with the national propor-

tion for that industry, thus indicating local specialisation. The economic base of a region relates to that group of industries primarily engaged in the production of 'basic' or 'export' goods to other regions, employment in locally consumed 'non-basic' goods and services being dependent upon the level of production and employment in export or basic goods and services. A relationship expressed as a proportion or multiplier between export or basic employment and local or non-basic employment can, therefore, be derived from a fairly simple analysis. This can then be applied to the likely future trends in the respective industries within the area based upon national forecasts, thus indicating probable total future employment. It should be remembered, however, that the ratio or relationship could change over time due to such factors as technological advance. Problems are also encountered in distinguishing between basic and non-basic industries.

The technique is also used, in conjunction with a comparative cost analysis, in determining those industries that might be introduced into an area with the aim of creating an economic base for future growth. This application is closely allied with the concept of growth 'points' or 'poles' which are locations ideally suited to the induction of new industries which would themselves generate further development.[4]

2. Input-output analysis is another technique available for the study of employment and is again closely associated with the concept of relationships between both regions and industries and the calculation of ratios or multipliers to assist in forecasting. The analysis aims to discover how much input to a particular industry is obtained locally from the area under study, and similarly how much output is sold there, and how much elsewhere. It is then possible to compare these results with other regions as well as with national figures and draw certain conclusions regarding future trends in the industry and its labour force. It might be, for example, that the input of labour in the industry was locally very much higher than the national average and likely to diminish proportionately with the introduction of automation. Another industry might prove to be heavily reliant upon sales to other regions and should be strategically placed

in an optimum location for 'export', thus increasing productivity, growth, and employment.

Input-output analysis detects and exposes the linkages and transactions that take place between industries and between areas. One major drawback is the lack of reliable information with which to construct the matrix that displays the relationships; it is both complex and costly to collect.

3. Technique for area planning (T.A.P.)—to overcome the problems of data collection this approach has recently been developed whereby the process of defining and examining linkages is considerably simplified. A distinction is made between major and minor industrial concerns and relationships are only identified for the major sectors where information is more readily available. H. Richardson describes T.A.P. as 'a mongrel technique, somewhere between an input-output model and an economic base study. It avoids the costliness of the former and the undue aggregation of the latter. Although it follows base analysis in giving exports primary consideration in the final demand sector, impact estimates from T.A.P. were found to fall within 5% of those resulting from comprehensive input-output studies. A T.A.P. study may be used either for projection or for evaluating the impact of alternative policies (e.g. the choice between promoting the growth of an existing firm, a new firm related to existing local activities, and a firm in an industry new to a region) on local employment or income.'[5]

4. *Others*—income statistics can be used to gauge an approximate indication of future employment. Total figures of estimated future national income are sub-divided into regional portions on the basis of how much each region can expect to share. Using forecasts of production and output per worker a projection of expected jobs can be obtained. Reliable information is once again the key to the success of this method, which is essentially a short-cut approach.

C. M. Law has described a means by which a similar approach to that employed in estimating future population levels can be applied to forecasting employment.[6] It is called 'growth analysis' and is founded upon the assumption that jobs possess a kind of birth and death rate which can be measured by area over time.

Another technique described as Industrial Complex Analysis

gives attention to the interrelationships that exist between industries. The location and production of a motor car industry, for example, will affect the location and production of many other related concerns, all gaining external economies from enhanced accessibility. A modified form of input-output analysis is used to examine the ideal location for the 'set' or complex of related industries and measure potential growth or decline and therefore prospective employment.[7]

Employment—references

1 Hunter, L. C., 'Planning and the labour market', *Regional and Urban Studies*, eds. Cullingworth, J. B. and Orr, S. C., Allen and Unwin (1969).
2 Jackson, J. N., *Surveys for Town and Country Planning*, Hutchinson (1963).
3 Hughes, J. T., 'Employment Projection and Urban Development', *Regional and Urban Studies*, eds. Cullingworth, J. B. and Orr, S. C., Allen and Unwin (1969).
4 Hansen, N., 'Development pole theory in a regional context', *Kyklos*, **120**, 1967.
5 Richardson, H. W. *Elements of Regional Economics*, Penguin (1969).
6 Law, C. M., 'Employment Growth and Regional Policy in North West England', *Regional Studies*, **4**, 1970.
7 Richardson, *op. cit.*

Further recommended reading

Beynon, T. G., 'A method of forecasting local employment', *Town Planning Institute Journal*, September, 1966.
Bracken, I., 'A basic model for population projection', *Town Planning Institute Journal*, December, 1969.
Needleman, L., *Regional Analysis*, Penguin (1968).

9   Housing

One immediate and immensely important characteristic that can be readily identified in respect of the housing market is its contentious and controversial nature. It is housing that gives shelter, security, privacy, investment, and personal identity. The town planner, being concerned with housing need and provision, valiantly strives to marry the two together. He is, however, beset on all sides by administrative, statutory, financial, social and political constraints. These are exemplified by the hodge-podge miscellany of legislation that relates to the problem, for since the Rent and Mortgage Restriction Act of 1915 there have been ten major Housing Acts, and more than twenty-five other statutes relating to rent control and security of tenure.

In attempting to reconcile the demand for, and supply of, residential accommodation the town planner must analyse:

(1)   The existing housing stock

a. Density—the various means of expressing residential density and their relative merits are described elsewhere,[1] but briefly it can be measured in terms of dwellings, habitable rooms, persons, or bedspaces per hectare. The purpose of surveying prevailing densities is to ascertain the degree of comfort that exists throughout the community, pinpoint the areas of need, relate the size of population to the provision of services, and permit the monitoring of a plan's performance.

b. Type of dwelling—it is important to know the range and variety of dwelling types within a particular area for they all have different characteristics and requirements. Most surveys should therefore attempt to assess the housing mix in terms of small or large blocks of flats; detached, semi-detached, or terraced houses; bungalows, maisonettes, caravans, boats, down to institutional accommodation such as old people's homes. One important factor that should also be taken into account besides the mere number of dwellings is their relative size. This should not only be calculated in number of rooms but also expressed in persons per square metre, thus giving a clearer indication of crude accommodation capacity and use. It is common practice to obtain information regarding the age of dwellings within a particular area under study. Different bases are employed for this purpose but pre-1880, 1880–1919, 1919–1944, and 1944 onwards are popular and easily applicable. It is interesting to note that due to early industrialisation nearly one half of the existing stock of houses was built before 1919, and that the average age of dwellings throughout the country is about fifty-six years.

c. Occupation—this is most generally gauged in terms of a household and the number of rooms available to them. One difficulty emerges in the very definition of a 'room' for different housing surveys have adopted varying measures. The Allen Report of 1965,[2] for example, whose principal concern was with the impact of rates on households, included bathrooms and garages which are usually ignored. The Rowntree Housing Study, also in 1965, excluded attics unless specifically used as bedrooms, and the Census has now changed its policy in respect of kitchens to include them as a room for the purpose of the survey irrespective of their size or use. This variance can lead to anomalies because, as Cullingworth points out, 'households who are forced through lack of space to use attics as bedrooms may appear to have more rooms than smaller households in identical accommodation. Conversely, households small enough to eat in a kitchen may appear to have more rooms than larger households who eat in a living room.'[3]

Once again the measures of persons per dwelling and persons per habitable room have been found inappropriate in assessing overcrowding. A more sophisticated approach is provided by the Social Survey which views not only required capacity of accommodation but also takes account of sex and age separation. The statutory methods of judging overcrowding are very much more arbitrary and solely relate the number of rooms in a dwelling to the permitted number of persons, with some allowance for the size of the room. With the increasing rise in the standard of living, statutory measures fail to keep abreast with popular attitudes towards acceptable accommodation. The legal definition of overcrowding, for example, is set at over two persons per room, an exceptionally low standard when the Greater London Council aims at achieving under one person per room.

With the present housing shortage under-occupation has become as significant as overcrowding in assessing the overall allocation of accommodation. Whereas the 1960 Housing Survey of England and Wales indicated that only 0·6% of households were statutorily overcrowded, 10% of dwellings were found to be under-occupied.[4] Moreover, on the night of the 1961 Census nearly 4% of all dwellings were vacant and with annual additions to the housing stock running at below 2% this represents a significant factor in the housing crisis.

Another factor that should be considered when analysing the nature and degree of occupation is the form of tenure, whether it is owner-occupied, rented, municipally owned, or tied to employment. Although it is often difficult to ascertain when conversion or a change of use has taken place within a dwelling, the consequence of such action has considerable repercussions upon planning policy in terms of the provision of services and facilities. In this context many authorities are experiencing great difficulty in forecasting future community requirements with the explosion in higher education and the demand for student lodgings.

d. Physical condition—at a time when there are nearly two million 'slum homes' in this country, representing approximately 12% of the total housing stock, and eight million persons require re-housing because their accommodation is obsolescent, it is scarcely surprising that overriding concern is directed to the quality of dwellings. Information regarding the condition of buildings is of consequence to the town planner in establishing his overall priorities, determining the nature and magnitude of the housing problem in his area, comparing it with the national picture, and enabling him to make decisions regarding alternative solutions. A detailed survey will require a set of objective criteria with which to assess standards of physical condition and permit comparison. J. N. Jackson in his book *Surveys for Town and Country Planning* cites the American Public Health Association manual as providing an excellent approach. This publication sets out a *Housing Condition Index* whereby a very wide range of varying factors including heating, lighting, sanitation, access and overcrowding are awarded points based upon acceptable standards. In this way housing deficiency is measured and recorded. The National Institute of Economic and Social Research undertook a 3500 sample survey of the physical condition of dwellings in England and Wales using a ranking basis of Good, Fair, Fair to Poor, Poor, and Very Poor. Not surprisingly a direct correlation between age and condition of dwellings was discovered.

A more significant relationship is that between external and internal conditions recognised by Professor Parry Lewis at Manchester University. His researches have led to the formulation of a Survey for Housing and Environmental Deficiency (SHED), which is based upon the hypothesis that the internal condition of a property and its respective amenities are reflected in the external condition. The advantage of this method is that an inexpensive external survey is sufficient to determine housing deficiency, although where possible a brief internal inspection is advisable as a safeguard against inaccuracy. It is further possible to attach a figure for repairs and improvement based upon the 12 point housing standard advocated by central government and employed in SHED. Parry Lewis found the cost in Manchester to be about £12 per point. From this the total figure can be obtained for bringing an authority's housing up to Housing Act standard, as well as figures for average improvement cost per house, per person, and per household adequately accommodated. The Department of the Environment now provides a similar Housing Condition Index which relies, perhaps too heavily, upon the expertise of the individual inspector undertaking the survey who is required to estimate the cost of repair.

Several surveys following comparable procedures have recently been undertaken by local planning authorities. Besides the actual condition of the housing stock they have also paid regard to the condition of the environment, a notoriously difficult concept to measure objectively, the information being obtained from the Census, particularly in respect of the provision of amenities, local authority housing returns which provide details regarding the legal criteria of 'unfitness', and rateable values which supply a measure of housing quality based upon tenure, condition, and location, possessing a common basis. Notable amongst them are the Teesside Study,[5] which adopted SHED as the basic model and applied to 75 environmental areas within its area, producing a programme of priorities for treatment; the Leicestershire Study[6] which instituted a field survey of dwellings awarding penalty points related to the cost of rectifying deficiencies whilst attaching great weight to the environment; and the Warwickshire Study[7] which rejected a cost based assessment in favour of 'an assessment based on socially-desirable weightings defining a level of environment', which took into account such aspects as car parking, noise, proximity of shops, schools, open space and public transport. A comprehensive base for formulating national and local housing policies incorporating an environmental survey and classification has been outlined by Buchanan[8] and awaits implementation.

The problem with almost any housing quality survey is deciding upon which particular factors merit attention, the way in which they should be measured, and the establishment of acceptable standards.

(2) Rehabilitate or redevelop?

Having conducted a survey of the existing housing stock and defined those dwellings or residential areas that are unsatisfactory, problematic in itself for 'satisfactory' can mean all things to all men, the next step is to decide upon the most suitable course of treatment. The decision whether to demolish and build anew, or to rehabilitate as an improvement area, or individually by means of improvement grants under the 1969 Housing Act, is one that has exercised the minds of town planners and economists alike over the last few years. This dichotomy, to refurbish or rebuild, has led to the development of a number of 'decision models', or evaluation techniques, designed to assist choice. Those proposed by Dr. Needleman, whilst at Sussex University, and Professor Schaaf of California University are very similar, and relate to 'least cost' criteria, whereby rehabilitation is selected if it proves cheaper than replacement, ignoring subsidies and bearing in mind that renewal is in fact only deferred. More recently W. Lean has put forward a slightly wider economic view whilst preserving the premise of least cost.[10]

An alternative approach that does not merely confine itself to an examination of cost but includes an appraisal of benefits has been propounded in the United States by J. Rothenburg.[11] A case study at the Pine Ridge Indian Reservation was undertaken incorporating a partial Cost Benefit Analysis appraising, on a before and after basis, the performance of a housing improvement scheme. The results showed that alongside normal direct returns there were great savings in the equivalent of social security payments, a reduction in medical expenses, a fall in absenteeism, and a rise in production in local industries. The study suggests that 'least cost' is not by itself always the best basis for judgement. Similar work has been done in Los Angeles, again discerning significant benefits that might often be ignored. The Cost Benefit Analysis approach has been applied in this country by Martin Horne in the Barnsbury area of North London with conflicting results depending upon whether the viewpoints taken are those of the local authority or the residents.

To investigate the advisability of rehabilitation, and devise an approach towards its assessment, the Ministry of Housing and Local Government undertook a feasibility study in 1966 at Deeplish, a nineteenth-century residential area of Rochdale. A mixed-discipline team of architects, town planners, valuers, surveyors, engineers, and sociologists prepared a report detailing their survey procedure and examining the implications of such a policy.[12] This study has supplied a preliminary framework for adoption and improvement elsewhere.

(3) Future provision of housing

Any calculations regarding future housing needs are inextricably bound in with population studies and projections. Not only is it estimated that nationally there will be a crude population growth, but increased household formation is also likely, and together these factors predicate a need for a further 1·3 million dwellings by 1981. Another factor that influences the demand for housing is the level and rate of growth of incomes. Due to the degree of government involvement in the housing market, and the limitations of economic models, it is difficult to be precise whether or not housing demand is more or less responsive to changes in income than other goods and services. On balance, however, it is likely that rising incomes will cause an increase in total expenditure on housing. Thus, as incomes rise the demand for housing will also rise. F. Pennance, in the Hobart Paper *Housing Market Analysis and Policy*, suggests that the demand for housing is responsive to both price and income changes.

Another determining aspect that the town planner should consider in surveying future residential demand is migration, which has the effect of increasing household formation in particular localities and of exacerbating regional housing problems. Housing demand is further stimulated by urban renewal, and if present slum clearance rates are maintained then an additional 750 000 dwellings will be required throughout the country by 1981 for this purpose. More and more houses, however, might fall into the categories requiring replacement due to obsolescence, higher standards, or comprehensive redevelopment. The town planner working at the local authority scale is required to translate these national traits into a local context.

Future provision is obviously not limited to the influence of the demand side of the market. The supply side is riddled with controversy, beset by political vascillation, stunted by lack of professional imagination, and constrained by a statutory straitjacket. Whilst on the demand side techniques of housing survey and analysis are becoming comparatively sophisticated and reliable, on the supply side, due to the complex interplay of social, economic, and political forces, they are virtually nonexistent. The effects of rent control legislation, building standards

145

such as those instituted by the Parker Morris Report, subsidising council tenants, density standards, public transport policy, credit availability, taxation, release of land, restriction on planning permission, and a whole host of other supply determinants can only be guessed at.[13] In the light of prevailing circumstances it becomes increasingly difficult to make a temperate statement on the subject.

The majority of those elements that exert authority over the housing market are determined as a result of political pressure or national economic policy and, as such, are outside the domain of the land-use planner. There are aspects which are relevant to the local scale, warranting attention by a local planning authority, and deserving of more extensive survey. These can be summarised as follows:

a. Survey of existing stock—as previously described, to ascertain its nature, range, location, environment, ownership, age, condition and occupancy in order to provide a basis from which to formulate policy.

b. Estimate future need—in terms of a programme linked to a time scale, taking into account migration, commercial, industrial and natural growth, household formation and urban decay. It might be necessary to decide, at a comparatively early stage, the most appropriate course of action for particular areas. Rehabilitation, with its inherent advantages of conservation of buildings of a special historic or architectural interest, preservation of existing densities, a minimum of disturbance to the indigenous population, no need to exercise compulsory purchase powers, the use of facilities already available and serviceable, and the distribution of the financial burden between the public and private sector, might be a more attractive proposition in certain circumstances to redevelopment, despite the advantages gained by planning afresh. It is also necessary to link the supply of house types with the demand for accommodation capacity. The 'three-bed semi-detached syndrome', supported by the entrenched bastion of financial reaction that supplies credit to the market, satisfies but part of the population who are forced to endure it.

c. Survey of land availability—given the present housing shortage a review of land use allocation, often designated and zoned

146

many years ago, is probably well overdue. A more positive approach to derelict land, land held off the market and a change in the parsimonious attitude towards residential planning permission that prevails among all too many planning authorities is urgently required.

d. Survey of existing densities and future potential might well indicate that minimum controls in peripheral urban areas are more expedient than maximum controls in central areas.

e. Survey of development agencies—having decided the amount of future housing required, the desired location, and the type, it is necessary to appraise the most suitable agency for building it. If private sector participation is sought a successful way of stimulating its involvement is by the preparation of detailed 'planning briefs' which set out the local authority policy in respect of the particular site, detailing such things as the level of permitted density, necessary access, car parking, materials, height and use. This can often save a great deal of time, and expense, and thereby renders the scheme more profitable to the developer, and the policy more viable to the authority.

It is always worth remembering that in any survey or technique applied to housing, a large measure of value judgement is introduced. Whose opinion decides such criteria as fitness, overcrowding, environmental deficiency, building standards, space standards, high-rise development, high-density construction and priority regarding land release? These highly evocative and controversial topics can all too easily be subjected to sophisticated technical processing, and presented with a falsely accredited aura of objectivity.

Housing—references

1 See page 293.
2 *Commission of Inquiry into the Impact of Rates on Households Report*, Cmnd 25/82, HMSO (1965).
3 Cullingworth, J. B., 'Housing Analysis', *Regional and Urban Studies*, eds. Cullingworth, J. B. and Orr, S. C., Allen and Unwin (1969).
4 Gray, P. and Russell, R., *The Housing Situation in 1960*, Central Office of Information (1962).

5 Wilson, Womersley *et al.*, *Teesside Survey and Plan*, HMSO (1969).

6 *Leicester and Leicestershire Sub-Regional Planning Study*, Leicester City Council and Leicestershire County Council (1969).

7 *Coventry–Solihull–Warwickshire: A Strategy for the Sub-Region*, Coventry City Council (1971).

8 Buchanan, J., 'Evaluation of Housing Stock and its Environment', *Town Planning Institute Journal*, September, 1971.

9 Lean, W., 'Housing Rehabilitation or Redevelopment', *Town Planning Institute Journal*, May, 1971.

10 Rothenburg, J., *The Economics of Urban Renewal*, Brookings Institution (1967).

11 *The Deeplish Study*, HMSO (1966).

12 Ratcliffe, J., 'Rent Control, The Francis Report, and the Housing Market', *Architect and Surveyor*, September, 1971.

Further recommended reading

Department of the Environment, *Area Improvement Notes*, HMSO (1971).

Donnison, D. V., *The Government of Housing*, Pelican (1967).

Merret, A. J., and Sykes, A., *Housing Finance and Development*, Longmans (1965).

Medhurst, F. and Parry Lewis, J., *Urban Decay*, Macmillan (1969).

Stone, P. A., 'Improve or Build—Economic Realities', *Official Architect and Planner*, February, 1970.

10 Offices

As society becomes more economically mature so the proportion, and therefore the importance, of tertiary or service employment increases. Although total employment grew by 20% between 1921 and 1951, office employment rose by 150% over the same period. The role of office development thus assumes a prominent position when allocating land among competing uses. Four basic types of office development can be distinguished, those providing local services, those directly associated with industry, those which represent the regional headquarters of large organisations, and those which provide national or international headquarters for similar concerns. As industry has moved out of town so offices have moved in; moreover, they have tended to locate in the South East where 35% of the country's total supply is to be found, and more particularly they have competed for space in London itself. It is difficult, however, to outline the surveys and techniques that surround the consideration of office development in the planning process for there are few types of survey and an absolute dearth of techniques.[1] All that is possible is a brief chronicle of the attitudes and policies that govern office location.

The origins of the boom in office development can be attributed to the economic expansion of trade and industry in the nineteenth century. Apart from a slump in the 1930's, reflected in a sharp decline in rents, and caused by an over-provision and a general crisis of confidence, the demand for office space has continued unabated. With the publication of the Barlow Report, and its view of employment as being a national problem and not a series of local ones, and the main solution being some form of dispersion, the scene was set for the next thirty years. The Report recommended the introduction of industrial development control which created a precedent to be followed at a later date in the sphere of commerce, and the Second World War witnessed a short sharp burst of decentralisation due to the threat of bombing, which despite dying out at the end of hostilities again set a pattern for future events. The Abercrombie Plan for Greater London published in 1944 hinted at the need for some measure of regulation and even dispersal, quickly followed by the New Towns Committee who shortly after the war advocated the relocation of some of London's offices in the proposed New Towns. Even now, however, they account for less than 2·5 million square feet in these areas. Under the 1947 Town and Country Planning Act commercial development was controlled by the usual devices employed in land-use regulation, namely zoning and density controls, particularly plot ratio and floor-space index.[2] The advent of comprehensive planning legislation in respect of office development led at the time to the chaotic situation caused by the exploitation by way of the notorious '3rd Schedule Loophole' whereby developers were allowed to replace certain buildings plus an extra 10% of the original cubic capacity. Modern office construction and design, however, permitted considerably more than 10% additional lettable floorspace to be achieved, and owing to the extraordinary compensation provisions included within the Act few applications, for what can only be described as excessive planning permission, were refused. The 3rd Schedule has been held directly accountable for the creation of 170 000 additional office jobs in Central London. Apart from this anomaly the general policy for directing the growth of the capital appeared contradictory, for on the one hand it propounded the relief of congestion while on the other it extended the zoning of areas for office location.

The now famous 'boom' in office development of the late fifties and early sixties was due to the release of pent-up demand caused by the war, the shortage of materials, building licence control, a reaction against general immediate post-war uncertainty, and the growing trend towards service industry investment. These forces all led to increasing central area congestion, the displacement of traditional central area uses, the exacerbation of regional imbalance and an increased pressure upon the green belt for the release of land. Admittedly some decentralisation of office users occurred but they were largely voluntary and perhaps even inevitable, caused by rising rents and land prices in the metropolis. Furthermore, a significant proportion of the moves were only made over a short distance, a large number of firms transferred to sites in Middlesex, and this period in the late fifties marked the beginning of Croydon's vast expansion. The areas zoned in the surrounding home counties as locations for decentralisation merely attracted additional companies to the South East, thus complicating the issue.

The failure of the London County Council in controlling the growth of office development led in 1963 to the formation of the Location of Offices Bureau, an agency designed to encourage the transfer of jobs out of London. Ironically the Bureau's address is Chancery Lane, London W.C.1. Devoid of statutory authority or adequate financial backing to provide inducements, its success has been strictly limited. Even the newly appointed Director recognised the task ahead, and admitted in a *Times* article, 'King Canute had the advantage over me—King Canute knew that if he couldn't stop the tide coming in, at least he knew that it would go out again.'[3]

In 1964 the now renowned 'George Brown Ban' was retrospectively introduced by the Control of Office and Industrial Development Act 1965 in a further attempt to rationalise office growth. It instituted the system of Office Development Permits, roughly similar to Industrial Development Certificates, which applied initially to all proposed development in the South East and Midlands over 3000 square feet. These permits were to be obtained from the Board of Trade and without which planning permission was invalid. The principal aims were to solve regional imbalance by attracting, or rather diverting, firms to development areas, ease congestion caused by office employment in Central London and increase the supply of houses by focusing the attention of the construction industry on residential building instead of commercial. The criteria for issuing an O.D.P. in the selected areas for control were that no extra employment should be created and that the scheme should be in the public interest. Initially it was envisaged as a temporary measure, rather like income tax, until a more positive policy in respect of office location and decentralisation could be formulated. The system has come in for a great deal of criticism, but it did provide a breathing space, although it probably contributed to the spiralling increase in rents that has occurred over the last ten years. In 1961 City of London office accommodation was letting at under £2 per square foot in prime positions, West End rents were under £1 and suburban and provincial levels were under 50 pence, whereas in 1971 the rents were about £15, £8 and £3 respectively. The introduction of permits has been vilified because it did not reduce congestion, demand increased unabated, firms made more intensive use of existing premises, there exists a continued pressure for prestige locations, and dispersal to the regions is not an acceptable alternative to many firms. In the period between 1964 and 1967, when an additional 35 million square feet of floorspace was constructed throughout the country, 56% was in the South East, and the next 'blessed' region was the North East with 10%.[4]

Location theory for industry might be unsophisticated but for offices it is primitive.[5] The policy underlying it is indiscriminate, inconsistent, tardy and heavily reliant upon trial and error. Too much emphasis is placed upon the existing stock and future supply without sufficient regard to the nature of demand. Virtually no attempt has been made to define which office functions are most appropriate to central metropolitan positions, which to peripheral positions and which to the provinces, and how a policy of decentralisation, if considered expedient, might best be implemented. Moreover, there is a strong political reluctance to offer the necessary incentives to reinforce such a policy, in marked contrast to industrial relocation. A further major obstacle to the establishment of a consistent approach towards the problem is the conflict that persists at all levels and between all agencies involved in the execution of commercial development policy. National strategy is at odds with regional, regional vies with the dominance of the South East, particularly the Greater London Council, and the GLC possesses a dissident relationship with its constituent Boroughs.

Another problem that presents itself within a rather topical context is the vast and widening differential between the level of office rents in London and those that prevail in other European capitals. Commercial accommodation in the centre of Brussels lets at around £3·00 per square foot, Zürich about £4·00, whilst in London similar offices let at £15. These extraordinarily high rates are largely a function of planning control, and it is possible that such a policy could detract from the expansion of London as a commercial centre. In the same vein, some economic planners advocate using London as a 'nursery' for cultivating office employment with the inherent location advantages permitting firms to grow in strength and productivity until they grow in establishment to such an extent where they benefit from decentralisation to a number of provincial centres, maintaining only a small headquarters staff in the capital. Again it is suggested that office development control could interfere with this process. Another flaw that can be identified in the present approach is the lack of flexibility and discretion that manifested itself in respect of applications for office development over central area railway stations where no extra land is required and little extra burden is placed upon local public transport services, and yet forty-three such schemes proposed by British Rail were frustrated by the introduction of the 1964 ban. Despite the apparent scarcity of techniques of analysis and surveys of future requirement, even those that have been undertaken have all too often relied on inaccurate data and thus spread further confusion over office location policy. For years planners had been working on the assumption that 15 000 additional jobs were created in London every year and all predictions, forecasts, and strategy had been based upon this figure. Not until 1965 and the publication of Census data which indicated a total of about 6000 per annum was the estimate found to be incorrect. The fault was due to the fact that National Insurance card returns were used as a basis for calculation and many firms with their administrative headquarters in London exchanged the cards there for employees working throughout the country. This fundamental error illu-

153

strates the danger of placing too much reliance on certain information systems.[6]

The Greater London Council have now formulated more realistic employment and floorspace targets to assist in long-term planning. The current 1972–6 targets are higher than previous ones, for it is now considered that jobs were being lost at too fast a rate. Two levels of criteria have been adopted to judge locational suitability; firstly at a strategic level which is directly concerned with the overall performance of the metropolitan economy, and has yet to be defined; and secondly at a local level which has regard to the special benefits that a proposed scheme will bring to a particular area, how it fits in with other buildings, relates to car parking requirements, road building proposals, what assistance it can given to larger developments of which it forms a part, and how it is situated in terms of accessibility for workers.[7] To this end they have selected twenty-eight strategic centres and six major strategic centres throughout London towards which development will be channelled. In the light of their plans the GLC have been criticised for pursuing what has been described as an excessively parochial policy, ignoring in effect national need and regional requirements.

As it is the number of employees commuting to work that causes urban congestion, and not the sheer bulk of office buildings, it has been suggested that control should be exercised over the number of workers and not the amount of floorspace. The GLC have taken this concept of capacity into account and aim at achieving an average of 216 square feet per worker by 1976. This represents a considerable increase over prevailing standards, which are about 160 square feet per worker, with the statutory minimum a startling 43 square feet. Such a worker density standard does not provide an ideal measure because of varying conditions of employment and the inherent difficulties likely to be encountered in enforcement, but it is a more appropriate yardstick than building bulk.

Due to the tremendous conflict that pervades the area of commercial location policy and the remarkable lack of continuity that exists, there is a pressing need to devise a more rational basis by which to assess the respective forces that dictate the demand for, and supply of, office employment and development.

A great deal more research into the very dynamics of office growth, the importance of central and metropolitan location, the nature and degree of linkages both between various office uses and between other land uses. If decentralisation is settled upon as a desirable solution to urban congestion then effective positive inducements must be made available and perhaps, above all, a clearer definition of responsibility for office development and location among the various levels of the administrative and political hierarchies must be made.

Offices—references

1 Economist Intelligence Unit, *Survey of the factors governing the location of offices in the London area*, Location of Offices Bureau (1964).
2 See page 301.
3 Sturgess, E., *The Times*, 10 October 1963.
4 Ford, A., Unpublished thesis, Oxford Polytechnic (1972).
5 Lind, A., 'Location by guesswork', *Journal of Transport Economics and Policy*, 1, 1967.
6 Ford, *op. cit.*
7 Cowan, P. and Hillman, J., *Planning for London*, Penguin (1971).

Further recommended reading

Cowan, P., *et al. The Office: a facet of Urban growth*, Heinemann (1969).
Wright, M., 'Provincial Office Development', *Urban Studies*, November, 1967.

11 Shopping

Until recently the vast majority of shopping facilities in this country were unplanned, like Topsy they 'just grew', sometimes by historical accident and sometimes by way of convenience. Now great attention is being directed towards the provision of shopping, its location, size and character. This is scarcely surprising when, although figures vary, it is considered that retailing commands an additional investment of around £220 million every year. This represents an annual expenditure of approximately £12 000 million or one-third of the gross domestic product, employs over 2·6 million persons, or one in every twelve workers throughout the country, and exerts considerable magnetism over other land uses. Because of the important role it plays in the national economy, the location of shopping has become the concern not only of local but also of regional and central planning agencies, and increasingly exercises the minds of geographers, economists, surveyors, developers and town planners alike. Apart from these economic aspects shopping provides a social function acting as a focus of the community, a meeting place, and generally contributing to the well-being of society. Over the last few years it has displayed a changing character, the corner shop is disappearing, the old high street parades straddling the channel of greatest traffic congestion are giving way to the planned, covered, pedestrianised centres adequately supplied with car parking, children's crèches and a wide range of other services.

Central place theory

Being essentially, through not exclusively, a central area function the assessment of shopping demand and the decisions regarding retail location have their roots firmly planted in central place theory. The origins of this theory are to be discovered in the writings of von Thünen, a nineteenth-century Prussian landlord, who propounded an 'isolated state' theory based on the concept of the economic rent to be gained from agricultural production. He constructed concentric rings of land use radiating out from the market place which were dependent upon, and determined by, labour and transport costs.

The theory was developed and applied to retail service activity in the 1930's by two German academics, Walter Christaller, a geographer, and August Lösch, an economist. They extended the notion of centrality, defining and detailing the importance of central places with reference to a series of complementary regions, examining the trade areas or hinterlands for a range of different goods and services. From their analysis they ascertained that different types of business have different conditions of entry, which they described as thresholds, some requiring larger minimum trade areas, or support population, than others. Put another way, consumers spent varying amounts on different goods and services and purchased them at varying intervals. From this they postulated a clearly identifiable hierarchy of central places. In fact they approached the problem from opposite ends. Christaller constructed his hierarchy from the strongest or highest order centre downwards, requiring all his lower order centres to take account of them in determining their own location. Lösch, however, built his hierarchy from the lowest order goods and services upwards, allowing a certain degree of manipulation of the location of centres to obtain an optimum hierarchy taking account of every level.

In this country a similar study, but this time employing more empirical information, was undertaken by Dickinson. He examined the existing pattern of centres in East Anglia, classifying them according to their function and establishing an index of the services they provided. Many other parallel studies have been tackled, not unnaturally, their principal finding being that time rather than distance is the major determining factor in location.

The shopping hierarchy

From these studies of urban hinterlands and the pattern of retailing that emerges from their analysis, a hierarchy of shopping centres can be distinguished. This hierarchy is liable to change over a period of time. As a result of less available shopping time through increased female employment, rising car ownership and therefore greater mobility, a growing proportion of families possessing deep freezers and thus an added incentive to bulk-buy, worsening central area congestion and increasing expenditure on luxury durable goods promoting the demand for comparison shopping, the exact nature of the hierarchy is currently experiencing considerable alteration.

Although different definitions of the hierarchy are to be found, the following is a widely accepted summation:

1. Regional centre—which generally supports a population in excess of 300 000 and contains many specialist services and a full range of department stores. The best examples are probably the major conurbations such as Bristol, Leeds and Newcastle. It is predicted that such centres are likely to experience a decline in trade owing to increased car ownership and worsening congestion, but that the severity of the decline will vary from centre to centre. Where the whole spectrum of alternative centres is available the regional centre receives approximately 15% of total consumers' retail expenditure, most of which is spent on durable goods.

2. Sub-regional centre—usually supports a population of between 100 000 and 300 000 and includes national department and variety stores such as Marks and Spencer, John Lewis and Littlewoods. There is still a strong element of specialisation, but more limited than that of the regional centre. Examples of this level of centre include Warrington,

158

Cheltenham and Portsmouth. Currently almost 40% of expenditure passes to the sub-regional centre, and if current trends continue an increasing proportion of spending on durable goods will take place at this level.

3. District centres—cater for a catchment area of about 50 000, sometimes less, and normally include a variety store such as Woolworths, a Boots, and supermarkets like Sainsbury or Tesco. There are few, if any, specialist services and examples of this type of centre can either be isolated towns like Hertford and Colchester, or found in the suburbs of large cities like Cowley in Oxford or Leith in Edinburgh.

4. Neighbourhood centre—often indistinguishable from the district centre, but can be as small as 12 shops serving a population of 10 000. The functions of the neighbourhood and district centre are tending to merge together with the result that between them they account for about 25% of total consumer expenditure and very much more if other levels are not present.

5. Local centre—consisting of a few shops supplying a population of up to 2000, but nevertheless accounting for up to 20% of retail expenditure.

It must be stressed that this picture of the hierarchy represents a general description only. The exact nature of the pattern of retail expenditure can vary considerably from area to area, as can the character and size of the centres. It often occurs that not all levels in the hierarchy are always represented within a region, in which case a regional centre might have to double a sub-regional and even district centre. To illustrate the point, an alternative hierarchy was outlined by G. M. Lomas in his study of retail trading centres in the Midlands as follows:[1]

1. First Order or Metropolitan centre namely, London
2. Second Order or Provincial centre such as Birmingham
3. Third Order or Regional centre such as Shrewsbury
4. Fourth Order or Local centre such as Bromsgrove
5. Fifth Order or Service Villages.

The types of shops that are to be found in any particular centre depends upon the population required to support them profitably in business.

The following table gives some indication of the necessary support populations for various trades.

Table 1 (a)

Trade	Population
Grocer	750–1000
Butcher	2000–3000
Baker	4000–5000
Greengrocer	4000–5000
Off-licence	4000–5000
Chemist	4000–5000
Newsagent/Tobacconist	4000–5000
Ironmonger/Hardware	4000–5000
Fishmonger	5000–10 000
Delicatessen	5000–10 000
Clothing	5000–10 000
Supermarket	20 000

Source: *Retail Site Assessment* by R. K. Cox, Business Books, 1968

Assessment of shopping catchment

Any analysis of the potential location for shopping facilities involves two basic assessments. First it is necessary to calculate the size, shape, and extent of the 'catchment area'. Secondly, consideration must be given to the degree of trade which any new development will capture or attract from competitors who depend upon the same catchment area, sometimes called the 'market penetration'.

The catchment area is that sphere of influence from which the vast majority of retail sales for a particular centre or development are derived. There are several techniques available to assist in its measurement, most of which mainly relate to 'generative' shopping locations, those which positively attract their own custom direct from residential areas, as opposed to 'suscipient' shopping locations which depend upon the impulsive or coincidental purchases by customers attracted by some other activity.[2] There are a number of underlying factors which affect the sphere of influence or catchment areas of any centre. These can be briefly listed as the size of the centre, the proximity of competing centres, the variety of trades provided, the general accessibility, the deficiency in other levels of the shopping hierarchy, the car parking facilities, and the availability of other services.[3]

The following techniques can be employed to calculate catchment areas:

Experience and observation—although this scarcely qualifies as a technique, certain locations lend themselves to ready assessment. New housing estates, for example, will normally require a small local shopping centre, the catchment area of which is often all too obvious to see. The only problem remaining is deciding upon the correct number of shops.

Accessibility—naturally, the nearer shopping facilities are to the customer the more attractive they will appear. Because of this it is possible to calculate the approximate boundaries of a catchment area for any particular centre by analysing the travel habits of the surrounding population. A map can be drawn from public transport time-tables showing the spheres of influence for the centre under consideration and for other competing centres. Because of the increasing importance of the motor car in determining shopping habits, the next step is to decide how much time people are prepared to spend in travelling to the centre by private car. This is called the 'drive time' and is normally measured during off-peak traffic periods. The catchment area is calculated by constructing a series of zones devised by drawing a line connecting points of equal 'drive time', these are called Isochrones and are commonly established for 10, 15, 20 and 25 minutes. It is important that speed limits are strictly observed, that a standard family saloon is used, and that the calculation is done, as previously stated, in off-peak periods, that is between 10.00 a.m. and 3.30 p.m. A roughly similar procedure can be carried out for public transport, always remembering to take account of the pull or attraction of other centres. Having considered the degree of car ownership, and thus the likely division between private and public transport within the respective zones, the total potential population within the catchment area can be gauged by reference to the current Census, or Sample Census of Population, updated and corrected as necessary. Once the total population of the hinterland has been established, the next step is to assess what proportion of trade will be attracted to the new centre of proposed development. This is described later.

Reilly's Law of Retail Gravitation—propounded by Professor W. J. Reilly in 1929 and stating that 'two cities attract trade from an intermediate town in the vicinity of the breaking point, approximately in direct proportion to the population of the two cities, and in inverse proportion to the squares of the distances to the intermediate towns'. This statement was expressed in the formula:

$$\text{Number of miles from City } A \text{ to the outer limits of its catchment area} = \frac{\text{Mileage on road to adjacent town } B}{1 + \sqrt{\dfrac{\text{Population of town } B}{\text{Population of city } A}}}$$

The 'attraction factor' used by Professor Reilly was population and the 'deterrence function' distance. These have been found to be inappropriate in assessing both catchment area and turnover. This again is examined later when considering market penetration. Reilly's Law did, however, provide a basis from which a number of more sophisticated techniques have been developed.

Consumer survey—by employing shopping questionnaires and enquiring of customers their address, frequency of visit, purpose of visit, mode of travel, and general preference for particular centres it is possible, by plotting their point of origin on a map, to establish in broad terms the extent of the catchment area. This technique is only suitable when assessing a new development within an existing centre; although similar market research techniques have been applied to proposed new centres they tend to be generally less reliable. To ensure a satisfactory degree of accuracy the survey sample should be comparatively large, at least 10%, which can prove expensive.

Assessment of market penetration

Having calculated the total population within the sphere of influence of a particular centre it is necessary to discover how much trade is likely to be attracted there. Taking the total effective population, the overall retail expenditure can be gauged by multiplying this figure by the amount spent on shopping per head of population, available from the *Family Expenditure Survey* published in 1971. This provides information on regional variation, the proportion spent on food items, and can readily be updated to current price and volume levels by reference to the *Index of Retail Sales* issued by the Department of Trade and Industry. Based upon these calculations an assessment can be made in respect of the share which any proposed development might expect, depending once again upon such factors as accessibility, competition, car parking, complementary services, and size. Naturally, the farther away the prospective customers the less inclined they will be to travel. Experience, and the analysis of comparable developments in similar situations elsewhere, will indicate the proportion of population falling within the hinterland that will be prepared to travel to the proposed centre. The percentage in question, and the rate at which it 'shades off' with distance, varies according to individual circumstances. Other factors that must be taken into account are such things as unemployment, socio-economic groups, car ownership, and future employment policy, which all determine the exact nature of retail expenditure within a locality.

Once total predicted expenditure has been obtained the need to translate this demand into a physical context, in terms of how much floorspace, in how many shops, to assist in formulating a planning policy for retailing, arises. This is achieved by the use of 'conversion factors' which simply express turnover per square foot of gross floorspace. They can be related to turnover per square foot of selling space, but this is of greater moment to the developer in the management of his property rather than to the town planner concerned with the physical extent of building.

These factors display a regional variation, being highest in the South East, relatively high in the North and in the Midlands, but much lower in the South West, South Wales, East Anglia and Scotland. They also tend to be higher in newly constructed premises, areas with a highly developed shopping hierarchy, and in town centres as opposed to suburban locations.

Other changing aspects of shopping also play a part in the steady rise of conversion factors: longer shopping hours, the

Table 1 (b)

Type	1972 Conversion factor per square foot gross	Average annual rate of increase
All goods throughout centre	£27	5%
Durables throughout centre	£16	4%
Convenience throughout centre	£31	2%
Single convenience goods shops	£36	2%
Single durable goods shops	£34	7%
Supermarkets	£50	5%
Department stores	£18	1%
Variety stores	£22	1%
Discount stores	£25	Unknown

Compiled from a number of sources

reduction of non-productive space and an increased proportion of expenditure on durable goods.[4] Although certain reservations have been expressed regarding the use of conversion factors they will provide a more reliable basis for trend projections than exists in forecasting employment, car ownership, population, and housing.

The potential trade for a new centre can be calculated by employing what is variously described as the 'vacuum', 'residual' or 'remainder' method whereby the total consumer expenditure going to other centres in the vicinity is assessed at first instance. The procedure briefly includes determining the prospective catchment area, gauging the total population by Census district, calculating retail expenditure by goods and socio-economic groups, allocating expenditure to more accessible and convenient centres, allowing for local traders' share, and estimating the potential trade remaining, for where positive the turnover will be available to the new centre, where negative the area is already overshopped.[5]

Shopping models

In recent years there has been a rapid advance in the development of sophisticated techniques that aim to assist in the assessment of the retail hinterland, the measurement of market penetration, and provide some explanation for retail land use location. These techniques are grouped together as shopping models. They seek to represent a real world situation in simple enough terms to permit examination of past and present shopping patterns and the prediction of future trends. Three basic categories of shopping model can be identified. First, those based on Central Place Theory which distinguish a hierarchy of centres derived from an appraisal of the purpose, frequency, and length of shopping trips. These have been developed from Walter Christaller's original work in respect of the location, size, and character of markets. Their main contribution is limited to supplying a general understanding of shopping habits. Second, those described as Spatial Interaction models which analyse the collective movements of large numbers of shoppers. These have evolved from Reilly's Law of Gravitational Retailing which merely established the 'breaking point' between two spheres of retail influence, useful enough in planning the provision of public transport services but inadequate when requiring a more accurate distribution of the trade area. Modifications have been devised providing more appropriate attraction factors such as floorspace instead of population, and a more reliable deterrence function, time in place of distance. Spatial Interaction models have also been constructed to account for competition between more than two alternative centres. Third are the category collectively known as Rent models which seek to explain in terms of land values the relationship between land use, shopping demand, and retail location.[6]

Probably the most popularly applied group are the Spatial Interaction models, all basically refinements of Reilly's Law and expressed as mathematical formulae. David Huff, for example, constructed a shopping model in 1963 that both took account of more than one centre, and, using floorspace and journey time, identified a series of 'breaking points' not only for different types of goods but also for varying frequencies of shopping trips.

He thus introduced a more sensitive and detailed examination of the probability of certain activities occurring. One of the first gravity models to be applied in practice was devised in 1964 by T. R. Lakshmanan and W. G. Hansen to help in formulating a policy towards shopping centres in Baltimore. Using Huff's model as a basis it considered the overlapping of competition and distribution of retail expenditure between competing centres. Variations of this approach have been employed in this country. In the study of a proposed 'out-of-town' shopping centre at Haydock a model was constructed to predict the future sale of durable goods at the new centre and indicate the effect it would have on existing centres. It demonstrated that if the new centre was built Liverpool and Manchester would eventually lose about 12% of their trade, Warrington, 46% and Wigan 41%.[7] Permission was not granted. The same principle has recently been applied in the London Borough of Lewisham, a complex situation involving the analysis of the distribution of retail expenditure between ten centres within metropolitan London. Using the cost of travel as the deterrence function, and total retail sales as the attraction factor, it attempted to gauge whether or not existing development proposals would lead to an excessive supply of shopping space.

Shopping models, by their very nature, can only be as good as the information available to them. They remain as partial techniques for they say little regarding the effect shopping habits have on other aspects of urban form.

Future changes

If retail expenditure continues to grow at the present rate, about 2·5% per annum, as seems likely, and if conversion factors behave similarly, rising on average at about 5% per annum overall, then it would appear that there will actually be a loss of floorspace. This does not mean that the development of shopping facilities will cease but that its location might change following the demolition of traditional centres and redevelopment elsewhere. The present policy pursued by the national multiple chains indicates a rationalisation of floorspace and outlets, with an increase in unit size and a continued transfer from counter

166

service to self-service. A factor which, in itself, enlarges the prime selling space, or zone A, from 1000 square feet to 10 000 square feet on average in central areas. The shift to supermarket domination is also likely to continue; it is anticipated that their numbers will swell from 3700 in 1969 to 6900 in 1975 despite the fact that the total number of shops is expected to fall from 196 800 to 155 000 over the same period.[8] It is further forecast that a growing proportion of total space will be given over to selling; mail order and automatic vending will expand, opening hours will be longer, shopping habits will change, and the pressure for out-of-town locations will increase. In view of all these changing factors a greater premium will be placed upon developing and applying accurate techniques for predicting retail demand and supply and determining shopping location. This assumes even more importance in the context of strategic planning on a regional scale where the hierarchy of centres plays a prominent part in influencing the siting of other activities. Perhaps a lesson is to be learnt from Denmark where an agency called the Institute of Centre Planning was set up under the Directorship of John Allpass to co-ordinate all the research directed towards planning studies.

Shopping—references

1 Lomas, G. M., 'Retail Trading Centres in the East Midlands', *Town Planning Institute Journal*, March, 1964.
2 Nelson, R. C., *The Selection of Retail Locations*, F. W. Dodge Corporation, New York (1958).
3 Cox, R. K., *Retail Site Assessment*, Business Books (1968).
4 Jones, R., *Vacant Space? Retail Floor Space Trends in the 1970's*, Polytechnic of Central London (1971).
5 Jones, C. S., *Regional Shopping Centres*, Business Books (1969).
6 NEDO, *Urban Shopping Models*, HMSO (1970).
7 Jones, C. S., *op. cit.*
8 Tanburn, J., *People, Shops and the 70's*, Lintas Special Projects (1970).

Further recommended reading

Capital and Counties Property Company, *Shopping for Pleasure 1969*, and *Design for Shopping 1970*.
Darlow, C., *Enclosed Shopping Centres*, Architectural Press (1972).
Multiple Shops Federation, *The Planning of Shopping Centres* (1964).
NEDO, *The Future Pattern of Shopping*, HMSO (1970).

12 Transportation

The greater the degree of specialisation, development and growth in society the greater the degree of dependence among urban activities and the greater the extent of movement between them. This movement or transportation has therefore assumed a paramount role in determining the location of activities and thus the use of land. Because of its impact and importance the measurement, guidance and control of the demand for movement and accessibility has become one of the major areas of concern for the physical land use planner. So much so, in fact, that a separate breed of transportation planners has emerged, equipped with its own theories, tools of analysis and techniques. The provision and management of transport facilities are among the most expensive of all urban services to cater for. They can only be properly designed if the present situation is fully understood and future requirements can be adequately predicted. Because of their complex and sophisticated nature, however, the treatment of this aspect of town planning is even more partial than many others dealt with in this book, providing little more than a glossary.

The transportation planning process

The essential format of the transportation planning process is based upon two fundamental assumptions. Firstly, that demands for movement are directly related to the various land use activities

168

that are pursued at both the origin and destination of journeys. Secondly, that a relationship inevitably emerges from these movement demands which can not only be readily quantified but also remains constant in the future. In this way, if the transportation planner can establish consistent quantifiable relationships between present day demands for movement and can also predict future land use activities, their nature, intensity and distribution, then by adroit application of current travel and land use equations he can further gauge future movement from land use activity forecasts.

A number of separate stages can be identified in the transportation planning process and whilst different authorities cite varying approaches the following is a convenient summation; surveys, forecasts, goal formulation, network design and testing, evaluation and implementation. Although it is but one stage in the overall process attention is primarily focused in this section upon certain inventories and the collection of data that are contained in the survey stage. Apart from making brief references in order to provide a general context the other stages are largely ignored, but can be followed up by consulting the list of further recommended reading supplied at the end of the chapter.

Surveys

As with any other planning process a clear understanding of the present is a vital prerequisite to a forecast of the future and the preparation of appropriate policy.

The first step in any survey is to carefully define the area of study, draw a suitable boundary around the significant catchment or hinterland of the area concerned and divide it into apposite zones. Although some external zones will be described outside the boundary to account for commuting or through traffic they will be, comparatively, much larger than the zones drawn internally within the boundary. All zones should be drawn up to coincide as closely as possible with Enumeration Districts so that demographic data can be related to transportation. The internal zones are further sub-divided according to different urban activities such as residential, commercial or industrial so as to assess more accurately the varying transport demands of alternative land uses.

169

The actual number of zones employed depends upon the degree of accuracy required and the budgetary constraints imposed.

Two main types of survey can be distinguished, those relating to land use activities and those relating to the pattern of movement between them. Although a host of major surveys relating to land use such as employment, commercial floor area and population, as well as those relating to the characteristics of movement such as the speed, volume and density of traffic, are undertaken, the principal inventory which frequently includes, or is classified according to these other elements, revolves around the Origin and Destination Survey. The purpose of this is to obtain information on traffic (a) that passes through the area having both origin and destination outside, (b) that which travels to the area having its origin outside and destination inside, (c) that which travels away from the area having its origin inside and destination outside and (d) that which travels within the area with both origin and destination inside. In this way the pattern of transport for the particular town or city can be identified, and the needs and priorities for alternative strategies can be established. Depending upon the type of traffic movement involved a range of survey techniques are available which can roughly be divided into Home Interview Surveys and Cordon Surveys.

Home interview surveys on a representative sample of the population can be carried out on either a personal basis or by means of a carefully prepared questionnaire. Besides collecting mere statistical information on the travelling habits of the local inhabitants they also provide an insight into the general characteristics and behaviour of households enabling conclusions to be drawn which can be incorporated into a transportation model at a later stage in the process. This technique provides very detailed information and is singularly successful in appraising the journey patterns to particular establishments such as factories, army camps or universities. It cannot be used, however, for collecting information regarding trips having origins outside the study area which can exceed 30% of total trips; its reliability depends heavily upon the expertise of the interviewer, a large proportion of non-work trips are all too often forgotten, and it is relatively expensive to mount.

Cordon surveys, sometimes called screenline surveys, are conducted on traffic routes at specially selected points permitting easy and comprehensive measurement. Cordons or screenlines should be so situated as to record inter-urban and intra-urban trips. Once again an interview approach is normally employed, either at the roadside or by issuing pre-paid postcards. With the full roadside interview all motorists, or, more usually, a predetermined proportion of them, are stopped at selected points on the various cordon lines and questioned about the origin, destination and purpose of their journey. Because of the inevitable delays involved, the consequent shortage of time for questioning and the reluctance and avoidance on the part of drivers, the results are not always reliable. The cost of mounting these surveys is also extremely high. The postcard questionnaire however provides a fairly cheap form of survey. The cards are handed out at check points along the cordon lines and filled in by the recipients at a later time, thus reducing delay to a minimum. The response rates vary but are generally around 30% which is an adequate base upon which to conduct an analysis. Data regarding the travel habits of persons using public transport can also be obtained from direct interview whilst they commute, or from questionnaires that they are asked to fill in either during or after their journey. In both cases response rates are likely to be very much lower than those from private motorists. The volume and length of journeys in the public sector is, however, comparatively simple to calculate from observation and ticket sales, but the actual origins, final destinations, and therefore real desire lines, are very much more difficult to compute. Detailed information relating to commercial traffic movements can be obtained from office interviews with firms based in the locality, and a similar procedure can be adopted for taxi-cab operators.

Cruder survey methods by way of simple traffic counts or the recording of vehicle registration numbers are available but rarely advisable except as checks and monitoring devices. Traffic counts, for example, which can be undertaken manually using Ministry Enumerator Forms or by employing continuous meters known as tally counters, record the overall direction and volume of traffic but only provide information regarding road capacity at a particular point. They say little about the beginnings or ends of

171

journeys and are therefore irrelevant in constructing 'desire lines', that is what the travel lines would be if straight line routes were provided, which are essential in plotting general policy.

Because the scale and location of car parking facilities can exercise a marked influence on the level and flow of traffic within an urban area and the availability of parking space can itself be a generator of movement, the management and control of parking becomes an important aspect of overall local planning authority transportation policy, and to ensure an informed approach a number of surveys are crucial.

To be in a position to plan for future provision a detailed record of existing facilities is essential. Plotted on a map, it should include private as well as public, temporary as well as permanent, and 'on' as well as 'off' street car parks. The road network should also be examined to make sure that no parking bays cause undue obstruction to the traffic flow. The information obtained from the transportation survey regarding the trip destinations gives a useful indication of the locational demand for car parks, and the distance motorists have to travel from their cars, once parked, can be gauged by use of questionnaire.

Once the planner knows how many parking spaces are available, and where they are, it is vital for him to ascertain the intensity of their use, and the length of time they are used for individual cars. The intensity of use should not only be measured at different times of the day to allow for commuting, shopping, or entertainment peaks, but also on different days of the week to allow for local markets, early closing and weekend trippers. The duration of stay is calculated to identify the relative proportions of short-term and long-term parkers.

From an appraisal of the parking demand of different land uses, how many employees require long-term facilities, how many clients require convenient short-term, and what degree of service traffic requiring access is likely, for example, an overall picture emerges. From this information a set of standards can be devised which apply to offices, shops, restaurants, theatres, hospitals and all other urban activities that generate traffic and demand parking space. Apart from describing the existing space available and the extent to which it is used, the survey results will also reveal any

172

deficiency or surplus in the system. One further aspect of conducting a survey regarding planning for parking provision is the location of car parks in respect of transport routes. The sudden uncontrolled disgorgement of large numbers of long-term parkers at peak hours onto important intersections can have disastrous repercussions on the performance of the road network.

Forecasts

Once an outline of the existing situation has been established forecasts are required to estimate what the transportation system for a particular area will have to cater for in the future.

In order to estimate future provision of transport services it is imperative to know the likely trends in population for the area under study. Not only does demand increase in absolute terms as population grows, but the number and length of trips made per head of population also increase. The techniques for predicting population growth have already been outlined but suffice it to say that they are subject to uncertainty.

Having conducted population projections it is possible to relate these to the other forms of human activity that constitute urban life and which require both land use provision and communication. This involves forecasting the future patterns of retailing, employment, leisure and education to provide some indication of the number of trips that will be created based upon an analysis of existing travel habits and prevailing trends. Once again the larger and more dispersed the urban structure becomes the greater the number and length of trips.

Apart from these general population and land use considerations it is essential that social and economic factors are taken into account to ensure effective forecasting. Even a change in the pattern of household formation can affect the demand for transport services, for as households increase so too do car ownership and total trips. In this country the change is now so gradual that it exerts little influence. Of some relevance, however, is the fact that richer residential areas, having a higher degree of car ownership, produce more traffic per head of population than do poorer residential areas. It is therefore advisable to take the socio-economic distribution of the population of a town into account when planning the provision of roads. Furthermore, the proportion of employed persons in a community can have a similar effect, particularly at peak hours at which time the transport system has to cater for its greatest capacity. It is therefore necessary to study the nature and characteristics of existing and possible future activity rates. In the same context it is worth giving some consideration to the length and pattern of the working day. Reduction in the number of working days, staggering of hours, introduction of shift work, shortened lunch hours and longer holidays all contribute to the overall level of demand for services, particularly public transport.

Another important economic aspect that determines transportation demand is the general level of prosperity. When a high level of economic activity is experienced a greater pressure is placed upon existing road space, and if the prevailing rises in the standard of living are maintained both car ownership and mileage are likely to increase.

Goal formulation

The clear and rigorous statement of goals and objectives is a vital part of any planning process. They are the criteria by which any scheme is framed and tested. In transportation studies they may take the form of relatively quantifiable aims such as achieving a certain benefit/cost ratio, minimising residential demolition, attaining certain capacities, removing through traffic from central and environmental areas, or even minimising the loss of human life from traffic accidents. Alternatively they may be related to the overall development plan in a more subjective manner such as revitalising public transport, minimising the disruption to the general environment, or maximising convenience and comfort. Whatever transportation plan is selected it must be shown to be the best in terms of the stated goals.

Network design and testing

Perhaps the most intricate and involved stage in the transportation planning process is the construction and simulation of possible networks or systems which meet future movement forecasts

174

within the broad objectives of the development plan. To assist in the design of these networks a large number of computer aided transport models have been developed. In essence a transport model simply attempts to describe the travel patterns of large numbers of people. In the light of existing information regarding land use activities, the movement between them, and projected trends within the study area the model examines the reasoning behind individuals' decisions to make journeys (trip generation) the probable destination of those journeys (trip distribution) the route they will take (traffic assignment) and the means of transport that will be used (modal split).

Significant improvements have been made of late in the development of comprehensive land use prediction models which seek to describe the location decisions of households, firms and other types of urban activity based upon the principle that such decisions are to a large extent dictated by the costs of overcoming distances which separate inter-related and interacting activities. The transport model, which is itself composed of the many sub-models relating to the generation, distribution, assignment and mode of movement, is therefore seen to be part of an integrated process of urban spatial interaction.

Evaluation and implementation

Such technical advances as those outlined above have permitted the transportation planner to create increasingly more realistic working representations of urban areas and to test various alternative plans by computer simulation, assessing their performance against prescribed objectives. It has been suggested that there are four ways in which transportation plans should be evaluated; numerical, checking the computational validity of forecasts; operational, assessing the potential stresses and failures that might occur in the system; environmental, gauging the aesthetic impact of any proposed transport plan; and economic, measuring the respective cash-flows and financial repercussions that result from particular plans.

Plans are of little value unless they are put into practice and yet the stage of implementation is possibly the most neglected of all in any planning process. Essentially it involves the co-ordination and management of public or internal agencies involved in the execution of the transport plan, the stimulation of private or external agencies, the control of resulting development, and the careful scrutiny or monitoring of the way in which the plan performs.

Although transportation planning has assumed a major role in determining the nature and function of urban development, it is essential that such studies are not seen in isolation, set apart from the other stages and components of the planning process. Being a comparatively complex discipline, possessing a range of seemingly sophisticated techniques, and achieving further deification by some due to the extensive use of computers, there is a danger that the policies and programmes for transport might dominate those of other land use developments. Fortunately, there has been increasing co-ordination of late between the various aspects of urban planning, and the knowledge, propagated perhaps by a systems approach, that everything affects everything else, ensures that the execution of the broad strategy and the relationship of the constituent parts receives continuous review and revision.

Transportation

Further recommended reading

Brierley, J., *Parking of Motor Vehicles*, C. R. Books Ltd (1962).

Bruton, M., *Introduction to Transportation Planning*, Hutchinson (1970).

Creighton, R., *Urban Transportation Planning*, University of Illinois (1971).

Lane, R. *et al.*, *Analytical Transport Planning*, Duckworth (1971).

Leeds City Council, *Planning and Transport: The Leeds Approach*, HMSO (1969).

Ministry of Transport, *Traffic and Transport Plans* Circular 1/68, HMSO (1968).

Wilson *et al.*, *New Directions in Strategic Transportation Planning*, Centre for Environmental Studies, Working Paper 36 (1969).

Wingo, L., *Transportation and Urban Land*, Resources for the Future Inc. (1961).

13   Leisure and recreation

In common with most other Western European and North American countries, Great Britain is having to cater for ever-increasing demands for recreational and leisure facilities. The process and its impact are described by Michael Dower in his book *Fourth Wave, the challenge of leisure*.[1] 'Three great waves have broken across the face of Britain since 1800. First, the sudden growth of dark industrial towns. Second, the thrusting movement along far flung railways. Third, the sprawl of a car based suburbs. Now we see, under the guise of a modest word, the surge of a fourth wave which could be far more powerful than all the others. The modest word of leisure.' Though often used in the same context, the terms leisure and recreation are not synonomous. 'Leisure is essentially the time one has free from income earning responsibilities and from personal and family housekeeping activities . . . Recreation, in any socially accepted sense, involves constructive activities for the individual and the community.'[2]

Five basic factors determine the demand for recreation:

1. *Population growth*—The population of England and Wales alone in 1951 was 44 million, it is now over 49 million, by 1980 it will be approximately 53 million, and by the year 2000 it will probably be in the region of 62 million. This indicates a 25% increase in under 30 years.[3]

2. *Changing work patterns*—The working week is now, on average, 41 hours long, whereas in 1950 it was 45 hours long.[4] It is

expected to decline by a further 25% by the end of the century,[5] due to increasing automation, and a different attitude to work. Paid holidays are becoming longer and more common, work sharing is a distinct possibility, and there is an increasing tendency towards the taking of second holidays in this country. The retirement age might be lowered, and even assuming that this does not occur, there will in any event be 33% more people above the existing level by the year 2000.

3. *Income*—It has been found that there is greater degree of participation in recreational activities by those in higher income groups,[6] and real income is expected to rise by about 66% in the next 30 years. Moreover, where previously leisure was the prerogative of the few, economic circumstances have dictated a change in the leisure and recreation patterns throughout all income groups.

4. *Education*—The group of people that indulge most in organised outdoor recreation are those pursuing a course of education.

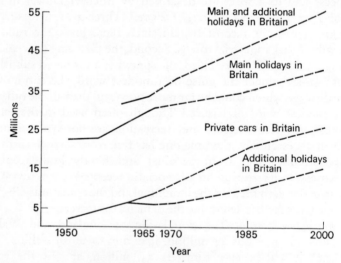

Fig. 22 Trends in holidays and car ownership

SOURCE: Robert Arvill, *Man and Environment: Crisis and the Strategy of Choice*

There is expected to be an increase of around 100% in the numbers involved in higher education by the year 2000.

5. *Car ownership*—Increased mobility means increased accessibility to recreation facilities. Driving itself is considered by many to be a leisure pursuit. Car ownership, which stood at 2 million in 1949, and 12 million in 1970, is predicted by the Ministry to reach an unprecedented 20 million by 2000. Although such estimates have always been subject to revision, there can be no doubt that a substantial increase is likely.

Planning and recreation

The problem of both estimating future demand for, and organising the requisite supply of, recreational facilities is further aggravated by the introduction of modern farming methods and the increasing unsuitability of the countryside for leisure activities. Open field systems, intensification, and industrialised methods leave little room to spare. A great deal of research has been recently undertaken in respect of the concept of 'recreational capacity' which has been defined as 'the level of recreation use an area can sustain without an unacceptable degree of deterioration of the character and quality of the resource or of the recreation experience'. In many ways it is similar to Professor Colin Buchanan's notion of environmental capacity for residential areas. Three main elements can be discerned that together constitute the overall concept. First, ecological, because the intense use of an area for recreational purposes can cause damage in the form of erosion and compaction of the soil which in turn can have far-reaching effects on the local plants and animals. Second, physical, for the sheer weight of numbers can produce the most horrific visual impact, as anyone who has watched the cancerous growth of caravans along our coastline will substantiate. Third, economic, because other aspects of society regulate use and fix capacity by application of market forces.

The planning profession is required to predict change and distinguish between fads and fancies currently in vogue and the establishment of any long-term trends. To this end the formation of the Countryside Commission is of inestimable worth, providing both a comprehensive appraisal of existing circumstances and continuity for change. Recreation, by its very nature, however, lends itself to a variety of interpretations. To some it represents the immediate environment around their homes where they can while away their leisure hours. There seems little doubt, however, that current residential design is not geared towards providing adequate space for solitude or for hobbies. To others it means an escape to the countryside for any one of a range of activities, and, as already mentioned, the availability of land and facilities is gradually being whittled away.

It can, therefore, be seen that a need exists to plan urban open space with greater attention paid towards recreational demand. It has been suggested that such provison falls into two basic categories:[7] the local park, where children can play, mothers meet and the older generation relax; this must necessarily be close to the home. The other is the park, less local in character, still accessible, which supplies facilities for the whole community, such as golf, sailing and swimming. A more positive approach towards the green belt could assist in catering for the latter, together with the further development of 'green fingers' or 'wedges' of land penetrating to the heart of built-up areas. The Lee Valley Scheme is an admirable pioneer attempt in this direction. A further accomplishment in the context of urban recreation would be the formation of a network of interconnecting footpaths linking open spaces, community centres and residential areas, alongside an improvement in canal towpaths and riverside walks.

Increasing pressures are being placed upon the countryside from both agriculture and rural recreation demands. The two forces are not, however, irreconcilable, they merely require careful planning. One approach put forward refers to the special development of recreational areas in addition to the use of farmland, whereby the poorer quality agricultural land could be transferred to leisure uses, being ideally suited because of its varied topography with trees, water, and varied flora and fauna. Furthermore, camping and caravan sites could be provided, picnic spots selected, sporting facilities made available, all fitting within an existing agricultural economy. These measures in poorer areas should strengthen rather than weaken the rural heritage.[8]

To promote a greater degree of consistency and continuity in the assessment of recreation demand a classification of constituent elements is extremely valuable. Although none has been applied in this country, an example is provided by the *Report of the Outdoor Recreation Resources Review Commission* published in the United States. This sets out six basic recreation area groups:

'1. High density recreation areas suitable for weekend leisure, managed for recreation and sited close to major conurbations.

2. General outdoor recreation areas designed for less intensive use, with a great variety of activities in a natural setting.

3. Natural environment areas with natural surroundings and basic facilities.

4. Unique natural areas with natural phenomena that can be studied without harm.

5. Wild areas managed to maintain their wildness, with no facilities.

6. Historic sites, protected from overuse and managed to encourage proper use without spoiling.'[9]

A more detailed classification has recently been devised by Max Nicholson and appears in his book *The Environmental Revolution*. Here in the form of a chart of human impacts on the countryside the whole range of recreation pursuits are listed under the activity concerned, the area or type of land affected, the nature of effects arising and their incidence.

Work of this nature provides a foundation for recreation planning. What is really required, however, is a national plan that would take account of all the various interacting aspects of recreation planning, the calculation of demand, the problem of supply; the protection of footpaths, green belt and coastline; the conservation of wilderness areas for peace and solitude; the development of disused railway land for leisure pursuits; the creation of farm trails as well as nature trails for educational as well as recreational purposes; the promotion of urban open space and linked footpath systems, and a whole host of other considerations. It virtually amounts to a national scandal that no land use classification for leisure and recreation exists, and whereas this country possesses the most sophisticated control over urban areas, no similar decisions regarding priorities and

181

associated regulation in the form of zoning or density restrictions are provided for rural areas.

Leisure and recreation—references

1 Dower, M., *Fourth wave, the challenge of leisure*, Civic Trust (1965).
2 Palmer, J. E., 'Recreational Planning: a bibliographic review', *Planning Outlook*, Spring, 1967.
3 Registrar General, *Census and Quarterly Returns*, HMSO.
4 Sillitoe, K. K., *Planning for Leisure*, HMSO (1969).
5 West Midlands Sports Council Technical Panel.
6 Pilot National Recreation Survey Report, British Travel Association (1967).
7 Curl, J., 'Towards a National Plan', *Official Architect and Planner*, August, 1969.
8 Wibberly, G. P., 'Land Scarcity in Britain', *Town Planning Institute Journal*, **53**, 4, 1967.
9 Hookway, R. J. S., T.P.I. Summer School, 1967.

Further recommended reading

Burton, T. L. (ed.), *Recreation Research and Planning: A Symposium*, Allen and Unwin (1970).
Patmore, J. A., *Land and Leisure in England and Wales*, Newton Abbot, David and Charles (1970).

14 Evaluation

Once the broad goals and objectives for a particular planning problem have been established, and alternative courses of action have been prepared, the next step is to test these alternative strategies, comparing their respective advantages and disadvantages. This testing process is described as 'evaluation' and is intended to assist the decision maker in selecting his final choice. As evaluation entails more than just a description of alternatives, the various constituent elements of the plan must be identified and subsequently measured. In conducting this measurement the town planner will need to be equipped with techniques that assist him in the task. Lichfield[1] suggests a distinction between testing and evaluation, stating that tests of various kinds are continuously undertaken throughout the planning process appraising such aspects as conformity to density standards, adherence to green belt policy, feasibility, consistency, and ability to solve the planning problems posed. The evaluation of alternative plans takes place after testing, and the technique employed should take account of the fact that a town or city is a complex organism with many, often divergent, interests. To cater for this, Lichfield[2] sets out ten criteria which an appropriate technique should satisfy. It should:

'1. Have regard to the stated or implied objective of the decision makers (which may or may not be the objectives of those for whom they are planning)

2. Cover all systems of urban and regional facilities which are encompassed in the plan
3. Cover all sectors of the community which are affected, that is those which should be included within the decision maker's concern
4. Sub-divide the sectors into producers/operators of the plan output and its consumers so that all the 'transactions' implicit in the plan are considered
5. Take account of all costs to all sectors, including externalities
6. Take account of all benefits to sectors including externalities
7. Measure all the costs and benefits in money terms
8. Facilitate the adoption of a satisfactory criterion for choice
9. Show the incidence of the costs and benefits on all sectors of the community
10. Be useable as an optimising tool with a view to ensuring the best solution.'

It is impossible to describe the entire range of techniques that present themselves for adoption. The principal methods of evaluation have been selected for consideration, most other approaches being derivatives of some form.

Cost benefit analysis

The technique of Cost Benefit Analysis (C.B.A.) has largely developed in response to requests for a more effective way of choosing between alternative policies in the public sector. It provides a practical way of assessing the desirability of projects and in doing so takes account of all the relevant and foreseeable consequences of a particular decision. It places particular emphasis upon the consideration and measurement of social costs and benefits as well as private costs and benefits, taking both a long and wide view.[3] In making a decision, for example, the individual entrepreneur considers only his own private costs and benefits but in pursuing a particular course of action which to him appears attractive he might impose a whole range of costs upon others not directly concerned. Conversely, there are certain services and facilities of a non-profit-making nature that both confer benefits upon large numbers of persons in the public sector as well as render other profit-making uses of land more profitable. C.B.A. is a means by which a longer and wider view of the full implications of respective strategies can be judged. It attempts to ensure the optimum allocation of available resources so as to maximise the welfare of the whole community.

It has a relatively long history, emanating in France in the mid-nineteenth century in the writings of Dupuit, and later Pigou, who were largely concerned with the utility of public works. It came into prominence in the U.S.A. at the turn of the century and gained considerable currency in the 1930's when it was applied to investment in the vast water resource projects undertaken as part of the 'New Deal'.

Prime consideration was given, however, to 'internal' cost and benefits, that is those directly concerned with the implementation of the particular project. The application of cost benefit analysis was broadened by the end of the Second World War when operating agencies included more and more 'secondary' costs and benefits, or, put another way, those repercussions external to the project under consideration. Greater attention was also given to the problem of assessing 'intangible' costs and benefits, those which defy ready quantification in a numerical form such as aesthetic or environmental factors.

Through time the major limitations are becoming increasingly evident. Above all the political or social character of many decisions distorts the true value of C.B.A., as does the very scale at which this technique is employed, for the greater the magnitude of investment the less accurate the analysis.

The primary considerations when undertaking a Cost Benefit Analysis are:
1. What costs and benefits are to be included?
2. How are they valued?
3. At what interest rate should they be discounted?
4. What are the relevant constraints?

(1) What costs and benefits are included?

The respective costs and benefits entailed in the various alternatives can be divided into *internal* or *primary*, and *external* or *secondary*. The identification and inclusion of primary costs and benefits is comparatively straightforward, but in accounting for the external effects of their actions undertakers of public investment projects should only consider those aspects that alter the physical production potentiality of other producers. They should not take into account any side effects that merely reflect in price changes of products or factors. The closure of a local bus service might reduce the catchment area for a regional shopping centre and cause a decline in retailing, thus imposing an external cost which should be included, but the fall in the shop rentals and the drop in the price of land for retailing should be excluded. If not it would amount to 'double counting'.[4]

One of the major difficulties encountered whilst conducting such an analysis is in defining the 'cut-off point', for proposals involving large-scale public investment tend to have a ripple effect spreading out from the centre and becoming increasingly more diffuse and difficult to identify.

(2) The valuation of costs and benefits

Once identified, the various costs and benefits must be valued. This should be done in terms of money value wherever possible, with annual sums being discounted back to a present capital value. Some components with a record of open market transactions easily lend themselves to valuation, for example rents, loans, and construction costs. Others, where no market exists, require a system of substitute or 'shadow' prices to permit financial appraisal. This system of 'shadow pricing' is popularly employed in the evaluation of time saving, particularly in respect of leisure time. The C.B.A. on the M.I. valued leisure time at various levels between 10p and 50p per hour and the Cambrian Coastline Study at 15p.

Grave problems occur when investment projects are themselves large enough to affect prevailing prices and values, further market imperfections such as the monopolistic control over certain factors may influence the prices for particular goods and services, thus hindering the calculation.

Taxes and controls can also affect the valuation of respective costs and benefits. It has, for example, been decided in many schemes to exclude the tax element in the estimation of fuel saving from road improvements. The tax foregone, however, must be recouped from another source—but with what effect!

Another aspect of the evaluation procedure relates to what are often described as the 'distributional' consequences. The schemes under consideration will often reallocate resources from one sector to another, some might gain, some might lose. The result might well have social, economic or political undertones. This redistribution of wealth involves other questions regarding the marginal utility of money, £1 in London is not necessarily worth the same in Sunderland. Similarly, £1 to a rich man cannot be equated with £1 to a poor man. Perhaps the most vexed and thorny aspect of valuation is in respect of those elements that defy financial quantification, the 'intangibles'. It has become fairly common practice to set these factors aside and consider them separately, either by merely listing or noting them, or by applying some form of crude weighting or ordinal ranking. This is very much the preserve of the politician or decision maker.

(3) The choice of interest rate

In order to reduce or discount the value of the various elements and their constituent cash flows through time to a common base, namely the Present Capital Value, it is necessary to adopt an appropriate rate of interest. Five basic approaches offer themselves for possible selection:

a. *The government borrowing or lending rate:* this presents a tax based riskless choice. It is popular and easily applicable, but used for expediency rather than accuracy. The actual rate has normally fallen between 4% and 6%, but is becoming higher.

b. *Social time preference rate:* it is thought that the very nature of public investment is to attach greater weight to the needs of the future by way of long-term planning than would the private individual who prefers to discount far away costs and benefits at a much higher rate of interest. In other words, individuals are often short-sighted about the future and government intervention is justified to 'give adequate weight to the welfare of unborn generations'. The Social Time Preference Rate is therefore established at a lower level, invariably about $2\frac{1}{2}\%$. Its selection is open to considerable criticism.

c. *First year rate of return*: whereby the net benefits obtained during the first year of operation are expressed as a percentage of total cost.

d. *The opportunity cost rate of interest*: this relates to the return that could be gained if the project were not undertaken and the capital were invested elsewhere. This has obvious attractions in cost benefit analysis but again is hard to establish accurately. Central government has often laid down guidelines as to the level of certain opportunity cost returns, and they have varied from 8% to 10%.

e. *Sensitivity analysis*: in order to explore fully the implications involved in the selection of any particular rate of interest, it is often advisable to undertake the evaluation and discounting procedure using several rates of return. This is known as 'sensitivity analysis'.

(4) The constraints

In tackling a Cost Benefit Analysis it is vital to recognise the various constraints that surround project evaluation. They can be conveniently grouped as follows:

a. *Physical*: one or more of the inputs might be in inelastic supply.

b. *Legal*: there could be many problems associated with rights to access, easements, restrictive covenants, acquisition, and delays due to legislative procedure.

c. *Administrative*: two or more conflicting authorities or agencies might be involved, or the method of implementation might be too costly or complex as in certain proposed road pricing schemes.

d. *Distributional*: the effect on personal incomes by their re-allocation might be contentious or unwise. It might affect regional policy, or other pricing policies,

e. *Budgeting*: as always!

f. Political: perhaps above all! It is, however, a factor that is hard to account for in an objective manner in conducting such an evaluation.

Some applications of cost benefit analysis

One of the earliest C.B.A.s undertaken in this country was the Motorway 1 study carried out jointly by the Road Research Laboratory and Birmingham University. It was largely experimental in nature and being retrospective it merely sought to investigate the problems inherent in the technique, attempting to establish some form of approach to deal with such contentious items as accident costs and social time preference.

In 1963 Foster and Beesley conducted a C.B.A. on the proposed Victoria Line Underground extension. This was considered necessary because if a conventional 'internal' balance sheet were drawn up the proposed line would have made a loss at existing 'subsidised' fare levels. When 'external' costs and benefits, such as time and cost saving, together with greater convenience and comfort on that and other routes, were included, however, the construction was justified. In discounting the various cash flows it was stated that they would have liked to have used the Social Time Preference Rate of Return or, failing that, Opportunity Cost, but in fact expedience compelled them to adopt the prevailing market borrowing rate of 6%, although other rates were tested.

One of the most interesting studies to tackle the evaluation of 'intangibles' was that undertaken by Professor Colin Buchanan in Newbury where he constructed an Index of Environmental Accessibility to take account of the intrusion of various levels of traffic upon the town.

Other Cost Benefit Analysis studies have been pursued in connection with rehabilitation in comparison with redevelopment, by Martin Horne in Barnsbury and by Rothenburg and Mao in the United States. In their various ways these have measured the wider consequences of housing renewal, examining the general effect on income, employment, health, welfare, police, education, transport, and so on. British Rail have recently conducted a pilot study in respect of rail closures based upon the Cambrian

Coastline service between Pwllheli and Machynlleth. Other recent uses of the techniques have concerned the appraisal of the proposed Morecambe Bay Barrage, the Greater London Council's urban motorway plans, the suggested Channel Tunnel project, comparing the relative merits of a tunnel crossing with a bridge, and, of course, the much vaunted, yet much vilified, Roskill Commission.

The value of cost benefit analysis

Whatever its shortcomings, the value of C.B.A. lies in the fact that it declares the hand of the planner and the decision maker, laying bare his objectives, criteria, and costing. It acts as a checklist for the professional, and at the same time sets the stage for public participation and criticism. There is, however, the grave danger of a valuable and essentially simple device becoming over-sophisticated and the means of evaluation becoming more important than the end.

The planning balance sheet

This technique is closely associated with Cost Benefit Analysis but was first put forward in 1956 by Professor Nathaniel Lichfield as a practical way of applying C.B.A. in town planning and development. The planning balance sheet sets out by identifying two broad categories of individuals or groups within the community, the producers responsible for introducing and operating the particular project, and the consumers who will be the recipients of its effects. Having determined the respective membership of these two sectors, the costs and benefits that accrue to them are compared and valued. Those that are capable of being assessed in money terms are entered into the Balance Sheet of Social Accounts, which is divided into Annual and Capital, Costs and Benefits. In that form, those that are considered to be intangible and defy monetary quantification are entered as I if capital items and i if annual, and similarly those that are measurable but because of time, expense, or lack of data are not measured are entered as M or m. If an increase over the existing

190

'do nothing' situation is envisaged then a positive (+) sign is employed; conversely, if a decrease is predicted a negative (−) sign is used. Some attempt is also made to gauge the degree of change between alternative plans by comparing the various elements one against another and arriving at either net advantage to one plan, or, where several alternatives exist, an order of preference. In more recent studies[5] a further sophistication has been introduced by attempting to rank or weight the various elements such as the relief of congestion or the displacement of population, and the affected agencies such as private and public vehicles or owner occupiers and council tenants. This practice of weighting or ranking involves a considerable amount of value judgement and political inference being injected into the evaluation, but if properly conducted can lead to far more realistic estimates.

Another problem that continually crops up in nearly all Cost Benefit Analyses is that of double counting, but the Planning Balance Sheet approach aims to eliminate not only double counting but also transfer payments and common items of cost and benefit at what is described as the reduction stage. The sheet used for reduction subtracts all items entered more than once, which are marked with an *E*, and all items of equal worth in each alternative; the remaining items are summed algebraically and reduced to a common form, either annual or capital.

As with other evaluation techniques the Planning Balance Sheet encounters difficulty in valuing those items which possess no market price, the inevitable intangibles, and further encounters the problem outlined previously in the appraisal of Cost Benefit Analysis regarding the selection of an appropriate rate of return for discounting public sector investment. The Balance Sheet does not, however, set out to provide a result for proposed schemes in terms of a rate of return or net present value, its inherent value lies in 'exposing the implications of each set of proposals to the whole community and to the various groups within that community, and also in indicating how the alternatives might be improved or amalgamated to produce a better result. The purpose of the approach is the selection of a plan which, on the information available, is likely to serve best the total interest of the community.'[6]

191

Goal achievement

This technique seeks to establish the extent to which a plan meets the original objectives set by the politicians. The most notable approach is that put forward in 1968 by Morris Hill in the evaluation of alternative transportation plans.[7] Hill's technique evolved from criticism of the Planning Balance Sheet for its tendency to classify all the costs and benefits of alternative strategies with no regard to the politics of a particular situation. He suggests that the goals and objectives of a scheme should be made explicit and that the alternative strategies be measured in terms of the extent to which they achieve them. The constituent elements of the plan, such as housing, employment and open space, are pre-weighted to indicate the political preference or priority attached to them. The various agencies or groups that will be affected by the plan are also weighted to reflect the political pressure they exert. In this way a matrix, or table, showing the relative performance of the weighted objectives and agencies is constructed. Subsequently social accounts are drawn up in much the same way as in the Planning Balance Sheet.

The most controversial aspect of this technique is the assessment of weights. Probably the most effective way of establishing these and incorporating them into the evaluation is by public participation and the use of questionnaires. This approach was adopted in the preparation of the South Hampshire structure plan when the goals and objectives devised by the professional planners and the political representatives were tested and in fact confirmed by a random sample survey of 3000 local residents. The results of this survey were used extensively in the evaluation of four major alternative strategies.

Although conceptually pleasing, *goal achievement* is very difficult to apply fully in practice, and its viability relies very heavily upon the validity of the weighting procedure.

Partial evaluation techniques

Because it is impossible to include all the repercussions of any particular planning proposal it can be said that to some extent all evaluation techniques are partial. In certain circumstances, however, owing to a shortage of funds, or the restriction of time, it may not be possible to attempt a full cost benefit analysis and resort has to be taken to a more limited approach.

Urban threshold analysis

This technique was first propounded by Professor Boleslaw Malisz in 1963[8] to establish certain boundaries for calculating economic growth in relation to long-range physical land use planning. It was originally formulated, tested and applied in Poland and subsequently in Russia and Italy. Over the last few years it has been successfully incorporated by the Planning Research Unit of Edinburgh University into a number of planning studies in Scotland, notably the *Grangemouth-Falkirk Regional Survey and Plan*,[9] and the *Central Borders Study*,[10] both published in 1968.

The theory upon which the technique has been devised is concerned with the initial investment costs required to overcome successive limitations in the urban development of a village, town or even region. Whilst not providing a comprehensive approach to planning it is intended to assist in the selection of alternatives and provide a firmer foundation for decision-making. Basically the theory suggests that towns encounter certain physical limitations to their growth. These limitations are called *thresholds*, and whilst not insuperable can only be overcome by exceptionally high injections of capital investment. Once this additional investment is made the average costs of development decline until the next threshold is encountered. In this way threshold costs can be described as variable costs, over and above the normal investment costs associated with urban development.

Three basic categories of threshold can be identified. Firstly, *physical* thresholds such as marshland, steep slopes or a river which restrict urban expansion. Secondly, *quantitative* thresholds imposed by the maximum potential capacity of public utilities such as sewage plant, drainage, water supply, or a road system. Thirdly, *structural* thresholds created by the internal structure of a town; for example, an increase in population might require an expansion in the existing shopping centre facilities where in fact no extra space is available, necessitating considerable expenditure to achieve a satisfactory solution such as multi-decking or expensive redevelopment of the surrounding area.

Although some degree of overlap is inevitable, these various thresholds come in different sizes and at different times in a town's expansion. The programming of the application of threshold theory and analysis to long-range town planning presents certain problems but in general certain advantages of using this technique have been distinguished.[11] It assists in defining growth potential and in assessing the most efficient alternative approaches towards future development by indicating, if various thresholds have to be crossed, the least-cost alternative. It aids in establishing the programme and priorities of public investment. It shortens the process of reviewing and revising development plans. Moreover, it can be used in the selection of regional growth points. Thus it provides, albeit in a more sophisticated cost-orientated manner, a technique that is not entirely dissimilar to the 'old fashioned' sieve maps which showed land physically difficult to develop, areas of high landscape value, agricultural worth, commercial woodland, water catchment grounds, as well as that land that could only be supplied with sewerage, drainage, or water with great difficulty and expense, and those areas that were relatively inaccessible. The preparation of threshold maps is described by Kozlowski in the *Town Planning Institute Journal* and that of sieve maps by Lewis Keeble in *Principles and Practice of Town and Country Planning*, from which the differences, if any, can be compared.

Despite the inherent advantages of threshold analysis in identifying the most suitable direction for future urban expansion certain reservations regarding its application have been expressed. It has been criticised for placing too much attention upon cost and not enough upon benefit, for stressing capital costs and playing down recurrent ones, and for ignoring some costs, such as accident and congestion costs, altogether. Further, there are a number of thresholds, particularly quantitative, that are extremely difficult to measure. Also costs may change over time relative to one another, development on flooded or steep land becoming suddenly much cheaper due to technological advance. Lastly, it

194

has been said that many thresholds exist, all interacting and virtually indistinguishable.

It is clear, however, that threshold analysis can play an important role in the evaluation of alternative planning policies, particularly as part of a wider cost benefit analysis, and in respect of focusing attention upon the suitability and availability of land for urban development.

Financial appraisal

Evaluation involves the choice between alternatives, and each alternative will possess a range and variety of respective costs and benefits, some of which will be quantifiable in money terms and others 'intangibles' which will defy such quantification. In any planning proposal there is likely to be a large element that can be costed. It is, perhaps, unfashionable to direct great attention to this aspect of town planning, but with an ever-increasing proportion of investment in connection with the 'built environment' being undertaken by public agencies, it is critical to be as precise as possible in respect of public moneys.

There has, in the past, been a distinct lack of harmony between the Financial Analyst and the Physical Planner. The one being an accountant, valuer, quantity surveyor or economist and concerned, in essence, with judging the relative 'cash flows' or prospective developments, how much revenue they will bring in, for what expenditure, at what time and at what risk. The other being an architect, planner, sociologist or engineer associated with design, aesthetic, social and environmental factors. These diverse disciplines, grouped for convenience into their two categories, often appear to be pulling in different directions. This is caused by their ill-conceived and poorly timed integration within the planning process. Financial appraisal is frequently introduced all too late in evaluation, being neglected in the preliminary investigation stage where it could save a great deal of otherwise abortive work. Moreover, it is the dilatory nature of its exercise that precludes it as a device for improving plan preparation and selection, and relegates it to the rather stigmatised position it at present occupies. It is, however, capable of assisting in the working up and improvement of proposed plans by indicating a more propitious development or funding programme. It can also expose, at an early stage, those elements that warrant greater consideration or alteration. It might, for example, be advisable to change existing public transport services to enlarge the potential catchment area of a new shopping precinct prior to development in order to render it commercially viable. An adjustment in the phasing of a town centre redevelopment to allow for early completion of shops and offices rather than civic buildings might so transform the cash flows of the scheme as to make a seemingly redundant proposal acceptable. Or a delay in landscaping by two or three years might elevate one alternative above another.

In tackling the financial appraisal conventional valuation methods are being replaced by Discounted Cash Flow (D.C.F.) analysis which differs only in being more sophisticated, more detailed, more time and risk conscious, and yet more flexible in operation. There are two basic methods of conducting a D.C.F. analysis. First, the Net Present Value method which calculates profitability by subtracting the present value of all expenditures *when they occur* from the present value of all revenues *when they occur*, employing an 'opportunity cost' rate of discount, that is the rate of return that could be earned by investing in the next best alternative. Any project that has a positive present value is basically viable, and the one displaying the highest net present value is, in purely financial terms, the most profitable. Second, the Internal Rate of Return (I.R.R.) or Yield method which employs the present value concept but seeks to provide an evaluation procedure that avoids the arbitrary choice of a rate of interest. Instead it sets out, by trial and error, to establish a rate of interest that makes the present value of all expenditure incurred in a project equal to the present value of all revenue gained. When calculated this interest rate is known as the 'Yield' of the investment. Having calculated the I.R.R. or Yield for each alternative they should then be compared with the cost of borrowing the capital. Any project or alternative having a return higher than the cost of borrowing is fundamentally viable, and the highest return is naturally the most financially attractive.

The evaluation of plans, projects, or development of any kind requires the actual tangible measurement of the constituent factors forming the scheme, together with an estimation of their future performance. Such estimates of future events depend largely upon an interpretation of what has happened in the past, and since experience shows that the pattern of past events is never exactly repeated, future predictions can be at best imprecise approximations. To be as accurate as possible, however, it is advisable to introduce a sensitivity analysis combined with a probability distribution which will explore, list, and examine the possible range of likely outcomes. This procedure is described in greater detail elsewhere.[12] Despite an entrenched reluctance in certain spheres to apply this approach, it does provide a significant improvement over conventional techniques. Furthermore, Financial Appraisal readily lends itself to adoption within the wider framework of Cost Benefit Analysis. Perhaps the most interesting example of a slightly different form of financial appraisal was the analysis of the performance, in terms of costs and revenues, of six English new towns undertaken in the late sixties by Nathaniel Lichfield and Paul Wendt.[13]

Evaluation—references

1 Lichfield, N., 'Evaluation Methodology of Urban and Regional Plans—A Review', *Regional Studies*, August, 1970.
2 *Ibid.*
3 Prest, A. R. and Turvey, R., 'Cost Benefit Analysis: A Survey', *Economic Journal*, December, 1966.
4 *Ibid.*
5 Lichfield, N., 'Cost Benefit Analysis in Urban Expansion: A Case Study: Peterborough', *Regional Studies*, 3, 1969.
6 *Ibid.*
7 Hill, M., 'A Goal Achievement Matrix in the Evaluation of Alternative Plans', *American Institute of Planners Journal*, 34, 1968.
8 Malisz, B., *The Economics of Shaping Towns*, Polish Academy of Science (1963).
9 HMSO, Grangemouth—*Falkirk Regional Survey and Plan*, 2, Edinburgh (1968).
10 HMSO, *Central Borders Study*, 1, Edinburgh (1968).
11 Kozlowski, J. and Hughes, J. T., 'Urban Threshold Theory and Analysis', *Town Planning Institute Journal*, February, 1967.

12 Ratcliffe, J., 'Uncertainty and Risk in Development Appraisal', *Estates Gazette* July, 1973
13 Lichfield, N. and Wendt, P., 'Six English New Towns: A Financial Appraisal', *Town Planning Review*, 40, 1969.

Further recommended reading

Hawkins, C. J. and Pearce, D. W., *Capital Investment Appraisal*, Macmillan (1971).
I.M.T.A., *Cost Benefit Analysis* (1969).
Laurie Carr, J., *Investment Economics*, Routledge and Kegan Paul (1969).
Merrett, A. J., and Sykes, A., *The Finance and Analysis of Capital Projects*, Longmans (1965).
Mishan, E. J., *Cost Benefit Analysis*, Allen and Unwin (1971).
Pearce, D. W., *Cost Benefit Analysis*, Macmillan (1971).
Peters, G. H., *Cost Benefit Analysis and Public Expenditure*, Hobart Paper, Institute of Economic Affairs (1965).

15 Other associated techniques

Gaming

With the development of a systems approach towards town planning, which attempts to distinguish the various activities that determine the nature of the human environment and understand their relationship, a range of associated techniques have been devised to assist in analysis and experimentation. The most notable of these is the construction of mathematical models to represent the real world in abstract but manageable conditions. One of their major drawbacks, however, is that they preclude the study of decision-making in situations of personal conflict. Most planning decisions are influenced in one way or another by political, social, economic or professional human attitudes and behaviour. To permit the introduction of individuals, agencies, and ideas into controlled and experimental conditions a number of 'games' have been conceived. These games are models or simulations of possible real-life circumstances which allow for interaction between individuals, thus portraying the politics of a situation.

The history of gaming has its roots in military training. This can be traced as far back as 3000 BC in China where the great military thinker and general Sun-Tzu simulated and played out his battle plans in a game called Wei-Hai, known today under the Japanese name of Go.[1] The French constructed games in the eighteenth century to familiarise cadets with basic military strategy, and the Prussians characteristically introduced a certain element of scientific method and rigour into their 'Kriegsspiel' which was extensively played throughout the nineteenth century.

Having found further service in the field of business management, it was not until the late 1950's that gaming was introduced into urban planning, and only in the last few years has it really established itself. It fulfils several basic functions, it is a method of self-teaching, it is widely used in training of all kinds, it can be employed in research, and it can be used for evaluation where numerative or quantitative techniques are inappropriate. It is therefore suitable on any occasion where it is necessary to replace the complexity of the urban scene with a simulation which allows certain representative features to be understood and recognised or where the study of phenomena by any other means might be dangerous, expensive or impossible.

One of the first urban planning games to be developed was the Cornell Land Use Game, or 'CLUG', which is still widely used, principally for educational purposes, and has provided the basis for many other games. Originally concerned with the study of land economics and location theory it has been expanded to include the effects of town planning, taxation, legislation and politics. Another, more sophisticated, game is 'Metro', which, based on a typical medium sized American metropolitan area, relied heavily upon the use of a computer, setting out to examine not only the economic but also the political systems and pressures influencing various sections of the community. The players adopt the roles of the politicians, professional planners, administrators, pressure groups and land developers. A number of mathematical models are built into the game and serviced by a computer which supplies information and projections regarding population, industrial growth, household distribution, voters' response to changing circumstances, crime rates, and development. These models also make allowances for the actions of the players during the game in their respective roles. A roughly similar, though slightly less complex, game is available in this country, called the 'PTRC'[2] game, which traces the growth of a medium sized county town, taking account of British town planning practice and procedures.

Apart from its educational function this approach readily lends itself to establishing and testing organisational and administrative structures by re-creating real-life situations in a practical manner. It has been used by local government in this country to test the introduction of corporate planning into an authority by speeding up the processes involved. One year's possible events were played out in a matter of days in order to search out any inconsistencies in departmental policy and structure and to identify the factors, agencies, personalities and pressures concerned.

As with so many other new techniques there is always a danger of too much importance being placed upon the method and performance of gaming, but it can provide a useful way of examining and understanding human behaviour and political decision-making and their effect upon town planning.

Models

A model is merely a simple reconstruction of reality that reduces the apparent complexity of the real world to something that the planner can adequately comprehend and cope with. It describes a system, and the relationship of the various activities or factors associated with that system. It is used in town planning to understand the forces that determine the size and nature of urban areas and the location of land uses therein. The planner uses the model to examine, and subsequently make statements about, the real world that will assist him in controlling and changing events in the real world. As models may be used to estimate unknown values of one variable, given a range of known values of other variables, it is essential in planning, if indeed the model is to assist in foreseeing and guiding change, to select variables which can themselves be controlled. In a shopping model, for example, floorspace is eminently suitable, future provision being dictated by planning permission. Some of the variables may not be directly measurable, such as the 'attractiveness' of a shopping centre. These variables are called parameters and can be adjusted to simulate a particular circumstance by assuming, for example, that while the attractiveness of a shopping centre is not directly proportional to its size, the larger a centre is the more attractive it becomes because of the wider range of goods offered. Although the precise value of the parameter is not known, trial calculations are undertaken and the results compared with actual figures. The procedure is continued until there is agreement and a satisfactory 'fit' is obtained. This process of introducing and adjusting parameters is known as calibration and testing. It is inevitable that the simplification implicit in model building involves some loss of aspects of 'real life'.

The development and application of the model building approach evolved because of a changing attitude towards the theory of urban structure. The traditional view of town and country planning is being subjected to considerable challenge, 'the merely morphological perception of the city that ruled the early literature on planning, whose signal features were size, shape, and density, have fallen to pieces'.[1] The advent of systems theory and its introduction into the planning process demands a more through analysis of the aspects, activities and agencies at play in society, and a greater understanding of their relationships and inter-dependence. Modelling introduces a greater degree of rigour into planning practice; despite the fact that it can still be highly subjective, it does permit a more precise examination, expose certain thought processes, require values to be placed upon items, declare the hand of the planner or decision-maker, aid communication, and facilitate comparison between alternatives.

Models divide themselves into different categories, depending upon their sophistication or purpose. Firstly they can either be 'partial', relating to only one form of activity or land use, or 'general', where more than one form of activity or land use are considered and their respective relationships simulated. Secondly, they can be classified as being descriptive, showing the existing situation; predictive, forecasting future trends; or prescriptive, examining alternative policies and deciding between them.

As with so many other 'technological advances' the construction of land use models was initially developed during the late 1950's and early 1960's in the United States of America, and was primarily concerned with the study of transportation. Although Reilly's Law of Gravitational Retailing, put forward in 1929, is essentially a simple model, the first land use models were developed and applied during the sixties. Probably the most comprehensive 'general' model is that devised by Ira Lowry for Pittsburgh.[2] This is really a set of models closely associated with economic base theory which assumes that 'the location of basic employment is independent of the location patterns of other activities such as non-basic employment and population, but that these other activities are locationally dependent upon basic employment. Therefore, the model assumes that population and non-basic employment can be uniquely derived from basic employment.'[3] In this way it distributes households to suggested residential areas, having taken into account where they must work, shop, and obtain other services. This model has been further developed by a number of social scientists—notably in 1966 by R. A. Garin,[4] who brought the technique even closer to economic base theory, the derived result being commonly referred to as the Garin-Lowry model.

In this country similar land use models have been constructed for the last five years. As Batty points out, the Garin-Lowry model readily lends itself to adoption in British planning practice.[5] It is the most comprehensive approach to date and singularly well suited to the 'structure' planning process established by the 1968 Town and Country Planning Act. Models have been devised at both sub-regional and urban scales. The former have been applied for Central Lancashire in appraising the designated site for a new town,[6] for Bedfordshire to evaluate alternative strategies, and for Nottinghamshire-Derbyshire,[7] Severnside, and Merseyside. The latter have all been developed at the Centre for Land Use and Built-Form Studies, Cambridge University, and relate to Reading, Cambridge, Stevenage, and Milton Keynes. All are derivatives of the Garin-Lowry model.[8]

The various inherent qualities of a land use model permit it to be used at several stages in the planning process. Firstly, at the analysis stage where it helps in setting down and clarifying the problems that present themselves in a manner that facilitates discussion. Secondly, in formulating a policy and designing the plan. Thirdly, in providing a most useful basis for comparing or evaluating alternative strategies. Fourthly, and perhaps more tenuously, in monitoring the plan's performance.

The vast growth in the development and application of land use models has been greatly aided by the advent of the high speed computer. Nevertheless a model is only as good as the information with which it is supplied. They tend, moreover, to possess a voracious appetite for data. A comparatively simple shopping model will require, for example, the following:

Boundary data

Population statistics

Existing retail expenditure in various categories of goods

Socio-economic structure of population

Total income of population

Future income of population

Definition of retail hierarchy

Car ownership rates, present and future

Proximity of competing centres

Travel distance, speed and cost

Trends in conversion factors

Existing sales

Existing floorspace

It is not intended to explain in any detail the mathematical working of a model, but to illustrate their nature a modified version of Reilly's Law, which attempts to establish the 'breaking point' between two retail spheres of influence, is described:

$$D_{01} = \frac{D_{12}}{1 + \sqrt{\dfrac{A_2}{A_1}}}$$

where D_{01} is the deterrence function expressed in distance, time, or cost between Town 1 and the 'breaking point'

D_{12} is a similar measure between Towns 1 and 2

$A_1\ A_2$ are the attraction factors expressed in sales, floorspace, or population of Towns 1 and 2

Although many problems exist regarding the construction and handling of land use models F. Stuart Chapin concludes his invaluable book on Urban Land Use Planning with this statement on their role: 'In larger urban areas and certainly in the major

204

metropolitan areas, planning agencies cannot hope to cope with the demands on their time and provide the kind of staff work for policy formulation that will be increasingly their responsibility to provide unless they avail themselves of these tools of analysis.'[9]

Linear programming

This operational research technique assists in selecting the best way of employing valuable resources in order to reach a desired state of affairs. This desired state of affairs or result is known as the 'objective function' and the degree of availability of the various constituent resources that are required to produce the result are called the constraints. The overall process is described as being one of optimisation. This approach lends itself to short-run problems when resources are comparatively scarce and fixed in supply and when the respective constraints can be easily identified. The result is obtained algebraically or, where the problem is extremely simple, graphically, and the technique is particularly well suited to computerisation when many hundreds of possible solutions consequent upon many thousands of resources can be examined in a matter of seconds.

This method of analysis, widely used in business management, has been employed in tackling regional planning problems where development has been restricted by the scarcity of one or more resource. Linear programming indicates the best way of applying all the available resources in such a way as to achieve the maximum return. One of the areas in which it has proved of considerable value is transportation planning where it is often necessary to minimise either the cost of travel or the time of journeys.

It has been further developed in Israel as a means of finding optimal solutions to overall planning problems.[1] As such it has been applied to the preparation and evaluation of alternative plans,[2] whereby one variable element of the plan at a time is allowed to change, all other variables are held constant, and a variety of combinations are tested in order to produce the best solutions.

In most planning studies, however, the number of constraints that have to be incorporated in the analysis is likely to be very high; moreover, they are rarely in a quantitative form appropriate to linear programming methods. In a similar way the 'objective function', or desired result, is itself frequently hard to define and operational research techniques of this kind cannot adequately handle non-quantifiable or intangible variables.

Gaming—references

1 Wilson, A., *War Gaming*, Pelican (1970).
2 Planning and Transportation, Research and Computation.

Further recommended reading

Feldt, A., 'Operational Gaming in Planning Education', *American Institute of Planners Journal*, January, 1966.
Meier, R. and Duke, R., 'Gaming Simulation for Urban Planning', *American Institute of Planners Journal*, January, 1966.
Taylor, J. and Carter, K., 'Instructional Simulation of Urban Development', *Town Planning Institute Journal*, December, 1967.

Models—references

1 Marsoni, L., 'On the use of models as tools for Planning', *Arena*, September, 1968.
2 Lowry, I. S., Model of Metropolis, Rand Corporation (1964).
3 Batty, M., 'Recent Developments in Land Use Modeling. A Review of British Research', *Urban Studies*, June, 1972.
4 Garin, R. A., 'A matrix formulation of the Lowry model for intra-metropolitan activities', *American Institute of Planners Journal*, **132**, 1966.
5 Batty, *op. cit.*
6 Batty, M., 'Models and Projections of the Space Economy', *Town Planning Review*, **41**, 1970.
7 Batty, M., 'An activity allocation model for the Nottingham–Derbyshire sub-region', *Regional Studies*, **4**, 1970.
8 Echenique, M., 'A spatial model of urban stock and activity', *Regional Studies*, **3**, 1969.
9 Chapin, F. S., *Urban Land Use Planning*, University of Illinois (1970).

Further recommended reading

Lanchester Polytechnic, *Gravity Models in Planning* (1970).
Lowry, I. S., 'A Short Course in Model Design', *American Institute of Planners Journal*, May, 1965.
Lowry, I. S., *Seven Models of Urban Development*, Rand Corporation (1967).
Wilson, A. G., 'Models in Urban Planning', *Urban Studies*, November, 1968.

Linear programming—references

1 Lichfield, N., 'Evaluation methodology of urban and regional plans: a review', *Regional Studies*, August, 1970.
2 Ben-Shahar, H., *et al.*, 'Town Planning and welfare maximisation', *Regional Studies* (1969).

Further recommended reading

Duckworth, E., *A guide to operation research*, Methuen (1965).
Morley, R., *Mathematics for Modern Economics*, Fontana (1972).
Yeomans, K., *Statistics for the Social Scientist: 2. Applied Statistics*, Penguin (1967).

PART THREE

Some aspects of town planning

16 Amenity

Conservation

With the unprecedented economic expansion, population explosion, and speed of technological advance of recent times, there are ever-increasing demands placed upon land for competing uses. These pressures often promote change, and change can imply the destruction of existing things and their replacement by new. This process is not always a welcome one for it may include the loss of features treasured by the community at large but in the hands of private individuals. It is therefore desirable to foresee, guide, and, where necessary, control the forces of change.

Urban conservation

Increasing attention is being paid to the significance and supervision of our historic and architectural heritage, for although change is implicit in urban life, economic forces are not always selective in their innovation and transformation of towns. The need to conserve that which is cherished is wide ranging and applies to individual buildings or parts of buildings, areas, landmarks, the atmosphere, and congestion.

Until a few years ago the approach towards urban conservation was limited and partial. Building Preservation Orders could be served on particular buildings and Tree Preservation Orders on individual trees. This would assist the local planning authority in determining its overall policy towards development and landscape as well as preventing the owner from materially altering the building or substantially affecting the tree. For their further protection, the Secretary of State maintains a list of those buildings which are not to be destroyed, these are Grades 1 and 2 on the Statutory List, and those which are not 'special' but are of sufficient merit to warrant consideration for preservation and are on Grade 3 of the Supplementary List. There are now over 120 000 buildings on the list and a continual survey is made for more that might be added. Only the Secretary of State has the power to list, but a local authority may still avail themselves of the Building Preservation Order procedure; however, its application is now limited to six months to allow for consideration of possible listing. If this does not take place no further Order may be served in respect of that building for twelve months.

Listing has been criticised for being insufficient, omission from a list ought not to condemn a building as without historic or architectural interest, though inevitably in practice it does so. Also that they are too specific, too individual, and not positive enough, particularly in terms of combating obsolescence.

Conservation areas
A more comprehensive approach towards urban conservation is provided under the Civic Amenities Act 1967 whereby local authorities are encouraged to define and declare areas with special character and quality as Conservation Areas. This no longer restricts attention to individual buildings but includes an appreciation of the character and appearance which deserves preserving or enhancing. This might relate to notable views or to buildings, which, though unexceptional in themselves, add to the general quality of the area; equally it might apply to park railings as well as to trees and shrubs, the principal aim being to prevent excessive intrusion by out of scale redevelopment. To date over 2000 such conservation areas have been designated. Perhaps in some areas too many have been identified and greater discretion might have ensured a greater degree of success. In certain towns virtually the whole urban area has been included whereas only

parts justify special treatment and there is a danger that the powers conferred by the Civic Amenities Act could be diluted.

In order 'to examine how conservation policies might be sensibly implemented' four historic towns of outstanding worth were chosen as subjects for pilot studies, Bath, Chester, Chichester and York, and for a short time a Preservation Policy Group was set up within the Ministry of Housing and Local Government to co-ordinate their efforts. Many of their recommendations are incorporated in the Civic Amenities Act and the Town and Country Planning Act 1971. Between them the resultant reports highlight the major aspects of planning for conservation.

Cost

Grants to assist in the improvement of historic buildings are available under the Local Authorities (Historic Buildings) Act 1962, the Historic Buildings and Ancient Monuments Act 1953 and various Housing Acts. It is true to say, however, that although residential values are often enhanced, individual private owners of commercial premises sometimes view the possibility of 'listing' or inclusion within a Conservation Area with fear and trepidation. One of the fundamental differences between 'conservation' and 'preservation' is that the former allows for change to occur within carefully controlled limits, the latter seeks merely to perpetuate the *status quo*. Conservation and economic viability are therefore not necessarily incompatible. A great many old buildings lend themselves to commercial conversion. In Oxford for example, a historic church was converted into a college library, and similarly, in Cambridge, a church was converted into public meetings rooms.[1] It is not always the case that the whole building requires conservation. The famous Nash Terraces in Regents Park have retained only their original façade, the rear and interior parts being completely rebuilt, and in Salisbury the medieval Staple Hall has undergone the remarkable transition to a cinema foyer.

Examples of economically feasible conservation where the forces of redevelopment are in evidence are comparatively rare, however, and if the private sector is to be expected to play a significant role in the future greater financial inducement will have to be provided. This could take the form of local authority

213

mortgages at low rates of interest and spread over a long period, or attractive sale and lease-back arrangements, or even a system of investment grants similar to that operated in development areas. Nathaniel Lichfield in *Economics of Conservation* has applied the balance sheet approach to conservation areas, and proposes a form of betterment charge to be levied on those uses such as hotels, restaurants, and tourists that benefit from the improvement or enhancement of the area. In whatever way it is provided the conservation of the country's national architectural and historic heritage cannot possibly be effected unless there are sufficient funds available, legislation alone is not enough.

Traffic

The terrifying impact of the motor car upon the character and environment of urban areas, and especially upon our historic towns, presents one of the most intractable aspects of conservation. It is a problem that begs innumerable questions and anything approaching adequate discussion is well beyond the scope of this restricted text. The visual intrusion alone, apart from the congestion and pollution caused by traffic in towns, detracts greatly from a satisfactory urban environment. Suffice it to say that in formulating a conservation policy there are certain factors that deserve special attention and this will inevitably involve:

a. identifying environmental areas—the policy must be selective, and a balance struck between those areas which merit treatment and the demands for an efficient transportation network within the town

b. exclusion of through traffic—if the motor vehicle is to remain as the mainstay of any urban transport system it is important to channel the longer movements from town to town and from one locality to another, on to effective and well designed distributor roads. Some environmental areas will attract considerably more traffic than others but the aim is to secure a suitable 'environmental capacity' above which danger, noise, fumes, vibration, and intrusion would be unacceptable. This level is likely to be considerably lower than the areas, sheer, capacity to pass vehicles

c. provision of a pedestrian network—in association with the

214

gradual removal of vehicles, and the provision of alternative car parking facilities elsewhere, it is essential to ensure that there are adequate pedestrian ways to, from and around chosen areas

d. provision of vehicular accessibility—some forms of traffic will 'belong' to the area, such as commercial vehicles required for servicing the buildings and the buses and cars of persons either employed in or visiting the area. The easier their access, the shorter period of time they will be present, and the less detriment they will cause. This facility will have to be measured against the danger of attracting extraneous traffic

e. provision of adequate off-street parking—the ease of parking may have a direct bearing on the prosperity of the area under consideration; therefore, priority must be given to the use most essential to economic viability. Whether this is the long-term office worker, the short-term shopper, or the resident will vary according to the circumstances

f. provision of attractive public transport—peripheral town car parks linked to a fast, frequent, and efficient public transport system are likely to prove essential to the future functioning of concentrated urban areas. Leeds are already operating a 'park and ride' policy and more towns will surely follow

The ultimate solution to the worsening problem of urban transportation probably lies in the adoption of a long-term, far-reaching, and more radical scheme such as flexible discriminatory road pricing at realistic marginal cost levels, or even the final sanction of banning the private motor car altogether.

Administration

Among the most important tasks in implementing a policy of conservation is the business of making available all the relevant information regarding grants, loans, advice and the obtaining of planning permission. The part to be played by good public relations and the inducement of more effective co-ordination and co-operation is vital to the speeding up of the process. The series of bulletins published by the Civic Trust entitled *Progress in Creating Conservation Areas* assists in this dissemination of information by outlining the policies pursued by many local authorities in a variety of circumstances. In the same vein there are a number of circulars and memoranda produced by the Ministry in respect of the Civic Amenities Act and the 1971 Town and Country Planning Act.

A popular device in implementing conservation policy has been the Article 4 Direction whereby deemed planning permission falling under the category of permitted development in the General Development Orders is withdrawn. The progress of more positive action is severely hampered by the paltry sum of £700 000 per annum which is all that is made available to the Historic Buildings Council towards preservation.

Amenity societies

These have a significant role to play and have been immensely stimulated by the formation and example of the Civic Trust. The trust was founded in 1957 by Duncan Sandys when only about 200 amenity societies were in existence; now, largely as a result of their efforts, there are over 700. Amongst the range of activities these societies engage in are the drawing up of conservation area proposals, representation on local authority committees, concern with improvement schemes such as tree planting, riverside walks and removal of eyesores, recommendations regarding the listing of buildings and consultation when listed buildings are to be demolished. They can even assist financially. The King's Lynn Preservation Trust has, for example, collected £120 000 for one conservation scheme alone, and £50 000 for another. One of the Civic Trust's first ventures was the 'facelift' of Magdalen Street, Norwich. What was previously a rather shabby shopping street was carefully and sympathetically refurbished. All the clutter of unsightly wires and sordid signs were removed, and the shop fronts were repainted using a harmonious colour scheme at little extra cost than would, in any case, have been expended by individual traders. The scheme, although only a skin-deep cosmetic treatment, was a success and demonstrated that a large number of separate interests can be unified in a common purpose if the right management approach is applied. A further example of the Civic Trust participation in planning for conservation was the memorandum submitted in February 1970 to the then Minister of Transport urging closer appraisal of the proposal for extra heavy lorries on existing roads. In conjunction with other local amenity societies, the Trust itself carried out a survey, and a year later put forward a report containing thirty specific recommendations relating to the legislation concerning the use of these monster vehicles. The report and recommendations were instrumental in the Department of the Environment's decision not to sanction their use at that time.

A comprehensive policy for conserving the urban environment cannot consider buildings and areas of architectural and historic interest in isolation, but must have regard to all the forces of change, and recognise the priorities for action and the competence to implement them. Conservation must therefore form part of the overall planning process and lay claim to its rightful place in the structure plan. A lesson can be taken from France where Malraux's Law of 1962, which combines national, regional and local agencies in providing for the comprehensive restoration of every historic urban site in the country, is paying handsome dividends. Despite certain financial problems the French appear to have mastered the art of integrating the past with the present whilst maintaining an eye to the future. They tackle the problems of rehabilitation, redevelopment, traffic congestion, pedestrian-isation, local industry and the social infrastructure in relation to conservation as a totality. Our own policy in this country is perhaps too negative in character and we could well remember that positive forward planning is the surest way of avoiding conflict. Equally important in conserving our urban environ-ment is the control of new development in terms of advertising, materials, height, car parking, traffic congestion, air pollution and high building.

Rural conservation

Over the centuries the face of the English countryside has undergone drastic changes due to increasing areas of land being put to agriculture, the advent of widescale sheep grazing, the development of Great Britain as a naval power, and the onset of enclosure. The first discernible movement to preserve the countryside developed in the nineteenth century, probably as a reaction against the urban squalor consequent upon the industrial revolution. The Commons, Footpaths and Open Space Society was established in 1865 and was eventually responsible for securing the Rights of Way Act 1932. The Royal Society for the Protection of Birds was founded in 1889 and again initiated the pressure that finally accomplished the setting up of sanctuaries under the Protection of Birds Act of 1954.

In 1907 the National Trust was formed to promote the cause of conservation and empowered to receive and manage land and estates in the interests of our national heritage. It is now the third largest landowner in Britain, possessing 120 000 hectares of land and several hundred miles of coastline. One of its most recent and popular campaigns has been 'Enterprise Neptune' launched in 1965 with the object of raising £2 millions to safeguard vast stretches of coastline. Another organisation that exerts considerable political pressure on rural conservation matters is the Council for the Preservation (now Protection) of Rural England which was founded in 1926. In 1970, European Conservation Year, the CPRE set up a number of working parties to look at various aspects of the rural environment. One of them, for example, looked at the vexed problem of transmission cables and power lines and recommended that the electricity generating boards should be made to take professional landscaping advice, set aside a fixed portion of their annual budget for visual treatment, adhere to amenity clauses in their articles of establishment, consult with local authorities whose areas might be affected, place more power lines underground, and spend larger sums of money on the design of equipment.[2] How much influence they have in determining national policy is hard to say, but anyone who has experienced their advocacy or attracted their wrath, particularly at local public inquiries, will vouch for their efficacy as a 'watchdog' of private interest.

The largest landowners in the country are the Forestry Commission who hold 1·2 million hectares of land and were set up in 1919 to rectify the appalling rape of the forests that had occurred during the First World War, and to build up a stock of timber for the future. This they have done, although it is inconceivable that we shall ever provide for our own timber requirements, and thankfully the Commission have time at last to consider the quality of the countryside as well as the quantity of wood, and are tempering their policy of covering our hillsides with a chequerboard of green.

National parks

A growing concern and interest for the countryside and for leisure pursuits between the wars gave rise to the National Parks and Access to the Countryside Act 1949. The aims of this act were conceived in the work of the Wildlife Conservation Special Committee in 1945, which recommended greater research in conservation and advised in favour of the acquisition and management of special areas of scientific importance, together with the Dower Report on National Parks in England and Wales 1945, and the Hobhouse Report of the National Parks Committee 1947. The act aimed at:

'1. The preservation and enhancement of natural beauty in England and Wales and particularly in the areas designated as National Parks or Areas of Outstanding Natural Beauty, and

2. encouraging the provision or improvement, for purposes resorting to National Parks, of facilities for the enjoyment of them and for the enjoyment of open air recreation and the study of nature.'

There are now ten National Parks like those of Snowdonia, the Lake District, Dartmoor and the North Yorkshire Moors, and nearly thirty Areas of Outstanding Natural Beauty.

The Act also created the Nature Conservancy which was set the task of establishing and managing nature reserves as 'living museums' as well as pursuing long-term scientific research. At approximately the same time the Town and Country Planning Act 1947 and the Agriculture Act of the following year pledged to maintain 'a stable and efficient agricultural industry' but which had the effect of sterilising the countryside into its existing pattern. Development Plans only prepared detailed proposals for urban areas and rural planning in the fifties was seen only in terms of village planning, the provision of services and the girdling of towns with green belts to prevent urban sprawl. Even now rural planning and legislation in respect of conservation is almost non-existent, and where it does occur, it is at best extremely fragmented. The countryside is all too often seen as a backcloth for urban development and the various Town and Country Planning Acts adopt a largely preservationist policy towards it; even the Planning Advisory Group Report virtually ignored the problem.

Table 2

Summary of statutorily protected land, England and Wales, 31 December 1969

	Square miles	Square kilometres	Percentage
Total land area	58 349	157 124	100·00
10 National Parks	5258	13 618	9·02
25 areas of outstanding natural beauty	4291	11 114	7·35
19 green belts	5709	14 786	9·78
66 national nature reserves	129	334	0·23
	15 387	39 852	26·38
Less areas in more than one category	522	1353	0·89
TOTAL	14 865	38 499	25·49

Times are, however, changing and the 1965 Countryside in 1970, conference indicated a growing awareness of the need for a concerted approach. The very fact that 89 different organisations were represented demonstrated an increasing interest. A like minded Labour Government established the Ministry of Land and Natural Resources which was charged with wide-ranging responsibilities relating to the study and control of land use, including commons, National Parks and water resources. For the first time the overall jurisdiction for the distribution of land among competing uses was placed under one authority. Almost concurrently in 1966, the Natural Environment Research Council was created to co-ordinate the work of organisations concerned with life and earth sciences. Shortly afterwards the Countryside Commission was formed following the publication of the Countryside Act (1968). The Commission have succeeded the National Parks Commission and their terms of reference are extended to 'review, encourage, assist, concert or promote the provision and improvement of facilities for the enjoyment of the countryside generally, and to conserve and enhance the natural beauty and amenity of the countryside and to secure public access for the purpose of open air recreation'.

They also aim to liaise with a number of other agencies in the field of rural conservation, such as the British Travel Association, the British Waterways Board, the Nature Conservancy Council, the Sports Council and the Forestry Commission, for the purposes of research and the formulation of a common policy. The Countryside Commission is further empowered to give grants towards the creation of country parks.

Despite the fact that the Ministry of Land and Natural Resources was abolished in 1967 its duties were incorporated in 1969 within the Department for Local Government and Regional Planning under Richard Crossman who was rather grandly referred to as the 'environmental overlord'. Its functions are now within the sphere of the Department of the Environment where a even wider perspective is permitted.

The movement towards an integrated planning policy towards urban and rural conservation is well under way. As the second Countryside in 1970 conference observed, there are still major influences demanding scrutiny and subsequent action, particularly in respect of recreational demands and the changing nature of the agricultural industry. There is also the need to reconcile the seemingly insatiable demands upon our water, timber and mineral resources, as well as alleviating the monotony of an expanding prairie landscape. Perhaps most important of all is the need to understand the ecological effects of an industrialised society.

Derelict land

Whereas preservation implies no change, conservation is associated with positive action and controlled change. The avaricious exploitation that befell the country's natural resources as a consequence of nineteenth-century industrialisation has left us with a legacy of dereliction accumulated over years of past neglect. Any policy of conservation must therefore concern itself with the thorny problem of derelict land. The landscape is pockmarked with spoil heaps and wasteland as a result of coal-mining, iron working, quarrying and chemical extraction. The gravity of the situation has prompted the government into action. Since 1964 every local authority has been required to make and return an annual assessment regarding the amount of derelict land in its area. This is defined as 'Land so damaged by industrial or other development that it is incapable of beneficial use without treatment, but not land which has become derelict from natural causes, such as marsh land.'[3] Also excluded are certain classes of man-made dereliction. In 1970 there were 96 697 acres falling within this classification.

The North has the worst problem, particularly in those counties where coalmining predominates, although the National Coal Board, albeit in the shadow of Aberfan and atoning for past misdemeanours, is attempting to remedy the situation. Even in the South there is no escape from the despoliation of modern industrial needs, as witnessed by the cavernous holes gouged out of the Thames Valley in the lustful search for gravel. At least these craters readily lend themselves to 'after-use'. They can be filled with refuse and returned to economic use, or put to recreation pursuits like sailing or water ski-ing. With no central authority responsible for the management of reclamation programmes the task of administration becomes enormous. The very number of local government units militates against an effective policy. In Lancashire alone there are 18 autonomous county boroughs and 109 county districts, which makes co-ordination an intricate affair.

The other major stumbling block is that of cost. Reclamation for alternative commercial uses averages out at between £1000 and £3200 per hectare, but if just cosmetic treatment is applied, that is planting, screening and generally tidying up, it can be as little as £750 per hectare. There is, as such, no obligation upon local authorities regarding the restoration of derelict land but it is a course of action strongly urged by the Minister. To this end there are a number of sources from which grants may be obtained. The Mineral Workings Act 1951 assists the financing of the reclamation of Midlands ironstone fields by imposing a levy upon every ton of ore extracted. The Industrial Development Act 1966 makes a grant of 85% in Development Areas where the land is to be returned to industrial use. The Local Government Act 1966 offers a grant of 50% over the whole country while the National Parks and Access to the Countryside Act 1949, besides giving local authorities specific powers to acquire land in need of reclamation, always provided that it is within a National Park or Area of Outstanding Natural Beauty, also makes available a 75% grant. More recently, where the Civic Amenities Act 1967 has prohibited 'dumping', the Countryside Act 1968 gives grants for the removal of disfiguring objects. Moreover, the Local Employment Act 1970 has instituted a crash programme in Development, Intermediate, and Derelict Land Clearance Areas aptly called 'Operation Eyesore' under which 85% grants are available in Development Areas and 75% elsewhere.

The total cost for nationwide reclamation is of course difficult to calculate. Estimates vary from £35 million[4] to as much as £100 million,[5] but somewhere around £50 million to £60 million appears to be widely accepted. As an annual sum this represents something in the region of £5 million, not, one would consider, an extortionate amount. The principal impediment in the field of finance is the procedure known as 'after-value' whereby the value of the intended use of the land, after it has been reclaimed, is deducted from any grant that is actually given. This does not, however, apply where the land is to be used for amenity purposes.

Despite these drawbacks a number of local authorities have displayed a notable sense of urgency in attacking the problem. In the forefront are Lancashire, Durham, and the West Riding of Yorkshire whose tasks are probably the most Herculean of all. In the Midlands Stoke on Trent were the 1971 winners of *The Times* and Royal Institution of Chartered Surveyors Award for land reclamation with a project that converted a 128 acre spoil heap into an attractive recreation area for cycling, horse riding, walking, football, pitch and putt and boating. In the South, Haringey London Borough Council, transformed what was previously a disused sewage farm and pig farm into an adventure playground.[6]

Apart from the question of cost, a certain hostility has been encountered in areas where reclamation of derelict land has been proposed. An inverted civic pride appears to exist, or more probably an attachment to the past. Whatever the explanation, it is a lesson to the town planner that he should not assume that one particular policy is always appropriate to all of the people all of the time. Even if it is appropriate, good public relations, careful explanation, and gradual acclimatisation are of paramount importance.

In 1970 only 1460 hectares of derelict land were restored out of a 'hard-core' total of 38640 hectares throughout the country. Furthermore, it has been estimated that every day an extra 4 hectares are added by existing processes.[7] We are merely keeping pace. In order to achieve anything approaching an effective programme of reclamation a far more radical policy is called for, but unfortunately it holds a lowly position in the financial priorities of local authorities. It has therefore been suggested that the method of 'after-value' should be discontinued, 100% grants should be made available, a levy similar to that introduced under the Mineral Workings Act 1951 should be applied on a more comprehensive basis, and to co-ordinate efforts a Central Agency for Derelict Land should be established.

Inland waterways

The British have always preserved a *penchant* for 'messing about in boats', not only at sea but also on the network of inland waterways that criss-cross the country. Their construction was caused by the pressure for improved internal bulk transportation at the onset of the industrial revolution. The first step was the development of rivers in the eighteenth century to render them navigable. Shortly afterwards followed the tentative pioneering attempts at canal building by such enthusiasts as the Duke of Bridgewater. The potential was quickly recognised and a network of canals known as 'the Cross', linking the four main river basins of the Trent, Mersey, Severn and Thames, soon sprang up. This was followed by the establishment of East to West routes based upon the coal and iron areas of Yorkshire, then from Yorkshire to Lancashire. Next, with the growth of Birmingham, there evolved a complex of canals in the Midlands. An almost nation-wide system was created by the building of the Grand Union and Grand Junction Canals which fused them all together. This all occurred in a relatively short period of time, and the 'golden age' of canal development was ended by the advent of the steam engine and consequent railway boom. By 1820 over 2000 miles of navigable waterway had been constructed and very little has been added since.

Although concern over canals was voiced around the turn of the century, it was not until the First World War that particular attention was paid to them. A Departmental Committee on inland waterways in 1920 and a Royal Commission in 1930 both advocated a rationalisation and further investment in certain canals which were still considered to be commercially viable. Virtually no action was taken, however, until the Second World War when they were placed under direct central govern-ment control, and in 1948 the responsibility passed to the British Transport Commission who undertook a survey and classification of existing canals. They grouped them in three categories, Grade 1 which possessed scope for commercial development, Grade 2 which were to be retained and run at an 'adequate level of efficiency,' and Grade 3 which were to be converted into water channels or allowed to relapse into dereliction.

With their other problems, which were frequently given a higher priority, the British Transport Commission were even-tually not deemed to be the most appropriate authority for administering canals. This function was passed in 1963 to a specially constituted British Waterways Board who were faced with an increasing deficit and charged with the duty of keeping it to a minimum. In persuance of this objective the Board formed a Commercial Division which was to manage those waterways which appeared capable of carrying relatively heavy freight traffic, as well as handling a fleet of barges, warehouses, docks and estates. Almost at the same time in the mid-sixties realisation dawned regarding the recreation potential of canals. To cater for this the Transport Act 1968 divided the other supposedly non-commercial canals in Cruising Waterways and Remainder Waterways.

Commercial Division waterways

Freight transport in the United Kingdom is heavily dependent upon inadequate and congested roads, therefore, with ever-increasing demand for the shipment of goods there will inevitably be an expansion of existing systems, both road and rail. Perhaps canals have as yet an unrecognised role to play. Three-lane motorways cost, at the very least, £1 million a mile to construct, £27 000 per mile a year to maintain, and carry about 24 million tons per mile every year if devoted solely to goods traffic. Four-track rail routes cost £600 000 per mile to build, £38 000 per mile to maintain and also carry about 24 million tons per mile a year. Canals, if constructed to International Standard specifications, also cost £600 000 per mile to build, £24 000 per mile a year to maintain and again carry about 24 million tons a year. Because they can be almost exclusively devoted to freight, and are not subject to the same degree of interference from other users as road and rail traffic, canal freight works out at 2·30p a ton per mile including carriage at both ends of the journey, whereas road and rail cost 3·39p and 2·85p a ton per mile respectively.[8] The social cost incurred by noise, fumes, vibration and visual intrusion is also considerably lower. Although the Board is currently losing approximately £2 million a year, a strong case can be made out for future capital investment in canal development, particularly in the light of entry into the Common Market, for Europe possesses advanced, standardised barge-linked freight systems.

Recreation

Water has always proved an attraction for recreational purposes and with over 2000 miles of canals throughout the country there exists an exciting source of untapped potential. Canals cannot only cater for boats but also provide facilities for anglers, walkers and picnickers. The British Waterways Board undertook a study of non-commercial inland waterways and in 1967 they published a pamphlet entitled *Leisure and the Waterways* in which they stated, 'for 200 years the canals have blended into their urban and rural surroundings, with each canal importing its own characteristic influences upon its particular environment. Almost suddenly, a decline in use has given way to a time of rapid development for leisure and amenity. This imposes special responsibility on the canal authority . . . to ensure that aesthetic and environmental standards are enhanced.'

In their quest to intensify the use of existing canals and reopen redundant ones the Board have invoked the help of local authorities, waterway societies, and canal-based industrialists and have undertaken a number of joint schemes. These are largely based upon the Cruising Waterways. One notable example in the centre of Birmingham at Farmers Bridge won the City Council a Civic Trust Award. Great support for restoration, maintenance and development of navigable rivers and canals is received from the Inland Waterways Association founded in 1946, as well as a number of smaller local associations.

The signs are favourable, in 1970 half a million people used the inland waterways in some form or another, and the revenue from licences and tolls rose from £70 000 to £170 000 between 1962 and 1970. The Remainder Waterways, those not in the Commercial Division or designated as Cruising Waterways, still remain a problem, for it is cheaper to restore a canal than to close it permanently because it still requires management. For this reason the Board are anxious to hand over the responsibility for these Remainder Waterways to local authorities for the purposes of drainage and water supply.

Despite a resurgence in interest for inland waterways, a national policy for canal development is still required for co-ordinating their efficient use, conservation, commercial and recreational balance and publicising their availability. It is also to be hoped that canals will not suffer if government proposals to establish Regional Water Authorities are implemented and jurisdiction for them changes hands.

Amenity—references

1 Ward, P. (ed.), *Conservation and development in historic towns and cities*, Oriel (1968).
2 Aldous, T., *Battle for the Environment*, Fontana (1972).

3 Ministry of Housing and Local Government, Circular 55/64.
4 Countryside in 1970 Conference.
5 *Hunt Report on Intermediate Areas*, HMSO (1969).
6 Aldous, *op. cit.*
7 Hawkes, D., 'Environmental Improvement', *Daily Telegraph*, 30th July 1971.
8 Ellis, C., Unpublished thesis, Oxford Polytechnic (1972).

Further recommended reading

Arvill, R., *Man and Environment*, Penguin (1969).

Barr, J., *Derelict Britain*, Penguin (1969).

British Tourist Authority and the Countryside Commission, *Historic Houses Survey* (1970).

Countryside Commission, *The Coastal Heritage*, HMSO (1970).

Hoskins, W. G., *The Making of the English Landscape*, Penguin (1970).

Ministry of Housing and Local Government, *Conservation Studies on York, Bath, Chester and Chichester*, HMSO, (1968).

Patmore, J. A., *Land aud Leisure in England and Wales*, David and Charles (1970).

Stamp, L. D., *Nature Conservation in Britain*, Collins (1969).

Worskett, R., *The Character of Towns*, Architectural Press (1969).

17 Resource planning and pollution

It is hardly possible to read a paper or switch on the television these days without being regaled about the latest chapter in the sorry saga of man's despoliation of his own environment. The frightening explosion in population growth, the pillage of the earth's natural resources, the contamination of the air, the creation of agricultural wasteland and infertile dustbowls, the poisoning of the waters and the gradual extermination of much of the world's flora and fauna are but a few of the chilling episodes in man's lustful drive for growth and productivity. A growth that appears to place greater emphasis upon quantity rather than quality. Many of these modern tragedies do not directly fall within the sphere of responsibility of the physical land use planner; many, however, do, if not wholly, then in part. The very development, management and maintenance of the built environment claims a large proportion of the effort and output of the nation's manpower and resources. The extent of these claims from construction industries alone has been estimated at approximately one-eighth of the gross national product.[1]

Population

The demand for resources is determined by the size and distribution of population and the nature of human activities. It can

229

fairly be stated that we now face a situation of pollution by over-population. The world total population which, it has been esti-mated, stood at approximately 5 million in 6000 BC, 500 million in AD 1650, 1000 million in AD 1850, 2000 million in AD 1930, and now stands at around 4000 million[2], is beginning to demonstrate those Malthusian properties that were scorned for so long. The time in which it takes to double is now down to about 35 years but in undeveloped countries, where 40% of the population are under fifteen years old and a phenomenal decline in the death rate is being experienced, it is as low as 20 years, compared to that in developed countries where if falls between 50 and 200 years. Although the situation is less severe in the United Kingdom it is nevertheless predicted that the population will double about 140 years hence.[3] The birth rate might have declined since the extraordinary immediate post-war levels, but it is still running at a relatively high rate, which, when coupled with the longer life expectancy in England and Wales of 69 for men and 75 for women, produced statistics for growth that defy complacency.

The general level of population and the factors that determine

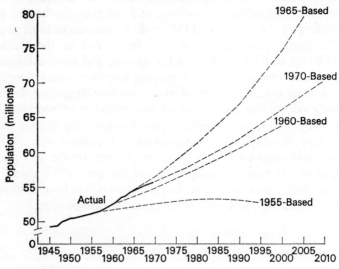

Fig. 23 Actual and projected total population of the United Kingdom
SOURCE: *Population Projections 1970–2010*, HMSO, 1971

it are thankfully not considered suitable areas for the town planner to exercise judgement. Probably the only effective controls that exist in this country are tax concessions or family allowances. Experience in France, albeit in the opposite direction, has shown how powerful these measures can be. There exists, however, a great political reluctance to employ them to any great extent in combating the menace of over-population. As opposed to influencing growth the planner is concerned with comprehending, predicting, and catering for it. The surveys and techniques available in this task have already been described, suffice it to say they are not faultless. In 1946 the population forecast for the United Kingdom at the turn of the century was placed at between 28 and 44 million, in 1964 it was calculated to be about 73 million, and it is now thought that it will reach 64 million.

The changing distribution of the population is also an important factor in the management of the country's resources, particularly when 80% of the inhabitants live in towns, 37% residing in the seven major conurbations, and the process of urbanisation places increasing demands upon these resources. It is the imbalance and distributional inequality of Britain's resources, both real and financial, that are inextricably bound up with the emergence of regional planning. As the continued high standard of living depends upon increased productivity and increased productivity requires the use of additional resources, the taxing and stretching of the nation's assets behoves the town planner to devise more and better ways of understanding and predicting population growth, and thus aggregate demand.

To tackle the situation on a universal basis it has been suggested that 1974 should be designated as World Population Year with the accent on providing pressure, publicity and education regarding the problem of uncontrolled population growth. Such a programme should involve the improvement of the demographic aspects of the planning process.

Agriculture and forestry

A recent and drastic transformation, whose scale and intensity virtually amounts to a revolution, has overtaken British agriculture. In a country where there is only just over one acre of agricultural land for every head of the population, land is quite naturally considered a scarce resource and great premium placed upon its efficient use. With over three-quarters of the land given over to farming, which, with an annual output amounting to £2500 million supplying half the population's food requirements, remains the nation's largest industry, even though it now employs only 3% of the labour force.

The advent of mechanisation and the introduction of industrial methods, stimulated by economic pressures and supported by government subsidy, has led to a sudden change in the face of the countryside. Farms have got fewer and larger, and fields have become more expansive, particularly in the Eastern Counties where arable farming predominates. A more efficient and scientific approach had led to increased densities of stocking, higher yields of produce, and better conversion factors of foodstuffs. Production has more than doubled since the 1930's and the present rate of productivity, running at approximately 1·3% per annum, is more than sufficient to keep pace with the 50 000 acres lost every year to urban encroachment.[5]

These cheering performances in agricultural production are but the harbingers of accelerating problems in rural resource management, themselves associated with the technical advance and intensification of farming. The increasing use of antibiotics in the development of factory farming could eventually endanger human health. The extensive application of artificial fertiliser and pesticides could cause untold repercussions. For instance, a satisfactory level of organic matter in the soil is considered to be about 8%; it has now declined to around 3%, which necessitates further artificial treatment, thus perpetuating the decline, and winding the vicious circle tighter and tighter. Resistant strains develop and residues appear in the final product. The delicately balanced stability in the natural order of things, or 'eco-system', is tragically disturbed, often with unforeseen and irreparable results. Heavy applications of fertiliser ultimately find their way into lakes and water courses, inducing weed growth to such an extent that they become choked and stultified. This process is known as 'eutrophication'.[6] In addition the tearing up of hedgerows, destruction of thickets, and felling of trees, all to promote efficiency, can deprive a variety of wildlife of their natural habitat,

The effect of removing hedgerows, currently at a rate of 5000 miles a year, is succinctly described by Allaby[7]: 'Hedges and trees play a crucial role in the water economy and their removal may affect drainage. They provide shelter for the soil and crops, as well as for animals. Wind speed is reduced to zero on the lea side of a hedge for a distance equal to twice the height; for a distance equal to twelve times the height of the hedge, wind speed is halved. In this sheltered area moisture is conserved in the upper layers of the soil and the soil temperature is higher.' They also act as invaluable windbreaks, preventing the erosion of topsoil, which is already becoming a serious problem in the East Midlands and East Anglia. This is one area, in fact, where the town planner, with his powers of conservation, is equipped to act, if the local political climate allows, and if he dares!

Another aspect of the countryside which merits attention is that portion given over to forestry. Currently this amounts to 1·8 million hectares, representing approximately 8% of the total land surface, only three-quarters of which is managed. This figure falls well below those of the other members of the Common Market which average out at around 22% each.[8]

Being one of the few renewable resources, as well as permitting pulping and recycling, the production of timber would appear to warrant encouragement, especially in the light of the exhaustion of many other mineral sources. To this end nearly 32 000 hectares a year are freshly planted, of which the Forestry Commission undertakes about half. Thankfully the dull conformity of the unnatural chequerboard layout, and the monotonous planting of single species so diligently pursued by the Commission, is giving way to a more imaginative and aesthetically pleasing policy.

A report made in 1972 to the Secretary of State for the Environment on the management of natural resources made several recommendations in respect of agriculture and forestry. These included the discontinuance of 'cosmetic pest control', that is the saturation of crops with pesticides to make them appear more attractive, the abandonment of hedgerow removal grants coupled with incentives for tree planting, the expansion of forestry, and perhaps above all the inauguration and development of research programmes into the long-term effects of modern agricultural methods.[9]

The atmosphere

Probably one of the most apparent aspects of pollution is the desecration of the air we breathe. As a predominantly urban and industrialised society the problem is one of long standing. London has suffered from choking smogs since the twelfth century, and this despite the existence of more drastic measures of control, for it is recorded that an inhabitant was executed in the fourteenth century for burning coal and making too much smoke.[10] The period since the introduction of the 1956 Clean Air Act has seen the amount of smoke disgorged into the atmosphere fall from 2 million tons per annum then to 800 000 tons now.[11] The chief culprit, where smoke is concerned, remains the domestic chimney, which is directly responsible for 85% of the total. The situation, which varies throughout the country—being worse in the North and in South Wales—continues to improve with the switch from coal to other forms of central heating.

Another contributory source of atmospheric pollution is industrial production. Apart from the emission of smoke, 5 million tons of sulphur gases and 1 million tons of grit, dust and ash are pumped into the air every year. As well as the power to designate smokeless zones conferred under the 1956 Act, local authorities are now responsible under the Clean Air Act 1968 for preparing a policy to combat the continuing problem of air pollution. This includes the control of the emission of dark smoke from industrial premises. Furthermore, certain industries with a propensity for such emission are required to register under the Alkali Acts whose regulations and standards are enforced by an inspectorate charged with the duty of ensuring that these concerns adopt the 'best practicable means' of preventing or minimising pollution. A stipulation that lends itself to wide interpretation. The government proudly boasts that private sector industry has spent nearly £400 million over the last ten years in an attempt to clean the air it has defiled. The costs imposed upon society by atmospheric pollution have been calculated to be in the region of £350 million every year. The position regarding industrial airborne waste does, however, appear to be improving.

A very different picture emerges when considering the degree of pollution caused by the motor vehicle. Although the actual

234

level is still comparatively small in comparison with industrial processes, the motor vehicle, which manifests itself as millions of separate mobile chimneys murderously close to the ground and perilously approximate to pedestrians, presents a major pollution problem, as anyone unfortunate enough to be caught in an Oxford Street traffic jam will surely testify. Every year a horrifying 6 million tons of carbon monoxide gas containing 3000 tons of lead are discharged into the atmosphere, a large percentage

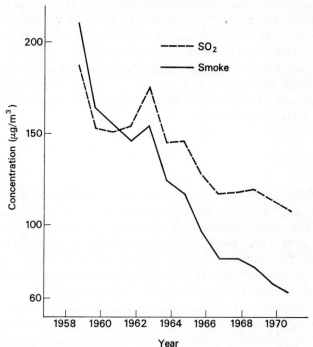

Fig. 24 Sulphur dioxide and smoke concentrations in the United Kingdom 1958–1971

of which must occur in centres of population. Although measures are being taken to reduce the lead content of petrol, the 15 million cars currently on the road are expected to rise to 22 million by 1980 and 32 million by the end of the century—what then?

These factors appear to emphasise the importance of pursuing a more positive approach to the problem of urban transportation as previously outlined.[12] There also emerges a need to formulate a comprehensive policy towards the planning of space as a complete entity. The physical land use planner is well accustomed to allocating land among competing uses, zoning activities to their most appropriate location, and controlling movement between them. It seems a logical progression to take account of the environmental forces above, as well as on, and below, the ground. This idea would involve an understanding of prevailing air currents and 'air sheds', which are defined as 'areas where air currents come together and flow in such a way as to create a zone of distinct character'.[13] This form of survey would then permit 'air-zoning' as a complement to land use zoning. A further remedial course of action would be the imposition of fines, levies, and charges upon the perpetrators of noxious substances, pitched at a level that would not discourage economic activity, the proceeds of which could be devoted to research on the development of cleaner processes.

Water

As with so many other natural resources the demand for water continues to grow, the current annual rate of increase being about 3%. The figures relating to future predictions vary enormously but it does appear possible that demand will have doubled by the end of the century. A recent government publication places current consumption at 55 gallons per head per day, half of which is used for domestic purposes and half for industrial.[14] Although this country appears richly endowed with rainfall, sometimes too much so, the supply is seasonal and unevenly distributed, where water is plentiful population is sparse. Nevertheless with an average daily downpour of 40 000 million gallons and a total demand of 25 000 the situation has obviously not reached crisis point. The United Kingdom, however, possesses fewer untapped sources of supply than almost any other European country and with increased demand, as well as the regional and seasonal variations, the proper management of water resources merits considerable attention.

The increase in supply is likely to be achieved in a number of ways, the tapping of new sources beneath the ground, increased reservoir construction and capacity, an extended network of pipelines, the re-use of water through the purification of sewage and effluent, the cleansing of river water and the introduction of vast barrages across estuaries such as the Dee, Wash, Solway Firth and Morecambe Bay, coupled with desalination techniques. It is envisaged that these latter developments could carry toll roads across them to assist in defraying their cost. It also appears probable that eventually domestic water will be metered and a charge made according to the amount consumed, in the same way as now occurs for industrial and irrigation supplies. It is worth noting, however, that with an advance in purification systems, recycling procedures, and coastal location of industry requiring water facilities, there are the first signs that the demand for water could well slacken over the next twenty-five years.

The responsibility for the administration of the nation's water resources has recently been transferred to ten specially created all-purpose Regional Water Authorities. For the first time all hydrological processes, water supply, sewerage, rivers, and canals, will be considered together. This should greatly enhance the supervision of recalcitrant local authorities regarding the disposal of untreated sewage in rivers.

The most urgent and critical problem that commands attention is the appalling condition of the rivers. The pollution from animal manure slurry, pesticides and fertiliser, as well as domestic sewage and industrial waste, has reached the alarming proportions where some rivers consist of 75% effluent, being little more than open sewers. Admittedly, since the 1951 and 1961 River Acts came into force the total mileage of grossly polluted rivers has decreased by 25% but there are still approximately 5000 miles that are in an unsatisfactory condition. The Acts introduced legislation whereby any discharge of effluent directly into rivers must be authorised and is subject to controls in respect of its volume, temperature and composition. Investment by industry in installing equipment for treating waste has substantially increased but at only £25 million per annum it is still far from being adequate. Over three-quarters of domestic sewage now also receives some form of treatment demonstrating that modern technology can cope; the situation is not irreversible, but the necessary finance, legislation and enforcement must be forthcoming. Moreover, to check the effectiveness of these measures a continuous monitoring system is required. Regard should not only be paid to the rivers but also to the seas and oceans of the world, which are themselves in danger of being turned into vast cesspits, having already been denuded of large areas of underwater forest, the habitat of marine life, and possible future source of nutriment.

Power

The hallmarks of an industrialised society are said to be energy and communication, and even communication requires energy. The consumption of power can also be used to compare relative levels of economic activity; the United States, for example, uses the equivalent of 9·4 tons of coal per person every year, whereas in Western Europe the figure is 3·1 tons, in Eastern Europe 1·5 tons and in the rest of the world 0·5 tons.[15]

This country is currently experiencing a fantastic boom in production of energy and almost cut-throat competition exists between the various power industries. The mechanisation of coalmining, the new and exciting discoveries of oil and natural gas and the development of nuclear reactors have all contributed towards a widescale reduction in prices. It is estimated that by 1975 oil will be the major source of power in the United Kingdom

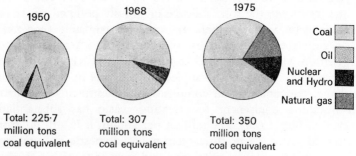

Fig. 25 Changing patterns of primary fuel consumption

SOURCE: Michael Chisholm, *Resources for Britain's Future*

with 42% of total production, natural gas will provide around 14%, nuclear power and hydro-electricity will supply approximately 11%, whilst coal will have declined to approximately 34%.

The many assessments that have been made regarding the likely duration of the world's remaining resources vary enormously. Some estimates predict that fossil fuels will last only another 80 years, others suggest that oil will only be economically available for a further 30 years, and still more maintain that reserves will be in supply for at least the next 150 years. Whatever the case may be it is fairly certain, however, that before the end of the century man will consume more natural resources in the production of energy than he has at any time in the past. With the inevitable decline in stocks, and the increasing costs of extraction, it seems reasonable to expect that alternative sources of power will have to be found, as well as more efficient methods of using the existing ones. This will probably include the harnessing of the winds, tides and sun. It is the town planner's task to foresee the character of future sources and be in a position to guide the location of their industrial plant, understand their effect upon urban structure, control the impact of their design and layout, and cater for their waste products.

Minerals[16]

Not including coalmining, the extraction of minerals can be divided into two convenient categories. Firstly, 'sedimentary', the working of lime, chalk, limestone, clay, sand and gravel used extensively in the construction industry and therefore in part responsible for the employment of 1·3 million men and the annual turnover of £5000 million. Secondly, 'metalliferous', including the winning of iron, tin and lead, forming a small proportion of the whole, but greatly encouraged in an attempt to reduce the heavy dependence upon imported metals. Together, the extraction of these minerals accounts for a gross annual turnover of £300 million per annum.

The degree of control exercised over the winning and working of minerals by town and country planning is very much greater than that over any other natural resource. The very nature of the extractive process with a predominance of open cast workings, the tremendous generation of traffic, the scars left by finished operations and the unsightly deposit of waste products, commends it to supervision within the sphere of environmental planning. Despite a certain amount of criticism to the contrary, a great deal has been achieved in regulating the way in which the working of minerals is pursued and the extent of landscape deterioration that is involved. As the industry falls exclusively within the private sector of the economy, unlike other resources, the principal control is the need to obtain planning permission. Within the planning permission can be incorporated a number of conditions relating to road access, screening, level of production and, perhaps most important of all, restoration. Many worked-out sand and gravel pits are easily adapted to alternative uses; for example, the filling in with waste and refuse followed eventually by residential development. A popular, and commercially attractive, 'after-use' in some river valleys has been the flooding of exhausted pits and the introduction of recreational pursuits such as angling, water ski-ing and sailing. Other sites, particularly metalliferous, can be returned to agriculture, forestry, or developed as wildlife sanctuaries. Some exciting and imaginative adventure playgrounds and recreational complexes have been established on what were previously mineral workings and slag heaps.

The wider problems of land dereliction are more fully discussed elsewhere,[17] but there still exist problems regarding the use of an ever-diminishing supply of mineral wealth. In this context certain recommendations have been put forward in an attempt to formulate a national policy. These include the need for further research into the development of alternative materials and processes, particularly in respect of the construction industry, more extensive recycling of metals, increased offshore mining, even further planning control and enforcement over mineral working, and the setting up of a Derelict Land Agency to supervise the task of reclamation.

Noise

The solitude of life is increasingly disturbed by the unseen, and largely intangible, atmospheric pollutant—noise. The aural invasion produced by motor vehicles, aircraft, industry and other human activities is fast becoming more than a nuisance and begins to assume the proportions of a major health hazard, both physical and mental.

Probably the most intrusive is that produced by motor traffic, which, when one considers that the amount of horsepower on the roads has doubled over the last seven years, is scarcely surprising. Following the 1963 Wilson Committee on noise and subsequent road traffic acts, fairly strict standards regarding permitted noise levels of individual vehicles have been laid

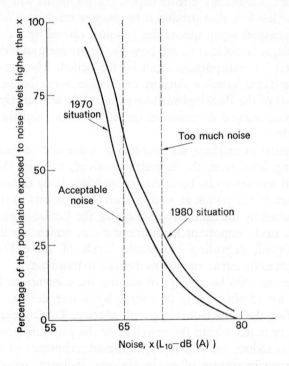

Fig. 26 Traffic noise exposure of the urban population in 1970 and 1980

down. The standards are being made even more stringent in respect of vehicles produced from 1973 onwards. It is not always possible, however, to ensure that this legislation is fully enforced;

the equipment is expensive and the task time-consuming. Moreover, these regulations and standards do not apply to streams of traffic, and the incessant drone produced by the sheer volume carried on urban motorways is a far more serious problem than the occasional individual miscreant.

Another major contributor to the disquiet of modern society is aircraft noise. Excluded from control under the Noise Abatement Act (1960), the advent of supersonic flight further threatens public privacy. The Air Navigation (Noise Certification) Order of 1970 has introduced standards for future types of aircraft to ensure that the noise from supersonic jet flights will be about half the level of that produced by present machines. Although these measures again ignore the problem caused by the volume of traffic, it is difficult to see how the desire for tranquillity and the need for transportation can be reconciled. The decision to site the Third London Airport on Maplin Sands instead of in the heart of the Buckinghamshire countryside was largely due to the environmental degradation caused by noise, and the public antipathy that this aroused.

To assist in tackling the problem of noise and to maintain a watching brief over the agencies involved, a Noise Advisory Council was set up in 1970. An independent body consisting of members of the public as well as accredited experts in the field, but chaired by the Secretary of State for the Environment, it has already made important recommendations, which are likely to be adopted, regarding acceptable levels of noise borne by residents unfortunate enough to front on to motorways.

There are two basic ways of solving the contentious issue of noise, by eliminating it at source by better design, and by separating the noise from the people affected. The latter approach falls very much within the province of the planning profession, who can reduce the impact by improved techniques of location and layout in respect of roads, airports, industry, schools, and housing. The setting of standards, the use of noise protractors, the zoning of land use activities with an appreciation of noise, and possibly the introduction of 'noise control areas' similar to those relating to smoke control, could all assist in ameliorating the situation.

Town planning and resource planning

The ability to strike a balance between economic efficiency and environmental amenity is the art and science of modern town planning. The planner is not just a conservationist or 'land accountant' but also an arbitrator of conflicting pressures and demands upon land and other resources. He is concerned with establishing and working towards long-term objectives, ensuring continued growth with progressive improvement. It is, therefore, encumbent upon him, in the preparation of a development plan, to undertake a survey and compile a record of such existing resources as coal, iron, water and power and also to promote an understanding of their availability, future demand, priorities for use and expected life. Moreover, he must be in a position to exercise control over their employment, condition and impact upon society.

In order to achieve this the nature and training of the physical land use planner must change. He must have regard for space and time as well as form. He must cultivate a knowledge of the human and economic, as well as built, environment. In other words he must adopt and develop a more comprehensive approach towards the environment, perhaps not individually but certainly as a profession. To implement his plans and policies, and to ensure their full perspective, a greater degree of co-ordination and co-operation is required at all levels of government and between all agencies active in society. Pollution, for example, is no respecter of boundaries. To be effective, therefore, the planning process needs to be more flexible, better conditioned to respond to ever-changing social, economic, and political circumstances. In addition, to eliminate contradictions and anomalies in a policy a more closely integrated approach between local authority departments and their constituent professional staff is called for.

Resource planning and pollution—references

1 Stone, P. A., 'Resources and the Economic Framework', *Developing Patterns of Urbanisation*, Peter Cowan (ed.), Oliver and Boyd (1970).

2 Ehrlich, P., *The Population Bomb*, Ballentine (1968).

3 *Ibid.*

4 See section on Population survey and techniques, page 121.

5 Edwards, A. and Wibberley, G., *An Agricultural Land Budget for Great Britain*, Wye College (1971).

6 HMSO, *Natural Resources: Sinews for Survival* (1972).

7 Allaby, M., 'British Farming: Revolution or Suicide?' *The Environmental Handbook*, John Barr (ed.), Ballentine (1972).

8 HMSO, *Natural Resources, op. cit.*

9 *Ibid.*

10 Department of the Environment, *The Human Environment. The British View*, HMSO (1972).

11 *Ibid.*

12 See section on The urban transportation problem, page 264.

13 Richardson, H., 'Economics and the Environment', *National Westminster Bank Quarterly Review*, May, 1971.

14 Department of the Environment, *op. cit.*

15 HMSO, *Natural Resources, op. cit.*

16 *Ibid.*

17 See section on Derelict land, page 221.

Further Recommended Reading

Aldous, T., *Battle for the Environment*, Fontana (1972).
Arvill, R., *Man and Environment* (1969).

18   Planning and public participation

Public or citizen participation has recently become an 'idea in good currency' and provides a watchword to both professionals and politicians involved in the planning process. A basic lack of communication exists between the planner and the planned, one that is exacerbated by an ever-increasing technical sophistication and the persistent use of professional jargon. Incomprehensible American articles on the very subject of participation amply portray the problem.

By its very nature land use planning affects every member of the community, albeit to varying degrees. In allocating the use of land and promoting future change, it determines the value of land, creating, apportioning, and redistributing wealth.

Because of this a veil of secrecy is often drawn over the preparation of plans and the choice between alternative strategies, until all is suddenly revealed in the final decision. The planning process in general, and the preparation of development plans in particular, has always appeared remote to the individual citizen, that is until he suffers an adverse decision in respect of his own property, or receives a notice to treat prior to compulsory acquisition, or finds an urban motorway spawning outside his window. Planning, therefore, is frequently stigmatised by its aspects of control, regulation, and intervention, bearing the brunt of personal and political attacks caused by poor communication and understandable self-interest.

245

The 1947 Town and Country Planning Act displayed supreme indifference to the need for discussion and consultation within the constituent community during the period of plan preparation. Its only gesture to participation was the limited quasi-judicial procedure of consideration of objections and representations before submission of the plan to the Minister and its publication as a *fait accompli* following approval. Thereafter, the legal right of dissent was restricted to certain persons who suffered an adverse planning decision or proposal.

The Planning Advisory Group, set up in 1964 to review the future of development plans, had as one of its main objectives 'to ensure that the planning system serves its purpose satisfactorily both as an instrument of planning policy and as a means of public participation in the planning process'. In their report they stated that a better public understanding of both the general aims of planning policy and the way in which it affected the individual was required. They also pointed out that because of the esoteric nature and technical detail of statutory plans this amounted to a major public relations task, calling for a great deal of careful thought and preparation, together with skill in presentation.

The 1968 Town and Country Planning Act, now re-enacted in the 1971 Town and Country Planning Act, attempted to incorporate these laudable objectives. A conflict, however, presented itself, for on the one hand there was the desire for greater consultation between the public and the planning agencies, whilst on the other there was the need for quicker decisions in the planning process. The government of the day endeavoured to reconcile these twin aims without seriously detracting from either by:

1. the devolution of responsibility in certain areas from central to local government, from local government to its appointed officers, and from the Secretary of State for the Environment to his Inspectors
2. providing that a local authority in drawing up a structure plan, and consequent local plans, give 'adequate publicity' to their survey, report, and policy and 'adequate opportunity' for public representations which should be taken into consideration in preparing the plan

246

3. depositing the plan for public inspection prior to submission and adoption
4. requiring the Secretary of State to be satisfied that the necessary steps to ensure full consultation have been taken

As a corollary to the 1968 Act the government commissioned a report concerning people and planning (the Skeffington Report) headed by the late Arthur Skeffington and published in 1969. Its terms of reference were to 'consult and report on the best methods including publicity, of securing the participation of the public at the formative stage in the making of development plans for their area'.

Many of its recommendations are couched in the most general of terms, which reflects the controversial yet universal nature of the subject and the implicit difficulties in establishing an acceptable procedure for citizen participation. It refers, for example, to the fact that 'people should be kept informed throughout the preparation of a structure or local plan for their area' and that they 'should be encouraged to participate in the preparation of plans by helping with surveys and other activities as well as by making comments'. It does not examine in any great depth the methods by which this can be achieved.

At a more practical level it did, however, propose the appointment of Community Development Officers who would assist in securing a greater degree of involvement from all sections of the community. Also the introduction of Community Forums to provide an opportunity for local organisations, agencies, and inhabitants to discuss local problems. It envisaged these forums and officers positively stimulating interest and concern to such an extent that formation of neighbourhood groups would result.

The report acknowledge that increased participation would probably mean increased planning blight. The 1968 Act itself, by way of 'strategic' structure planning, could with its 'broad brush' daub blight over a far wider area than did previous legislation, even though it might be a thinner coat. This might be acceptable if our laws in respect of compensation for injurious affection were adequate and equitable. The exposure of the decision-making process throughout all its stages could well extend the range of blight by the very consideration, through participation, of various alternatives. The uncertainty that goes

247

hand in hand with the flexibility generated by structure plans could be aggravated by any delay in the preparation, and particularly publication, of local plans. A serious temptation to local authorities unwilling to determine and define the exact area and degree of blight.

Another case militating against the adoption of continuous participation is that such deliberations can severely detract from early and viable implementation of particular planning and policies: witness the Piccadilly Circus debate and the Greater London Development Plan Inquiry. Such, perhaps, is the price of democracy.

Consultation and co-operation at all times on all matters, by all people, is probably an unrealistic ambition. Wholehearted and collective public action might be most appropriate to what can best be described as 'one-off jobs', such as the Stansted affair, the Cublington controversy, or the Homes before Roads campaign, where community involvement amounts to a reaction against planning proposals and an expression of concern that questions policies and priorities. It is much harder to incite interest in either the day-to-day decisions of development control or the determination of overall local government strategy.

One way in which an individual may demonstrate his displeasure at a particular planning decision is to lodge an appeal with the Secretary of State who will afford the 'aggrieved person' an opportunity to be heard in front of one of Her Majesty's Inspectors at either a local public inquiry or by written representation. This does not apply, however, to 'third parties', that is those persons affected by a planning proposal or decision but having no legal interest in the land subject to the decision; their rights are greatly curtailed, having at best what has been described as an administrative privilege to be heard as opposed to a legal right. The only exception to this is where the application for planning permission relates to what is described as 'un-neighbourly' or 'Clochemerle' development which must be advertised, at which time third parties are permitted to make written representations to the local planning authority. They are not, however, entitled to appeal if permission is subsequently granted. Although it can be argued that any relaxation of the rules that govern the rights of third parties would inevitably lead to a serious overloading of the planning appeal system, and, because it is comparatively inexpensive, give rise to abuse by vexatious litigation, nevertheless, a large proportion of the population still find themselves seriously disadvantaged. Examples of such circumstances can be found in the notorious 'Chalk Pit' case where a certain Major Buxton, whose house and land adjoined proposed chalk workings, discovered that he had no legal right to appeal or even to be heard at a local public inquiry, and again in the case of Gregory v London Borough of Camden where, although a local planning authority inadvertently granted permission for the change of use from a convent to a school without following the correct development plan amendment procedure, Mr. Gregory, whose property was materially affected, could not legally object.

Public participation is currently all too often synonymous with the mounting of exhibitions, the display of colourful maps and magnificent models, the delivery of professional talks, the showing of informative films, the holding of public meetings and the carrying out of questionnaires. These techniques, valuable in their own way, provide but a partial approach to the problem. Citizen involvement needs to be more closely associated with the identification of interest groups and the actual making of decisions that affect the local community, as well as consultation, education and information. In this respect the Greater London Council are taking steps to stimulate a greater measure of community action, and in this context the establishment of the Golborne Community Council, which attempts to reflect more accurately the varying views of different sectors of a local community and assist in policy making for the area, is a valiant experiment.

One sphere that readily lends itself to fuller exploitation in terms of public participation is the wider employment of the mass media. With the introduction of local radio, the relatively healthy state of local newspapers and the existence of regional television programmes, there is tremendous potential for both the dissemination of information and the expression of opinion to a far greater degree than presently is the case. Much progress has been made in this direction in the United States of America, due perhaps to the higher level of scepticism that is directed towards local government administration.

249

A neglected field for the practice of participation is at that evaluation stage in the planning process where certain techniques implicitly have a bearing upon the way in which decisions have been taken; particularly in connection with the handling of the social content of the development plan. The use of Cost Benefit Analysis in general, and the application of the Planning Balance Sheet and the Goals Achievement Matrix in particular, compels the professional planner and the political decision-maker to outline their strategy, define it in detail, and declare their hand, by attaching values to component parts of alternative schemes. This exposure of policy and judgement sets an ideal scene for citizen participation. An example of this was demonstrated at the evaluation stage of the South Hampshire structure plan undertaken within a comprehensive programme of participation and subject therefore to the pressures that such public involvement exerts.

In formulating the broad goals of their policy and establishing a procedure by which to judge alternative plans, the positive involvement of interested groups and organisations was attempted by South Hampshire based upon discussion, consultation, survey and questionnaire and employing extensive use of the local press and other media to publicise progress. One obvious problem emerges from their experience and that concerns the very nature of the goals themselves and the difficulties in attaching priorities to them. Two of the eight goals were *image*, that is the need to give a particular identity to new development in various parts of the area, and *flexibility*, the ability of the respective plans to adapt in the light of changing circumstances. It is hard enough for the professional town planner to comprehend the full significance of these goals and distinguish between them, let alone to expect the average lay man to do so.

Apart from the current trend towards innovation regarding this controversial topic there are other existing agencies of participation available, such as the Parliamentary Commissioner or Ombudsman, despite his limited powers, the various consumer associations, residents' groups, members of parliament and a host of organisations such as the Council for the Protection of Rural England, The Royal Fine Arts Commission and the Automobile Association who each, in their own way, promote the interest of their membership. It is perhaps worthy of note that the most vociferous and active citizens, those who tend to involve themselves in participation, are normally quite capable of representing themselves in any case. The problem is to stimulate concern amongst the 'silent', unrepresented, majority.

Planning and public participation—recommended reading

American Institute of Planners Journal, July, 1969.

Broady, M., *Planning for People*, Bedford Square Press (1968).

Committee on Public Participation in Planning, *People and Planning*, HMSO (1969).

Cullingworth, J. B., *Town and Country Planning in England and Wales*, Allen and Unwin (1970).

Dennis, N., *People and Planning*, Faber and Faber (1970).

Hall, D., 'The Participation Experiment', *Town and Country Planning*, September, 1969.

Housing and Urban Development Department, *Citizen Participation Today*, Conference proceedings, Chicago, H.U.D. (1968).

Reynolds, J. P. (ed.), 'Public Participation in Planning', *Town Planning Review*, July, 1969.

19 Planning and land values

In a society of ever-accelerating social, economic and technological change a complex and sophisticated urban pattern is bound to evolve. Inherent within this structure are the cross-currents of conflicting personal, political, and philosophical pressures. Perhaps the principal area where these divergent forces collide is that concerning land. The disputatious elements of tenure, proprietary interest, speculation and social need have entangled to produce a monstrous legislative morass, riddled with anachronism, befuddled by anomaly and founded upon obscure theory.

Private and public land uses, though related and interdependent, vie for dominance, and though the value of one is inextricably bound in the fate of the other, they lie in uneasy harmony even in the planner's presumed dispassionate design.

Land value

The initial study of the concept and development of the theory of land value has been confined almost exclusively to North America. The problems implicit in managing the wealth that accrues from land, and the implementation of a social and economic system that administers the equities of land ownership, and reconciles the public and private interest, are very much more related to our own experience and circumstance in the United Kingdom.

Concern with land and its associated value dates back to the eighteenth century and has its origins in David Ricardo's theory of agricultural rent. Ricardo, himself a man of considerable property, pointed out that land as a factor of production has two unique characteristics. First, it is limited in quantity, and second, its existence is fortuitous, being a free gift of nature and owing nothing to man's enterprise. The monetary return to the owner was due, therefore, to demand and not to his individual labours. The different values on varying plots of land was caused by an intrinsic qualitative advantage, for in his view the 'corn was not high because rents were high, but rents were high because corn was high'.

Von Thünen, a German economist and incidentally another wealthy landowner, echoed Ricardo's analysis and developed it a stage further by demonstrating that the yield from land was not simply a function of fertility or fortune but was also dependent upon the distance and transport costs to the market. Land in close proximity to markets would be used intensively and in connection with those products having high transport costs and demanding centrality. Von Thünen thus showed that rent more usually arose out of a locational, rather than an intrinsic, quality of the land and this advantage with regard to a market only exists because someone has created the market.

This is even more clearly demonstrated when one examines the relationship in terms of urban land, for where Von Thünen and Ricardo were principally concerned with agricultural land, all plots in a given urban area are of approximately the same quality, their function being basically that of support. Probably the earliest, and still one of the most succinct, analysis of the determination of urban land values was that set forth at the turn of the century by R. M. Hurd who asserted that 'since value depends upon economic rent, and rent on location, and location on convenience, and convenience on nearness, we may eliminate the intermediate steps and say that value depends on nearness'. Thus the pattern of urban structure is largely a result of a continuous struggle to maximise proximity or accessibility and minimise friction or transportation. In combination these forces aim to minimise cost, thus producing a situation where all urban activities compete for sites where costs are lowest. This process of competition, and the resultant 'bidding' that takes place in such a climate, leads, in an unrestricted market, to the activity which can most successfully exploit the locational attributes of a particular site, obtaining and occupying it. In effect these activities are 'bidding' away their economic rent, and it is the level of economic rent that determines the level of land values.

The very purpose of town planning, however, it to ensure that the welfare, efficiency, and productivity of the community as a whole is maximised, not just the return to a particular activity on a particular site. The regulation, intervention, and guidance exercised on behalf of the community through its planning powers establishes the nature and degree of accessibility and the location and strength of markets. This is especially true in this country where land is a scarce commodity, suitable and available undeveloped land is virtually non-existent and the majority of urban growth takes place within the city through the process of redevelopment. In such circumstances, therefore, where the economic rent accruing from land is largely publicly controlled some will gain while others lose.

Betterment/worsenment

It is first advisable to explain the terms *'betterment'* and *'worsenment'*, and clarify the relationship between them. Betterment is the increase in the value of land which accrues to the owner of that land as a result of the action of others, often public authorities. Where a decrease in the value of land due to the action of others occurs it is described as worsenment, and on those occasions when payment is made to mitigate the hardship of this loss it is described as *compensation*. The philosophy that underlies the contentious concept of the collection of betterment stems from the notion that being a community-created value it is fortuitous or unearned; moreover, large portions of it must be rendered up to ensure adequate measures of compensation are made available to alleviate the incidence of worsenment. The philosophical and political arguments are lengthy, tortuous, and beyond the scope of this text. They are, however, cogently summarised by Palgrave in his *Dictionary of Political Economy*, who defends the recovery of betterment as follows:

'. . . that persons benefited by public expenditure should contribute to such expenditure to the extent of the increased value of their property, and this not only if the improvement effected by the local authority was carried out for the purpose of conferring a benefit on such property, but also if the resulting benefit was purely accidental, the expenditure having been undertaken for a totally different purpose'.

Although certain individual and locally applied attempts to collect betterment were made in the murkier undocumented depths of the Middle Ages, and again in 1662 by Charles II who attempted a recover a portion of what was then described as 'melioration' regarding the increase in value due to London street-widening schemes, the recent legislative history can be traced back to the advent of the rail-building boom of the last century.

With the widespread application of compulsory purchase powers, and the general incorporation with acquisition of a standard code for compensation embodied in the Lands Clauses Consolidation Act 1845, combined with a common practice of awarding an extra 10%, or more, above normal purchase price to account for the 'forced sale', there came a realisation of the increases in land values elsewhere as a result of public undertakings and a pressure for collection. It was not until 1895, however, and the Tower Bridge Southern Approach Act of that year, that any betterment provisions were enacted. The scheme was very limited and merely allowed the London County Council to make a levy on the annual increase in value of properties immediately benefiting from the authority's road improvement works. It was also unsuccessful.

There were several other similar Acts which found their way on to the Statute Book around the turn of the century, whilst at the same time a strong current of feeling in favour of the introduction of some form of site value rating which failed to find sufficient parliamentary support. In 1909, however, the first comprehensive attempt to tackle the vexed question was included in the Housing, Town Planning Etc. Act which permitted local authorities to impose a 50% Betterment Levy on properties that had benefited as a result of one of their planning schemes. The following year saw the introduction of a far more sophisticated and comprehensive measure under the auspices of the 1910 Finance Act which introduced four types of duty on land, which were:

1. Increment value duty—a levy of 20% on the increase in value of land upon conveyance
2. Undeveloped land duty—at the rate of $\frac{1}{2}$d in the £ every year on the site value of undeveloped land
3. Reversion duty—a tax of 10% payable by the lessor on the value of the reversion at the end of the lease
4. Mineral rights duty—5% p.a. on mineral working rents

Due to the problems of valuation and administration all four were abandoned by 1920.

All this time the courts were awarding the '10% bonus' to allow for forced sale in cases of compulsory purchase. In 1919, however, the Acquisition of Land (Assessment of Compensation) Act introduced the 'Six Basic Rules' which still form part of the procedure by which compensation is assessed. The main effect was to abolish the 10% rule and establish open market value as the appropriate level. The Law Society have recently advocated a return to the pre-1919 situation, a clear admission, perhaps, of our failure to adequately reconcile proprietary interests and returns from land with the requirements of comprehensive planning.

Until 1947 the only other major change in the provisions of the 1909 Act was the raising of the rate of levy from 50% to 75% by the Town & Country Planning Act 1932. In 1943, however, an expert committee under the chairmanship of Lord Justice A. A. Uthwatt produced a report on Compensation and Betterment which still represents probably the most exhaustive study on the problem to date. The principal recommendations were:

1. that the development rights in undeveloped land should be vested in the state. All future land required for development would be compulsorily purchased at a value reflecting its existing use, and leased back at full open market value, thus recouping betterment
2. if the land was 'dead-ripe' for development, plans having

been prepared for it, it should still be acquired by the state but compensation would be full development value

3. developed land would only be acquired as and when necessary for planning schemes. The level of compensation would be assessed at full open market value as at 31 March 1939, thus, hopefully, discouraging excess speculation

4. a levy, for example 75%, would be imposed upon all increases in the value of land as from a particular date, with five-year revaluations

5. central government grants should be made available to local authorities to assist in the redevelopment of central areas

In making their recommendations the committee had taken account of several problems that surround the issue of betterment/worsenment. Firstly, defining the amount of the increase in the value of land that was attributable to direct public policy, and not market forces, was problematical. Secondly, the valuation of respective interests was difficult. Thirdly, if compensation was to be paid for restriction development might 'shift' elsewhere, and so one authority might collect betterment whilst another was forced to pay worsenment. Fourthly, if compensation was to be made in full for restriction in development, the actual worsenment might 'float' over many properties and owners' claims would exceed actual damage. For these reasons the recommendations have a pragmatic rather than philosophical approach to the problem.

The 1947 Town & Country Planning Act, which draws heavily from the Uthwatt Report, and a White Paper on *The Control of Land Use* published in 1945, has become established as a major landmark in land use planning, and is exhaustively documented elsewhere. In order only to achieve continuity, therefore, the principal enactments are listed below:

1. planning was made subject to central control

2. *all* development rights were vested in the state

3. planning permission was required for all development, and a charge was made on the difference between the existing use value, and the developed value, of land

4. existing use value was established as the basis of compensation for compulsory purchase

5. a Global Fund of £300 million was set up to compensate those persons who lost existing development value. The total sum claimed amounted to £376 million, which after allowing for 'floating' value would appear to be a remarkably accurate estimate

For a number of reasons, including the shortage of materials, and the general restriction of development, as well as the 100% Development Charge, the land market was stultified following the 1947 Act. A return to Conservative government resulted in the Town and Country Planning Acts of 1953 and 1954 which abolished the Development Charge, extinguished the Global Fund converting the claims for loss of development rights into Unexpended Balances of Established Development Value, but anomalously still restricted the compensation for compulsory purchase to existing use value only. This anachronistic and manifestly unjust state of affairs whereby a dual level of values existed side by side was rectified by the 1959 Town and Country Planning Act which re-established an open market value for land compulsorily acquired. This Act was subsequently consolidated in the 1961 Land Compensation Act which still prevails.

The only other major piece of legislation that has 'entered the lists' and tilted at the twin problems of compensation and betterment was the Land Commission Act 1967. This ill-fated enactment arose from a pledge in *Signpost for the Sixties* which reflected the general concern in the steeply rising cost of land. In brief, it sought to ensure that sufficient land was made available for development at the right time, in the right place, at the right price; and to ensure that a substantial proportion of development value created by the community returned to the community. Again sufficient detail is available elsewhere but suffice it to say that if the Commission had not been stigmatised with its betterment collecting duties, and plagued with the optimistic hopes of political punditry, it might have fulfilled a valuable role as a land-dealing agency.

We are then left with only two general measures currently in force which remotely approximate to a levy on betterment,- Capital Gains Tax at 30% where applicable, and the provisions of S.7 of the Land Compensation Act 1961 in respect of 'off-set'.

258

Although at the time of writing the government is contemplating the introduction of a land-hoarding tax.

Alternative solutions to the betterment/worsenment problem

One immediate solution is to do nothing, but to allow the fortuitous and unrestricted reallocation of land values due to public authority activity, wherever and whenever it occurs. In respect of betterment this is virtually the current situation, with the burden falling upon no one but the planning agencies. The corollary to this, however, is that no compensation for worsenment should be paid, which is obviously politically, and perhaps morally, unacceptable. The authority responsible must therefore, in effect, pay a double cost. This policy must inevitably detract from efficient and effective land use planning. The remaining variety of positive alternatives ranges from the arbitrary application of partial taxes, charges and levies, to immediate and comprehensive nationalisation of land. The following text briefly represents the majority of suggested reforms.

(A) Nationalisation

The principal problems that beset the viability of land nationalisation as an acceptable solution are the political implications of endeavouring to change the whole character and tradition of land ownership and tenure in this country; and the financial repercussions implicit in the payment of vast sums of compensation that might be unleashed upon the economy in any transitional arrangements introducing nationalisation.

1. Total nationalisation—Despite the inherent financial difficulties, and the political stigma, it would at least provide an instant panacea to the betterment problem. The task of valuation, however, would be stupendous and there is no reason why the process should not be made more gradual.

2. Unification of the reversion—This would avoid the problem of massive payments of compensation, for it would convert existing freehold tenure into long leaseholds of approximately the same value, which upon subsequent effluxion would revert to the state. It thus has the same effect as nationalisation but

mitigates the political and financial impact. The Uthwatt Committee made reference to such a scheme in paras. 348 *et seq.* whereby 'all land in Great Britain be forthwith converted into leasehold interests held by the present proprietors as lessees of the state at a peppercorn rent for such uniform term of years as may reasonably, without payment of compensation, be regarded as equitable, and subject to such conditions enforceable by re-entry as may from time to time be applicable under planning schemes'.

3. 'Lifing'—A scheme incorporating the unification of the reversion was proposed by *Socialist Commentary* in 1961 and described by Lichfield in *Land Values* in 1965. In this system all buildings would be surveyed and given a 'life' of up to 80 years depending upon their physical condition. Undeveloped land would be given a 'life' of 80 years subject to rent reviews and building leases granted upon development. During the statutory life of a building an increased rental would be levied by the state to reflect any change in value. Leases could be conveyed as would normally be the case, and for changes of use or upon redevelopment new leases could be arranged with revised rents. At the end of the lease the building would belong to the state, and compensation would be limited to the original site value plus 50% of any site value increase. There have been many criticisms of this scheme and it probably compares unfavourably with the Uthwatt proposals.

(B) Partial solutions to the betterment/worsenment problem

1. The unification of development rights—The purpose of this scheme is to vest all development value in the state whilst leaving land in the ownership of individual owners to change hands at existing use value, and was the basis of the 1947 Town and Country Planning Act. The chief criticism levelled at this method is the stultifying effect it can have on development, particularly if a change in political control and associated repeal is expected. Moreover, although all betterment is collected, the administrative problems concerning the assessment and payment of compensation are not reconciled.

2. Land management and levy—Similar to the recent Land Commission, whereby some central authority is charged with the responsibility of co-ordinating land development in this country. It would be vested with powers of compulsory purchase and exempt from any tax, charge, or levy, thus placing it in a favourable position and capable of ensuring a steady supply of land coming on to the market, particularly in crisis areas. Once again worsenment is neglected and betterment collection is only partial and the higher the level of levy the greater the discouragement of development.

3. Site value rating—This scheme is a principal plank in the party political platform of the Liberal Party. It has its roots in the Ricardian theory of economic rent, Adam Smith had proposed a tax on the returns from land, John Stuart Mill put forward a programme for taxing 'The future unearned increase of the value of land', and in 1879 Henry George advocated a Single Tax on Land, intended to replace all other forms of taxation.

Site value rating is essentially an annual tax on the site value of land. It is not levied on any improvement to the land, but is based on the optimal use to which the land can be put. It is, therefore, maintained that landowners would be encouraged to release vacant land because they are taxed on its development potential irrespective of whether or not the development has taken place. A similar argument is advanced in respect of re-development. It is also stated that the burden of the rate will fall upon the landowner since he is the person who receives the benefit of site value, but this idea is open to debate. The proportion of betterment collected depends upon the level of the site value rate decided upon. Revaluations would occur at appropriate intervals as with the present rating system, at least in theory. In one guise or another this approach has been adopted in New Zealand, Australia, Jamaica, Denmark and South Africa.

The major difficulties inherent in such a scheme are as follows: the revaluations tend to be postponed; the valuation task might be extremely complex, although the Whitstable study undertaken in 1964 to test the viability of site value rating proved otherwise; the decision as to 'optimal' use might be open to question and review leading to uncertainty, blight and conservatism; and the problem of worsenment is poorly covered.

4. Other proposals—Several reforms have been suggested that relate to improving the existing codes, particularly in respect of compensation for worsenment. Firstly, the Greater London Council have indicated a desire to extend their powers of acquisition to property that falls outside the line of any proposed scheme, but is so seriously affected that it cannot be disregarded. Also to acquire property that is required for environmental purposes in connection, for example, with redevelopment schemes. Further, to carry out, or make grants to owners towards the cost incurred in carrying out remedial works such as sound-proofing.

There is a strong current of opinion urging reform of the present law relating to compensation for injurious affection when no land is taken. The Chartered Land Societies Committee in 1968 proposed that this area should be subject to the same rules as those when land is taken, and that the individual compulsory purchase order might define lands not taken to which the rules could apply. In effect this merely provides for an extension of the line, arguably on a more arbitrary basis. They also recommended that claims for injurious affection might be delayed for up to two years to determine the real impact of any scheme, disturbance payments should be extended, interest-free grants for house purchase should be made available to displaced owner occupiers forced to buy more expensive accommodation and the qualifying categories for blight should be widened.

These are all recommendations of considerable merit but relate to an existing and perhaps inadequate code. With the proportion of national income spent on public works increasing yearly and the magnitude and degree of land use planning becoming ever more sophisticated and extensive, it is perhaps time to consider the full repercussions of neglecting a fundamental solution to this vexed and thorny problem.

Planning and land values

Recommended reading

Chartered Land Societies Committee, *Compensation for Compulsory Acquisition and Planning Restrictions*, C.L.S.C. (1968).

Hall, P. (ed.), *Land Values*, Sweet and Maxwell (1965).

Justice, *Compensation for Compulsory Acquisition and Remedies for Planning Restrictions*, Stevens (1969).

Pennance, F., Housing, Town Planning and Land Commission, *Hobart Paper 40*, Institute of Economic Affairs (1967).

Turvey, R., *The Economics of Real Property*, Allen and Unwin (1957).

20 The urban transportation problem

Hall, P., ...
...
Transport, K., *The benefits of ...* Allen and Unwin (1971).

The need for transport is an integral facet of everyday life. There is no escape from it, everybody is concerned and to some degree everybody is affected. It plays a dominant role in determining the scale, nature and form of our towns and cities. Its efficiency contributes largely to the level of productivity, economic growth and thus the standard of living. Its character greatly impinges upon the solitude of life, and yet its presence provides the life blood of the community.

Motoring gives great pleasure to large sections of the population, and contributes enormous sums to the Treasury by way of taxation. In a country where over 80% of the inhabitants live in towns and where there are 2·5 miles of road for every square mile, the highest proportion in the world, the continued and growing presence of the private motor car is rapidly becoming incompatible with urban life. With an increasing population expanding urban areas, rising car ownership, greater demand for space by every method of transport, ever-inflating traffic peaks getting sharper and sharper and growing competition for land from every quarter, the situation continues to worsen.

The problems inherent in any urban transport system, be it car, train or bus, are therefore pitched into the tumult of public controversy and subject to the vagaries of political, economic, and social expediency. These impediments severely limit any truly objective analysis or comprehensive solution capable of immediate implementation.

With circumstances reaching such critical proportions it is possible to discern for the first time a certain public reaction against the dominance and intrusion of the motor car. The recent debate that raged around the Greater London Council's road proposals, the emergence of political pressure groups like the Homes Before Roads campaign, and the action of a number of hard-pressed but realistic and imaginative local planning authorities indicate a changing attitude. Nearly ten years after the publication of Professor Colin Buchanan's timely warning regarding the environmental impact of *Traffic in Towns*[1] the first glimmerings of sense are starting to appear. Two principal approaches present themselves in the struggle to cure the cancerous incursion of the car, which the Americans describe as 'auto-sclerosis', into our towns. First, planning restriction, and second, economic charging, both fully cognisant of the fact that there can be no such thing as a town without traffic, both equally designed to remedy the malaise and promote urban efficiency.

Planning restriction

This approach is very much the domain of the transportation and physical land use planner, and although traffic management in its many forms has been employed for years there still exist areas for improvement.

Banning of cars

Probably the most difficult, politically, though not administratively, to implement. Having placed a total restriction upon the entry of private motor vehicles into central areas problems arise in deciding whether or not there should be exemptions, and if so for whom; doctors, midwives and the police spring immediately to mind as worthy causes, but what about builders, plumbers, window cleaners and milkmen? The line would be extremely hard to draw, and the repercussions hotly debated. A mounting pressure exists, however, to rehabilitate cities for pedestrian use and to permit them to return to fulfilling their proper function as civic and cultural centres. An alternative to the rather drastic solution of total prohibition would be partial restriction during certain hours and in this context it should not be forgotten that congestion is not just a twentieth century problem, for even in first century Rome wheeled traffic was restricted to the hours of darkness to combat this menace.[2]

New road construction

Although travel times can sometimes be shortened, and average speed increased, building new roads as a solution to urban congestion and environmental degradation is rather like printing more money as a cure to rising inflation. More roads tend to generate more trips and thus exacerbate the situation. Aldous[3] highlights one paradoxical contribution that major urban road construction has made towards the battle for the environment. It concerns the outcry that accompanied the development of Westway in London where public interest was focused upon the real social cost imposed on the neighbouring communities by such a scheme. He suggests that society owes a great debt to the engineers and politicians who pushed through the proposals, unconsciously awakening unparalleled public concern regarding the future of towns and their traffic.

Park and ride

This is a description of what potentially could provide one of the easiest, most attractive and least expensive answers to the problem. It involves the construction of multi-storey car parks unobtrusively, yet conveniently, sited at major transport terminii or route intersections on the periphery of towns or central city areas where land is relatively cheap. From these points a fast regular public transport service would convey the erstwhile motorist to his destination in town, relieved of the frustration, worry, and cost of central area parking. Leeds have already introduced such a system with outlying car parks linked with the centre by a mini-bus service which appears to be enjoying considerable success. Leicester envisages car parks built above their transport terminii, and the prospect of this technique being applied to London, with generous parking facilities being strategically placed at the end of motorways and alongside Underground terminii, presents tremendous scope.

Parking control
The number of cars entering nearly every conurbation in the country continues to increase, and at a much faster rate than the provision of parking space. The chances of a motorist finding a meter within a reasonable time in London are now placed at seven to one against. The supply of more spaces would assuredly lead to the generation of more traffic. Whilst one answer is to increase charges, another is to introduce selective control whereby the commuter, who is the prime culprit of the diurnal chaos, is actively discouraged from indulging in his long-term parking. Several local planning authorities are operating a system of 'shoppers only' car parks which remain closed until 10.00 a.m. and shut again at 4.00 p.m., thus denying access to the car-borne office worker.

Separation of traffic
This involves the provision of separate lanes for public and private motor vehicles. Although it has operated abroad for several years the scheme was first fully introduced in this country in Reading. A one-way traffic management scheme was put into practice with the buses running in their own lanes against the flow of other vehicles. A measure of its success is demonstrated by the fact that journey times have been reduced by around 40%, accident rates are down, and the number of passengers carried is up. Certain inherent difficulties would be encountered if this approach were comprehensively applied in all towns; street widths, numerous intersections, and complicated route patterns all detract from its viability. It has the merit of lending itself to partial introduction where circumstances are favourable. London already has several bus-only lanes and contemplates many more.

Better management of existing roads
The present transport network is capable of carrying a greater capacity with improved and more flexible planning. The designation of 'tidal flow' lanes, such as the one across Magdalen Bridge, Oxford, which employs movable bollards, carrying traffic one way in the morning and the other way in the evening, can facilitate movement. Similarly certain routes can be restricted

to one-way traffic for part of the day only. During the various railway strikes London-bound commuters were pleasantly surprised by the efficacy of one-way radial routes at rush hours. Another method of improving the capacity of the existing road system has been developed with the installation of computer-controlled traffic lights which take account of actual, and often unpredictable, traffic flows and adjust the timing and sequence of lights accordingly. Experimental schemes pioneered in Glasgow and Kensington improved the flow of traffic by 16% and 9% respectively.[4]

Improved public transport system

The alleviation of congestion caused by private motor vehicles is the improvement most sought after by public transport operators. Meanwhile, certain other steps can be taken to ensure a more efficient and satisfying service. The introduction of yearly, quarterly, and monthly season tickets together with the sale of 'rover' tickets on buses has been extremely successful on the Continent, particularly in Sweden. Early fears regarding a loss of revenue proved groundless, for takings actually increased. Moreover, the changeover to one-man buses is made a great deal easier with fewer people requiring change and causing delays. Other suggestions for improving the public transport system include the use of two-way radio sets in buses in order to identify and sometimes avoid hold-ups, moving pavements to connect transport interchanges, a separate elevated reserved track system that would accept and automatically control both private and public vehicles, monorails which can be designed to economise on valuable urban space and computer-controlled dial-and-ride taxi services which can be operated on a very flexible basis to meet the demands of passengers.

Changing working conditions

As previously indicated it is the work-bound commuter and the consequent rush-hour congestion that lie at the heart of the urban transportation problem. Some social scientists firmly predict a radical change in the nature, scale and location of future employment,[5] a kind of second industrial revolution. The first signs can already be discerned. In Japan several large companies, thwarted by congestion and the detrimental environment of city centres, have reversed the normal patterns of work, installing two-way television in employees' homes, any essential personal contact is conducted at home. The results have been increased productivity and enhanced leisure time. Another interesting innovation, this time from Germany, is the voluntary and flexible staggering of working hours under a system known as *Gleitzeit* or 'sliding time', whereby workers are permitted to arrive and leave at times of their own choosing within two-hourly limits at the beginning and end of the day, being paid according to the number of hours worked. This method of spreading the impact of peak hour travel has already been introduced in this country and represents a useful contribution to the overall problem.

Economic charging

In any economic appraisal of the provision of transport services it is immediately apparent that there is a serious imbalance between demand and supply. Not only is there a general excess demand and limited supply of services and stock, but it is also exacerbated at certain times and in certain places.

The result of this disequilibrium is congestion, associated with a loss in efficiency through reduced accessibility and, more often than not, a deterioration in the quality of the urban environment. Thus we are presented with a 'Buchanan's Law' situation whereby the degree of accessibility, the quality of the environment, and the cost of providing transport services are all interrelated, for instance, if the environmental standards are held constant then the degree of accessibility depends upon the amount of money spent on transport services; if the degree of accessibility is held constant then the environmental standard again depends upon the amount of money spent upon the transport services. This may appear to be a statement of the blindingly obvious, but it lies at the kernel of any appreciation of the urban transport problem, that is, the question is as much one of deciding priorities in the overall distribution of national resources as well as how effectively they should be spent once the decision is made. It should be recognised at this juncture that in Great

Britain only 1·30% of the gross national product is spent on roads compared with 2·48% in Japan, 2·23% in Germany and 1·47% in France.[6]

An underlying cause of the problem which merits considerable attention is the fact that urban transport is a rising cost industry, but unlike other rising cost industries prices have not risen selectively to choke off demand, particularly when one considers peak hour, and peak location, travel demands. The result is, of course, the commuting chaos of which we are all only too aware, due to the fact that supply cannot meet demand. The 'market solution' would be flexible discriminatory pricing, as for example with telephone services, where, after a basic charge, consumers are levied according to their individual use.

Before examining any form of pricing solution, it is necessary to look at the nature and form of the various costs involved in establishing an urban transport system.

Urban transport costs

It is possible to identify certain categories of costs, all conceptually quantifiable, which can be attributed to the use of roads. For example, some of these costs are private costs borne by the motorist, and some are social costs borne by non-motorists, rival motorists competing for road space, public services, the government, and the environment.

These costs can also be divided up into direct and indirect costs.

(A) Direct costs

Within this category there can be included initial construction costs of roads; associated capital costs, such as expenditure on snowploughs, gritters and other servicing equipment; maintenance costs; interest charges on capital; and ancillary servicing costs such as administration, lighting, signs, research and policing. If is fair to assume that the general consensus of opinion would agree that the motorist, as road user, should bear all of these

270

costs which arise as a direct consequence of his activity. In fact many motorists would advance the argument that in fact they do, and more besides, for in most years an amount approaching £1000 million is collected by the Exchequer in excise tax, fuel tax, and purchase tax over and above that spent on road building. It is arguable, however, that purchase tax cannot reasonably be included, for after all, it is levied on a multitude of other consumption goods, and one rarely hears demands from cigarette smokers, or drinkers, that the revenue from excise tax should be devoted to research on cancer or alcoholism.

(B) Indirect costs

Within this category are included accident costs, congestion costs, environmental costs, and alternative use value or opportunity costs.

(1) *Accident costs*
These are borne in general by the National Health Service and present delicate problems of measurement. It is an extremely difficult area to analyse in cost terms, for how does one assess the value of life or limb?

(2) *Congestion costs*
These are imposed by motorists on each other, but the effects spill over in the form of noise, exhaust fumes and visual affliction to the non-motorist sector. Briefly, after a certain level each successive vehicle which enters a traffic stream imposes cost in additional tyre, brake, and clutch wear, as well as extra petrol consumption and time losses, on all other vehicles already in the stream. At present the additional motorist only pays his own costs, which only rise very gradually for each successive motorist. Costs for the whole stream rise very much more rapidly as traffic increases. With a few rudimentary, and perhaps questionable, assumptions about motorists' valuation of time saving, one can quantify those marginal social costs on a congested road. For a private car the Road Pricing Panel suggested, some years ago, that these costs might be:

271

$$2p \quad \text{per vehicle mile at 20 mph}$$
$$5\tfrac{1}{2}p \quad \text{per vehicle mile at 15 mph}$$
$$17\tfrac{1}{2}p \quad \text{per vehicle mile at 10 mph}$$
$$\text{and } 30p \quad \text{per vehicle mile at 8 mph}$$

If, by some means, motorists were forced to pay this kind of marginal social cost, congestion would be considerably reduced as 'marginal motorists' left their cars at home, or travelled by a less congested route. It should, none the less, be emphasised that these congestion costs are borne by the motorist at present, but not equally or with any account of the optimum or best use of road space or individual's time.

(3) *Environmental costs*
These are largely ignored by many transport economists who maintain that they are not capable of measurement. This, however, is no reason for assuming their value to be zero which, when one examines an extreme case such as urban motorway flyovers, is manifestly not so. There is, perhaps, a need for some sort of scale similar to daylighting indicators, which would take account of noise, fumes, and visual intrusion.

(4) *Alternative use value*
Also described as the opportunity cost, this is borne by the community who, when allocating resources, one of which being land, to road uses, forego the returns which would be derived from the next best use of that land, and those resources. This opportunity cost of land is likely to be considerable in central urban areas and it can be argued that motorists should pay to ensure that this land devoted to roads is preserved in its transportation use. In so doing they would be identifying and taking into account the respective costs and revenues involved in their use of land and services, thus facilitating an efficient distribution of resources. This naturally assumes that motorists would adopt a rational approach towards their expenditure, utilities and preferences.

The price mechanism and the urban transport problem

It should now be clear that the construction and use of urban roads involves a whole series of costs, quantifiable in varying degrees, and falling on a number of different sectors. The motorist's traditional claim that he more than meets the costs is a dubious one. It now requires to be demonstrated why he should meet the costs he imposes personally and, if so, how best this can be done. One immediate argument might be the ethical one of equity, why should others be compelled to pay for the various costs that he, the motorist, has imposed or created? The economic viewpoint has pretentions to a more logical and useful rationale. That is, that the individual motorists should pay these costs directly when and where they arise, since only in this manner will the best possible use be made of available road space, and, in the long run, of the resources available for investment in transport.

An economic system, of which the price mechanism is one tool, is required to make some contribution towards the solution of two major problems. Firstly, the allocation of existing resources, amenities and products to members of the community in such a way that maximum social welfare is achieved, in whatever way that is defined. Secondly, the application of land, labour, capital and organisation towards the construction or production of new amenities, facilities, or capital goods to a similar end.

A traditional solution of these two problems has been the use of a price mechanism, with competitive markets and competitively determined prices for each product, paid out of individual personal incomes. Given that there are not too many additional complexities this is a highly appealing solution. Producers are free to enter a production market and produce goods on a maximum profit basis at a price that equals the cost of the last unit of output (Marginal Cost). If profits are known to be above a minimum reasonable return, other potential producers will enter the market, and additional investment will be undertaken until competition brings prices down to an equilibrium level. At the same time, consumers will purchase enough of each individual item to make equal the overall marginal benefits from spending an additional unit of income.

In any examination of the market for transport services and the propagation of a pricing solution it is necessary to look in more detail at the components and determinants of an equilibrium position, demand and supply.

Demand and supply of transport services

There are various forms of demand in the transport market and they all have, to some extent, differing requirements. The demand may be for services to work, during work or shopping or leisure. These purposes in themselves may be categorised as 'essential' or 'optional' and may be supplied by any one of a number of means of transport either private or public, that is, the Underground, British Rail, bus services, private cars, motorcycles, bicycles or footpaths.

Demand characteristics

Notable amongst the characteristics of demand is the increasing pressure at peak periods in terms of time and quantity together with the rapidly growing number of long journeys in urban areas. In analysing the demand for transport it is also essential to differentiate between actual 'revealed' demand and 'suppressed' demand. Hence a new road system may not solve a congestion problem because transport demand is not only determined by total population income, wealth, car ownership preference, distribution of population and working hours. It is also directly related to supply, and if there is such a highway improvement the 'suppressed' demand will reveal itself in the form of generated traffic.

In the long run excess demand might perhaps be eliminated by strategic or detailed land use planning, for example, new linear settlements, out-of-town shopping centres or commercial and industrial re-location. It might even be the case that individuals' travel habits might be altered, as could be working and shopping hours by cheap off-peak fares.

The immediate problems of excess demand that present themselves require more urgent action in the form of demand restraint, an admittedly short-term solution.

Supply characteristics

When considering the various elements that make up the supply side of the urban transport market it should be remembered that the individual owner of the private family saloon has a distinct advantage in several ways, despite the cost of congestion, namely, he has a far higher degree of flexibility and convenience, it is considerably more comfortable and scores heavily over public transport for short journeys.

When total mass movements of commuters are being examined, however, it is an inescapable fact that buses are eight times more efficient than the car and the Underground is four times more efficient than the bus.

In attempting to alleviate the problems caused by insufficient supply of transport facilities, it is possible to make marginal improvements in the short run by such means as adding extra coaches to trains or introducing short-haul bus services. Further, road transport may gain some initial benefit from traffic management schemes (for example, one-way systems, clearways or linked signals), but the overall gain may be minimal owing to longer routes being involved, generated traffic and environmental destruction. The short-run supply approach may thus be considered an inadequate stop-gap.

The traditional long-run approach to solving the problems caused by inadequate supply of urban transportation has been to introduce increasingly larger road building programmes. This was certainly true in the fifties; the Buchanan Report saw it into the sixties, although the need for traffic restraint was recognised; and the London motorway proposals suggest that the approach is still dominant.

Does increased roadbuilding help? There is the ever present problem that new roads generate new traffic and the vicious circle continues. Public transport is caught in a detrimental downward cycle of decline because new roads present new competition, a fall in revenues, higher fares, or a reduced service, and a subsequent reduction in demand. Private road traffic may gain initially with increased speeds (the average speed on the proposed London Ringway 1 will be 35 mph compared with existing speeds of 13 mph in Central London) but, owing to the longer journeys involved, a great deal of traffic may not, in fact, be diverted and real time-savings reduced. The environmental impact of new roads in urban areas is well known. The Crowther Steering Group to the Buchanan Report stressed the point that British cities were physically incapable of accommodating new roads on the American style.

One last important consideration is the very cost of road building programmes. Denys Munby estimates that realistic urban costs are in the region of £12 million per mile in inner areas and £2·5 million per mile in suburban areas.[7] Reynolds estimated that the cost of implementing Buchanan's proposals in *Traffic in Towns* for Leeds would be £90 million.[8] The magnitude of these costs warrants a far closer examination of the basic question as to whether such amounts of our scarce resources should be allocated to transport services, and, in particular, to road building. Improvement in public transport is the other alternative on the supply side and would appear to be a more attractive proposition. The capital costs are, relatively, much lower and the carrying capacities much higher (the Victoria Line, for example, cost £60 million for an eleven mile stretch which will carry 40 000 passengers per hour, whereas a three-lane motorway costing £12 million per mile in the same area will support 2400 cars per hour/per lane, say 10 000 persons per hour at 1·4 persons per car).

Public transport will not be able to compete against the private car effectively, however, until they are both placed on the same economic footing. That is to say, until the private car owner has to pay the full costs of his use, not just in general as an overall taxed amount, but in those areas and at those times where at present he is, to all intents and purposes, being subsidised by other motorists who are paying in excess of the costs they themselves impose.

Thus, although the traditional supply approach, mainly concerned with short-run traffic management and long-run road improvements, has undoubtedly a role to play, it has certain inherent drawbacks if used to the exclusion of all other methods.

At some stage demand must be controlled.

Alternative road pricing and charging methods[9]

The current method of charging

This consists of three main elements, purchase tax, annual road fund licences and petrol tax. The taxes, from the vehicle owners' point of view, are a rather crude form of charging for their use of the roads. Fuel tax or petrol tax serves as a rough-and-ready means of relating the charge to the amount of use made of roads. Annual licence fees and initial purchase tax do not deter motorists from the use they make of roads, except that they may have deterred some people from becoming motorists in the first place.

The present method of charging fails to cope with the modern traffic problem in a number of respects: (a) it fails to discriminate between those situations in which congestion costs of road use are high and those in which they are low, (b) the use of the fuel tax is a singularly haphazard method of relating the charge to the amount of use made of roads. Different vehicles have varying consumptions and there is no relationship between the levy and the location of the road and thus the costs imposed by the motorist, (c) the comprehensive employment of a fixed annual charge appears to have even less effect than the fuel tax in restraining congestion.

Thus the current taxation methods do not effectively constrain the use of roads in the right places at the right times. It is of value, therefore, to examine alternative, and more acceptable methods of limiting the losses due to traffic congestion.

Alternative indirect methods of charging

(a) Differential fuel taxes
It has been put forward that it would be possible to levy fuel taxes at different rates in different areas, relating the level of the tax to the degree of urban congestion. The economic advantages of using this method would be considerably reduced by the all too obvious possibilities of avoidance whereby motorists could take on, or acquire, stocks of petrol in low price areas. One further drawback is that it would also discourage traffic in uncongested areas and at uncongested times, these losses offsetting the gains in congested areas.

(b) Parking charges
These are dealt with in detail later.

277

(c) Differential licences

Licence fees could be varied either by area or by time. Annual, and even daily, licences have been suggested with the price being fixed at a level calculated to limit the volume of traffic at peak times to a predetermined amount. The principal difficulty inherent in the annual licensing system proposal is the probable high value which would give rise to theft, fraud and avoidance. The likely costs of administration to prevent these detractions would also be relatively high.

The daily licence has less practical difficulties than the annual one, being purchased daily or in monthly or yearly books and having much in common with the parking tax, with the added advantage, however, of applying to all traffic passing through a congested area, not just traffic whose destination is within the area. The daily licence may also be used for restraining peak hour congestion.

The disadvantages of the daily licence are that, firstly, there is no control over the owner of the most expensive licence passing and repassing through one or more congested areas, and secondly, the need for sharply discriminating boundaries inevitably results in inequity.

(d) Tyre tax

This could be used as an alternative to a petrol tax. Its main advantages are that tyre wear is a much closer measure than fuel consumption of the wear inflicted on the road by the vehicle, and also a better indicator of congestion costs because tyre wear increases at a greater rate than fuel consumption on congested roads.

The disadvantages of a tyre tax are mainly administrative and technical, including the large initial sums for tyres, the difficulties of finding the correct purchase tax on tyres in general and on different makes in particular. It would also tend to encourage the use of dangerously worn tyres.

(e) Others

Numerous other methods of road pricing, such as poll tax, clutch tax, property tax and rates, have been promulgated. It is unlikely, however, unless they are combined with other measures,

278

that they would noticeably reduce the amount of traffic on the roads.

All the aforementioned methods of charging are related to some other product or service more or less allied with road use. The best method perhaps is to charge directly for road use itself.

Direct charging for road use

Toll gates have long been used in different parts of the world and are, of course, still employed on bridges, tunnels and on foreign motorways. In respect of ordinary roads in urban areas they are costly, inefficient, and impede the flow of traffic, due to the large number of access points required.

Recently schemes have been proposed which would enable an authority to charge directly for the total costs, including congestion and social costs, of using congested roads in urban areas. Direct road pricing schemes can be divided into 'on-vehicle' systems and 'off-vehicle' systems. Both systems can be further divided into 'point pricing' and 'continuous pricing'. Under a 'point pricing' system vehicles would be charged as and when they pass fixed pricing points which activate meters of one kind or another. Under 'continuous pricing' vehicles would be charged for time spent within a particular pricing zone.

(a) On-vehicle point pricing
This incorporates a system whereby a meter carried on a vehicle would pick up electrical impulses from cables laid across a road at selected pricing points. The meters could either be of a type sold with a given capacity and exchanged when exhausted, or they could be fixed permanently to the vehicle and be periodically read and accounts settled at special pricing stations.

(b) On-vehicle continuous pricing
Vehicles would be charged according to the time or distance travelled in designated pricing zones. The meter fitted to a vehicle could be adjusted so that it expires after a certain length of time travelled in pricing zones.

279

(c) *Off-vehicle systems*

Identification devices on vehicles would activate a vehicle identification apparatus which would relay information to a central computing station. Unfortunately, at present, there are no truly reliable automatic vehicle identification systems, and the development of one is likely to be very costly. Another drawback is the need to make provision for pricing to stop as soon as vehicles leave the public highway inside the pricing zones.

It would, therefore, seem that 'on-vehicle' systems are preferable. In choosing between point and continuous pricing, the main advantage of continuous systems is the ease of collecting payment, which would seem to present serious administrative difficulties with point pricing. There are several merits of point pricing, however, that should be considered. Firstly, it would not create the same boundary problems which are inherent in any continuous pricing system; secondly, it could be employed for toll collection on bridges and tunnels; thirdly, persons living within pricing zones might be compelled to pay parking charges under a continuous pricing system; lastly, point pricing would not encourage bad driving habits in an attempt to reduce payment.

The fixing of prices

Under a direct road pricing scheme the price charged should equal the costs arising from the passage of each vehicle, principally congestion costs. The determined price should, of course, be based upon the level of congestion and the ensuing costs expected after the road pricing system has been introduced. There is a problem, therefore, to judge what effect different price levels will have on traffic volume and hence the cost of road use. Thus it is necessary to estimate the cost of road use for different traffic speeds on each road and to gauge the reaction of traffic to different prices. In the initial stages some measure of trial and error will be unavoidable to ensure that road charges are established at such a level that the optimum use of available road space is made.

The level of charges will also be affected by the system of road pricing employed. In a continuous pricing system, assessment should be made for areas large enough to be considered as zones. Under point pricing the most suitable level can be set according to the prevailing conditions on a far more local basis.

The ability to adjust the effects of road charging by moving zone boundaries is of some importance because, where a meter scheme is involved, only a few levels of charge would be available to meet the needs of every town and city in the country.

One problem that presents itself is the need to decide what is the optimum level of traffic. From an economic viewpoint the price, or road charge, should be set at that level which brings the volume of traffic down to those proportions where the cost imposed by those vehicles is equal to the revenue collected. Although in practice this may rarely, if ever, be exactly attained, calculations made for the Smeed Report suggest that considerable variations from the optimum price may be made with little loss of benefit.

Enforcement

A practical problem of introducing direct road pricing concerns the vexed question of enforcement. Meters would have to be designed so as to make tampering impossible, or at least impracticable. Special methods would have to be inaugurated to detect persons attempting to avoid payment by not activating their meters. The intricacies of enforcement would be greatly facilitated if motorists considered that paying for the use of roads was fair, equitable, and perhaps more economic. To a large extent this would depend on what use is made of the revenue collected from road charging.

Investment policy

Direct road pricing methods can also be used as a criterion for assessing investment performance in roads. In order to do this the highway authorities would have to adopt the attitude of a competitive service industry. It would be required to expand those sections on which profits were made, and to contract those where losses are incurred. The process of expansion would raise the costs borne by the highway authorities in the profit-making areas but at the same time it would reduce congestion and the associated costs. This reduction in congestion costs might necessitate a lowering of charges if the saving outweighed construction, environment, and other costs.

In practice the highway authorities are likely to find themselves making profits on some roads and losses on others, the flexibility of road pricing not being perfect. Despite this, direct road pricing gives a better indication of the demand for certain roads, and, therefore, is a greater aid in making investment decisions than are indirect methods of charging.

The economic consequences of direct road charging

The immediate effect of introducing a direct road charging system would be the reduction of traffic in congested areas, and accompanying increase in average speeds and reduction in running maintenance, and depreciation costs. This would produce net benefits to the community in the form of savings in paid working time of persons travelling in the course of employment, savings in fuel, and greater productivity from buses and commercial vehicles. It would also involve certain losses to other road users, but these were losses that were previously passed on to other motorists willing to bear their own costs. The magnitude of the benefits would, of course, depend largely upon the type of system adopted and its efficiency in operation.

Direct road pricing would also have the effect of inducing people to travel at cheaper times or by cheaper routes. Greater use might be made of vehicle capacity in both the private and commercial sectors. In the same way shoppers might make fewer but bigger shopping expeditions.

Another result of this charging method could be a redistribution of real income. The nature and degree of the change would depend entirely upon the way in which the proceeds of road charges were re-allocated. It would be divided between central and local government, and could be used for improving the road network, or for subsidising public transport, or it could go into general revenue accounts.

Public transport would also be affected in that the increase in commuters using their services, caused by the innovation of any road charging system, would incur losses on existing passengers in the form of overcrowding unless facilities were expanded. On the other hand, bus services would be improved in terms of speed and regularity; furthermore, fewer crews and stock would be required for the same level of service. There is unlikely to be any increase in fares with the introduction of road pricing.

It has been suggested that road pricing would result in cities suffering from a deterioration in the attraction of their central areas as regards population, commerce, and social amenities due to the fact that a large proportion of traffic would either be deterred or diverted due to high charges. The point to be considered, however, is: Would the restraint of motor vehicles due to road pricing have a more adverse effect on urban centres than the constraints imposed by congestion? The Smeed Report concluded that the efficiency of streets should increase and that no harm to city development should occur.[10]

Summary of road pricing

It was earlier explained that the fundamental problem of urban transportation is the imbalance between supply and demand in the provision of transport services, the result of which is congestion. Indirect charging methods do not relate the costs of road use created by individual vehicles to the price that their owners have to pay, and are therefore at a major disadvantage to direct road pricing schemes, which from an economic viewpoint seems to offer the best solution to the problem in the short-run, and also offers considerable advantages in the longer term. In the final assessment, however, other factors must also be taken into account. The idea that roads should be financed by a direct pricing method is not perhaps immediately politically expedient. The implementation of this system would be greatly facilitated if there is public confidence that the funds raised will in fact be used to maintain and expand the existing road network as appropriate.

One partially attempted solution, that of charging for car parking, requires analysis in greater depth to see if it can be employed as either a complementary or supplementary method of solving the urban transportation problem.

Charging for car parking

In this country, the regulation of car parking has been seen for some time as one of the principal methods of traffic regulation in city centres. It has been held that the restriction of parking also restricts the total amount of traffic venturing into cities and thus reduces congestion.

There is, on the other hand, a lobby which is in favour of providing free car parking in cites as an incentive to retail trade and commerce in general. The motorist, presented with this dichotomy, finds himself perched uncomfortably on the fence. He appreciates free parking, quite naturally, if it is available, but he resents the congestion to which his own presence in the central area is in part contributing. If this dilemma is to be solved at all, one must examine first principles once again and question the nature of the demand for car parking and the characteristics of supply.

It is unreasonable for motorists to expect free parking as a basic right, for parking space, like almost everything else, is a scarce resource. That is to say, there is not enough of it as people would wish there to be in an ideal world, and in this imperfect one it is highly unlikely that there ever could be.

Scarcity implies that not everyone who wants a good parking space can have it, or at least as much of it as he would like. Some method must, therefore, be found of allocating the quantity of parking space which is available. Also the amount of parking space that can be provided must be ascertained.

Demand

If wastage is not to be the result, resources should go to those who most need them or who can best use them. Demand, however, cannot readily be assessed in the absence of a price mechanism, for if a good is free, demand tends to infinity. Including pricing, there are three methods of allocating parking space, the other two being queuing and time limitation. These will be considered in turn.

a. Queuing—implies a fixed amount of parking space which is allocated on a 'first come–first served' basis. When considering a city centre situation this has grave disadvantages. To begin with there is no logical connection between the time of a motorist's arrival and the extent of his need of a parking place, it can be as essential to find a space at 3.00 p.m. as at 9.00 a.m. There is also the fact that the first people to get to the town centre are those for whom it is a place of work, who like to park their cars close by for the whole working day without, in all probability, making use of them during that period. Such users will impose further congestion at peak hours which delays other motorists and public transport services.

b. Time limits—are often preferred to queuing because they do eliminate the all-day parker. This method, however, tends to the opposite extreme, for it implies that the benefit to the actual group of persons who use the space in place of the all-day parker is necessarily greater than the single user. This is not always the case, for the purposes of that group of motorists might well be frivolous and the need of the all-day driver critically important.

The only way to measure effectively the value of parking space to an individual would be to find out how much that person is prepared to pay for it. Nor do time limits prevent congestion, indeed they probably exacerbate it. The greater the vehicle turnover per parking space the greater will be the volume of traffic proceeding either to or from that space. Also, the very fact that the time period allowed is usually short (20–30 minutes) means that any driver seeking a space and who is not initially able to find one will be tempted to continue circling the block hoping for a vacated parking bay. This phenomenon is known as mobile parking and greatly adds to congestion. It can also occur if the purpose of the visit, perhaps to a single shop, is of short duration and can be accomplished by a passenger whilst the driver circumnavigates the block.

c. Equilibrium pricing—is perhaps the only method of pricing which adequately allocates space and indicates whether or not more should be made available. There already exist certain forms of pricing but they are very imperfect and arbitrary. None of them are straightforward applications of the pricing principle, but exist as unfortunate hybrids of the three aforementioned means of parking space allocation. Off-street car parks usually combine pricing and queuing; on-street parking is often metered, a method which in its present form composes pricing, time limitation, and queuing.

Pricing only really works when it is equilibrium pricing, that is to say a price which roughly equates supply and demand. In such a situation the motorist knows that he has a high chance of finding a space at a known cost. If the price is too low, as it often is in local authority car parks, the motorist is placed at a great disadvantage since he knows he will have to pay for parking, but is uncertain of obtaining a place as excess demand is regulated by queuing.

The same is true of meters if they are underpriced, with the additional drawback that they are time limited. They also clutter the pavements, and present problems of enforcement, and associated costs, due to 'meter feeding'. If the motorist was charged an equilibrium price, there is no reason why he should not stay as long as he liked. He would, after all, be meeting the full cost of doing so.

Supply

At present, the absence of any pricing system which reflects the full cost of providing space, and the demand for space at a price which reflects that cost, means that there is no economic yardstick which an authority can use to determine whether or not more space should be provided. Such decisions are therefore based on intuition and tend to be somewhat arbitrary. This position of subsidised parking also hinders the provision of parking space by the private sector, for as long as public space is unrealistically cheap, private developers appear to be charging exorbitant fees when in fact they might only just be covering their costs.

286

The implementation of equilibrium pricing

An equilibrium pricing system would be one that ensured that parking spaces were occupied most of the time, without there being satisfied demand at the price charged. The system would therefore have to be flexible through time, to allow for fluctuations in demand.

If road pricing on either the point or continuous method was introduced meters could be adapted to cover parking. Parking meters as such would be unnecessary since there would be no need to time individual vehicles. In the absence of road pricing, parking charges could operate on a ticket basis. Single machines, giving change, would serve quite long stretches of streets and drivers could attach tickets to their windscreens to cover the relevant period. Excess (unpaid) stays should be the responsibility of the owner who could himself reclaim the surcharge from the driver, if other than himself.

Householders with frontage on streets and no garages could rent on an annual basis the bay in front of their property which would be hooded when they required it themselves. Otherwise it could be used by other motorists and the householder could collect the ensuing fees to contribute towards the annual rental.

The prices of road space as against parking space, if full pricing were introduced, would be adjusted in respect of one another in order to optimise the use of all potential vehicle space. G. Roth suggests that if the congestion cost of a lane of 10 parked vehicles was £1 per hour the parked vehicles should pay at least 10p per hour. If the spaces were still used at 15p per hour more space should be devoted to parking. If optimal use occurred at 5p per hour more space should be devoted to moving traffic.[11]

Conclusion

Although road pricing and parking charge systems appear complicated, they do in fact greatly simplify the overall problem of the congestion of the urban transportation network caused by the disequilibrium of demand for, and supply of, car space in cities and towns. They assist in ordering the priorities and increasing the efficiency of roads, provide a more stable foundation for operating public transport facilities, ameliorate the environmental pollution caused by congestion, provide a valid guide to local authorities as to how much space should be provided, establish an equilibrium as to the distribution of land to traffic *vis-à-vis* other uses, and not least there would be a fair and rational allocation of resources amongst the competing motorists themselves.

The urban transportation problem—references

1 Buchanan, C., *Traffic in Towns*, HMSO (1963).
2 The Tabula Heracleensis forbad the use of wheeled vehicles on the streets of Rome between the hours of 6 a.m. to 4 p.m. except for official business.
3 Aldous, T., *Battle for the Environment*, Fontana (1972).
4 Hart-Davis, D., 'Hell in Cities', *Sunday Telegraph*, 14 November 1971.
5 Hall, P., 'Transportation', *Developing Patterns of Urbanisation*, Cowan, P. (ed.), Oliver and Boyd (1970).
6 International Road Federation Conference, Geneva (1969).
7 Munby, D. (ed.), *Transport*, Penguin (1969).
8 Reynolds, D., *Economics, Town Planning and Traffic*, Institute of Economic Affairs (1966).
9 Roth, G., *Paying for Roads: the economics of traffic congestion*, Penguin (1967).
10 *Road Pricing: The Economic and Technical Possibilities* (Smeed Report), HMSO (1964).
11 Roth, *op. cit.*

Further recommended reading

Gwilliam, K. M., *Transport and Public Policy*, Allen and Unwin (1965).
Meyer, J. R., Kain, V. F. and Wohl, M., *The Urban Transportation Problem*, Harvard (1965).
Thomson, V. M., 'The Case for Road Pricing', *Traffic Engineering and Control*, March, 1968.
Thomson, J. M., *et al.*, *Motorways in London*, Duckworth (1969).

PART FOUR
Development and control

21 Planning standards

Having established the broad goals and objectives of the development plan for a particular area it is necessary to translate this overall strategy into specific land use and space requirements. The various professions concerned with the planning process have therefore devised a set of codes, regulations and specifications by which to judge the performance of the constituent elements that compose the plan, and to assist in the optimum allocation of resources. Thus certain standards are set to control the physical setting of the urban area and to contribute in ensuring safety, health, amenity welfare, convenience, efficiency and public interest.

Although no definitive or comprehensive list of standards exists, a widely acceptable range have emerged from a variety of sources. There are legislative standards such as the Building Regulations, the Use Classes Order, the Control of Advertisement Regulations and a host of local byelaws that relate to development. There are central government administrative standards, often the result of commissions, reports and committees, that advise, recommend, and guide local authorities in the implementation of their policy. These include the *Design and Planning Bulletins*, the *Development Plans Manual* and the vast number of memoranda, circulars and handbooks that again aim to assist both public and private development and planning agencies. There are also empirical standards, those gained from experience and observation in practice.

Zoning

Whether this device for expressing land use proposals is best described as a form of control rather than as a planning standard is a matter of conjecture; it is, however, desirable that it should be mentioned in the same context. Zoning is a method by which the development plan segregates parcels of land or areas of towns and ascribes to them broad classifications of appropriate use, for example residential, industrial, commercial or educational. Combinations of uses can also be indicated. A set of characteristic notations is provided by the Ministry to secure consistency among authorities in the preparation of plans, thus commercial uses are shown in blue, educational in red and open space aptly in green.

The indication of suitable land use by means of zoning is but one technique amongst many for influencing change and deterring non-conforming uses in this country. In the United States of America it provides the basic planning instrument and is called the *zoning ordinance*. Closely associated with the Ordinance is the *performance standard* which is based upon the use of different tests to determine whether or not a particular land use conforms with certain established basic criteria regarding aspects of locational suitability such as noise, fumes, pollution, glare, and congestion. This performance approach is intended as a more sophisticated and sensitive alternative to groupings like 'heavy', 'light' and 'general' manufacturing industries. It has yet to be applied in this country but its merits are enhanced with the increasing amount of research that is being undertaken on the measurement of noise, pollution, overcrowding and so on.

The designation and allocation of land for specific uses under the 1947 Town and Country Planning Act code tended to be static, rigid and all too often merely reflected existing land use distribution, whereas the 1971 Act sets out to create a more flexible yet positive framework for the distribution of resources at the structure plan level, and a more precise and certain indication at the local plan level.

Density control

It can be argued that the very basis of planning lies in the functional relationship between land and the various competing uses to which it is put. What is required, therefore, is some form of index which equates both the demand for, and supply of, land and allocates it in such a way as to ensure a maximisation of existing resources. To this end a range of density standards have been established relating to residential and commercial activities. Essentially, density is the amount of some factor divided by the area that the factor occupies. The resultant figure expresses the average intensity in that area. In the sphere of plan preparation, monitoring, and control there exist a variety of density standards in respect of different areas and different representative units of intensity within those areas. The following definitions are extracted from the Ministry publication *The Density of Residential Areas*.[1]

Residential density

Residential density is a system of measurement expressing in mathematical terms the number of people (population density) or the amount of housing (accommodation density) in a specified area of land. From this are derived several other measures which depend on what particular area of land is being measured.

Overall residential density
This is applied to a town as a whole. It is the residential population of the town divided by the number of hectares it occupies, regardless of how the land is used. It excludes undeveloped or agricultural land but includes industrial land, all public open space, all schools, and all other types of development. It is not generally used for local planning purposes but it does have a significance in national and regional planning where the intensity of development of one town can be compared with another. Today 175 bedspaces per hectare is considered to be a low intensity of development, 175–300 about average and over 300 high.

Gross residential density

This is applied to a neighbourhood as a whole, or what is described in development plans as a 'gross residential area'. It is the population of the area divided by the number of hectares, including all the land covered by dwellings and gardens, roads, local shops, primary schools, and most open spaces, but excluding all other urban uses such as industrial land, secondary schools, town parks and town centres. It is of no direct relevance in development control but is used in the preparation of development plans where areas of high or low intensity can be identified.

Net residential density

This is applied to a particular housing layout or zone on a development plan and is regarded as being a normal basis for development control. It is the population or accommodation divided by the number of hectares including dwellings and gardens, any incidental open space and half the width of surrounding roads up to a maximum of 6 metres but excluding local shops, primary schools and most open space and all other types of development.

There are several ways of expressing net residential density. It can be either done in terms of the number of people themselves or in terms of the accommodation they occupy, as follows:

a. dwellings per hectare
b. persons per hectare
c. habitable rooms per hectare
d. bedspaces per hectare
e. floorspace

The most accurate measure is thought to be bedspaces, as it most closely reflects the demand for accommodation, the way in which it is supplied, and the degree of overcrowding; as such it is frequently adopted in cost analysis work and in Cost Yardstick calculations.

Population density can be readily converted to accommodation density and *vice versa* by making certain assumptions about the average number of people occupying a separate dwelling, or a separate habitable room, that is a room that is normally used for sleeping or living in. This is called the *occupancy rate* and is used to gauge the level of overcrowding or under-occupation, with 'one person per habitable room' being widely applied as a

294

maximum above which overcrowding exists. Many authorities seek to attain a rate considerably below this with 0·75 being considered comfortable.

The residential density controversy

Over time, and from various sources, the main functions of residential density control can be listed under the following headings:

1. the preservation and economy of land use
2. to ensure scope exists for variety of development
3. to give reasonable minimum requirements for comfort and a satisfactory environment
4. to confine urban sprawl and prevent low suburban densities
5. to ensure an adequate provision of community facilities
6. to recognise and control both overcrowding and under-utilisation, aid decentralisation and control growth guiding both the location and intensity of new development

1. The preservation and economy of land use

The town planner is charged with ensuring that no more land is used for urban purposes than is absolutely essential, a great premium is currently placed upon the preservation of agricultural and other land in non-urban use. One of the most obvious ways of achieving this aim is to raise the density of urban development, and a great debate has taken place in recent years regarding the relative merits of various forms of high-density living. In this vein the Joint Parliamentary Secretary to the Minister of Housing informed Parliament in April 1962 that 'by raising the net density of an area from 24 persons per acre to 40 persons per acre, and the number of houses from 8 to 13 per acre it is possible to save 17 acres of land per 1000 population or enough to house another 500 persons'. This proportionately high saving only occurs, however, where existing densities are at the lower end of the scale, because in circumstances where it is raised from 484 persons per hectare to 551 persons per hectare there is only a saving of 0·73 hectares, for as the number of persons increases so too does the amount of land required for community facilities and services.[2]

In this context it is worthy of note that it is unlikely that densities can be increased in existing suburban locations, so that adjustments are limited to the replacement of obsolescent housing in the inner city, where densities are probably considerably in excess of development plan maxima, and new estates of the urban periphery where densities have been increasing anyway. It is a common fallacy that building high saves land, for the savings in site and public utility costs with high-density development are less than the rise in maintenance and servicing costs which arise from the use of high buildings.

Despite the Malthusian prophets of doom, the need to save land is perhaps not so axiomatic as is often asserted. Even in the highly urbanised region of London only about 30% of the total area is developed, and in the outer ring of suburbia, where the gross residential density is only about 5 persons per hectare, some 80% to 85% of the total area is under agriculture or woodland. It has been calculated that to replace the produce all of land lost to urban development between 1950 and 1970 it would require an increase in net output on the remaining land of only £3 per hectare, whereas intensification schemes had been yielding £10 per hectare in a 5-year period. Furthermore, output in terms of calories increased on average by nearly 2·5% per annum, or enough to offset in one year the expected loss of land over a period of 20 years. A further analogy often quoted is, on the urban scale of *Lebensraum*, that is 125 persons or approximately 30 families per hectare, West Germany alone could house the entire present population of the earth. At this same density the entire population of the United States could be accommodated on the Pacific coast with nearly everyone having a view of the ocean. About 70% of the population of the United States is now concentrated in urban and suburban communities occupying in total a little more than 1% of the nation's land area. Even in England only 4% of the land is occupied by as much as 40% of the people.

These statistics are rather trite and say little about the real problems and causes of urban congestion and the need for density standards. The matter is put into perspective by J. R.

296

James when analysing the merits of employing gross densities as a planning yardstick. 'One main aim is to economise the use of land, and this can best be done not by raising gross densities to high levels but by keeping it above low levels. To crowd development closely and to build high does not produce an important saving in land. On the other hand great savings are achieved by preventing sprawl.'[5]

2. To ensure scope exists for variety of development

The mere application of density controls does not of itself guarantee the nature and form of development. The results can, in fact, be disastrously monotonous and regular. It is only when these standards are enforced with a measure of flexibility and discretion that any variety or mix can be achieved. It is essential that whilst a net residential density is valuable as a guideline, the actual planning permission should take account of the physical condition of the site, the purpose of the dwellings, the architectural quality and all the other factors that dictate satisfactory development. Although an overall standard might be appropriate to a particular area it is likely that a range of densities above and below that mark, related to specific sites, might produce the best result.

This approach is further supported by the demand for different forms of accommodation based upon varied social need. Housing estates with their predominently two-storey three-bedroom dwellings appear to cater almost exclusively for the family with children under sixteen who, after all, make up but 40% of total households. Special provision, based upon a survey of requirements for each separate planning area, should therefore be made in respect of mixed development, because although the residential space needs of substantial communities are fairly similar, the space needs of individual households vary enormously.

3. To give reasonable minimum requirements for comfort and satisfactory environment

A stated consideration in implementing density standards is to achieve 'compactness without congestion' and 'spaciousness

297

without sprawl'.[6] The means of creating this and the resultant densities are matters of great controversy. Of recent years the 'high-rise, high-density' school of thought has tended to give way to that of 'low-rise, high-density'. The reasons why the slab and point high-rise blocks of the fifties and sixties have fallen out of favour become apparent when the advantages of low-rise construction are set out. The major benefits are as follows:

1. there is greater supervision of play space and therefore greater safety for children
2. there is more private open space
3. greater accessibility to the street is available to all. There is no dependence on lifts
4. two and three-storey high-density development can be introduced to existing street patterns and based upon existing services
5. there is greater speed of construction
6. it is generally more economic
7. a wider range of dwelling size can be built
8. phasing is easier, redevelopment can be undertaken piecemeal
9. it can be applied to smaller and narrower sites

It must be emphasised, however, that although density standards are fine for sorting out numbers of rooms, people, dwelling, schools and other services, the visual and environmental effects can be calamitous. They might give a measure of the intensity at which people live on land, but they do not provide a comparative basis of living standards or a measure of aesthetic control.

4. Confine urban sprawl and prevent low suburban densities

It has been maintained that around all towns 'there has been a tendency for villages and new settlements to grow haphazard and produce a spoiled semi-rural, semi-urban background, a "rurban" area which if linked in the envelope of the town will show a dropping of density which is not a healthy sign either for the town or the countryside'.[7]

298

The main problem, therefore, is preventing excessively low densities in suburban areas which can easily become 'grey areas' secluded from city services with populations too thin to generate public life. This proclaims the need for minimum controls as well as maxima, and a number of county planning authorities enact just such controls.

5. To ensure the provision of community facilities

It is important that dwellings should be conveniently sited in relation to shops, schools, open space and other land uses normally associated with the general convenience of residents. It has been asserted that without density controls it is quite impossible to ensure adequate provision of such facilities.[8] Although they might provide an invaluable check or yardstick, particularly in respect of new development, density levels rarely reflect actual intensity of occupation in existing areas. Other means of ensuring the provision of community services are therefore required. It can be argued that at higher densities there is an increased loss of private facilities and therefore further provision of communal facilities should be made, thus demanding a more complex relationship between density standards and public services.

In the United States they employ the zoning ordinance which governs land use, and an associated sub-division regulation which governs the design of streets and provision of utilities. Approval of sub-division design can control the layout of an area, and in some instances approval can also control the placing of community facilities such as schools, parks and playgrounds, since the large land developer is required to set aside certain portions of his land for such purposes. Professor Denman has suggested a similar method, which he describes as an 'amenity percentage', for use in this country, giving a more flexible approach to the problem.

6. To recognise and control both overcrowding and under-utilisation

There are several bases for the bulk measurement of accommodation as mentioned previously.

1. *The dwelling*—commonly used before the war but suffers from the fact that it does not indicate the actual amount of accommodation owing to the variety of house size and type that exists. It is, however, used in rural areas as a minimum standard.

2. *The habitable room*—the definition of what constitutes a habitable room can vary between local authorities. Also the size of rooms and occupancy rate can vary enormously depending as they do on socio-economic group and age. When applied the desired occupancy rate is used to translate habitable rooms per hectare into persons per hectare and *vice versa*.

3. *The bedspace*—although not always used as such, this base should provide an indication of use and intensity.

4. *Floorspace*—this is difficult to measure, unnecessarily precise, and again subject to wide variations in different economic and social circumstances.

As the Ministry point out, however, 'density control is often expected or believed to serve many purposes which in fact it can only accomplish within very broad limits, if at all. For example, overcrowding within dwellings cannot be prevented by density control since it cannot limit household size or determine living habits, although it can influence the number of people who can live in an area by controlling the number of rooms or dwellings.'[9] An argument could in fact be advanced that the converse is true, and that density control, by limiting the number of rooms or dwellings in areas of high demand for accommodation, stifles redevelopment and in fact causes overcrowding.

Certainly as an instrument for assessing overcrowding or under-utilisation the social survey provides a far better measure.

Commercial density

The purpose of establishing commercial density standards is aimed at achieving a form and distribution of commercial activity which allows the town centre, or urban area, to function at its most efficient level, ensuring a balanced pattern of growth, and acting as a guide for future new development. Once again there exists no common standard for measuring and controlling the intensity of shop and office use. There are, however, two very similar methods that are widely acceptable, the *floor space index* and the *plot ratio*.

The Floor Space Index (FSI)

This is based upon the total area of permitted floorspace expressed as a proportion of the site plus half the width of surrounding roads. It is intended to take into account the need to provide a system which allows for all the service facilities implicit in development such as roads parking, access and footpaths. Thus, if a local planning authority, having considered existing and potential traffic and pedestrian flows, and the availability of other services and utilities, would allow twice the equivalent amount of floorspace as that area covered by the site and half the width of the adjoining roads the FSI is said to be 2:1. The developer is then able to decide whether he will construct three storeys over the whole site, assuming the road widths are 50% of the site area, or six storeys on half the site or perhaps twelve stories on a quarter of the site. There will, of course, be other controls that inhibit his decision and dictate the final form such as daylight and sunlight factors, car parking, access, height and materials.

Plot ratio

This is mainly used in London and is similar to the floor space index but excludes half the width of the roads. It provides a more consistent standard for controlling development on individual sites, because where the FSI is employed corner sites might benefit unduly and become over-developed and these are often the locations where congestion is at its worst.

It can be said that both the floor space index and the plot ratio provide a comparatively equitable assessment between respective sites, prevent over-intensification, and work against spiralling land values. Conversely they do not relate the amount of space available with the use to which it is put: a large block of offices given over to insurance companies, with their vast personnel, places a very different burden in terms of urban congestion upon a town than does a computer firm with its few operators. Their application can also lead to awkward, ugly and inefficient design and in no way ties in with parking, space, or height standards. Furthermore, it does not differentiate between sites in the same area but has contrasting accessibility characteristics. For example, a case can be made out for permitting considerably greater intensity of development over and around transport termini as happens abroad.

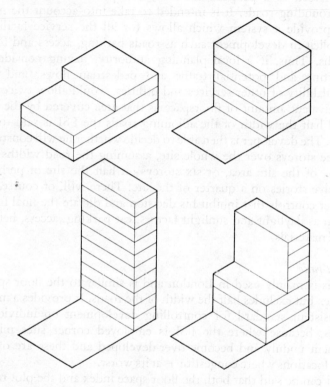

Fig. 27 Alternative methods of developing a site at a plot ratio of 2.5 : 1

An attempt has been made to devise an 'environmental standard' control of the bulk of buildings in central areas based upon the size, population, pedestrian space on the ground, and capacity of transportation.[10] The result is a formula which states the amount of floorspace in a building that can be permitted for a given amount of pedestrian footpath space fronting the building. A certain sophistication is added to existing procedures, but the amount of survey and analysis work involved detracts from its usefulness.

Industrial density

Unlike residential and commercial development no easily applied numerical standards exist for controlling industrial location, intensity and growth. Each case is judged on its individual merits. The principal constraints imposed are chiefly statutory, such as the Use Classes Order (1963), which distinguishes between various forms of industry such as 'light', 'heavy' and 'special', the various Acts that relate to development and employment which control industrial location, and the Factory Acts which relate to specific layout, design and construction of industrial premises. Some methods of quantitative assessment are mentioned in the following chapter on industrial site development.

Conclusion

Of necessity, density standards are negative in character. They cannot, of themselves, generate a development of a particular kind of character, although to some extent they can prevent improper or inefficient land use. Traditionally population density controls—those standards concerned with measuring the capacity of land in terms of persons—have been associated with residential development. More recently in the United States the notion of controlled population densities has been extended to the work areas of the community, the central business district and the industrial and commercial concentrations. In this extension of the concept, the criterion of density becomes the number of people present in an area during peak hours of congregation as opposed to place of residence. The densities are expressed in persons per million feet and provide a serviceable technique for the preparation, implementation and monitoring of plans.

Also in the United States they have initiated, under the auspices and direction of the Federal Housing Administration, a measuring device known as the Land Use Intensity Rating which is described as 'the overall structural mass and open space relationship in a developed property, which correlates the amount of floor area, open space, livability space, recreation space, and car storage space of a property with the size of its site or land area'. Its approach is not entirely dissimilar to gross residential density but it takes into account a wider field of planning factors, providing what is described as a more reliable and less variable standard.[11] It is interesting to note that the French award a 'density bonus' to schemes which in outline appear to have potential aesthetic quality.

Finally, great concern has always been given by planners and planning authorities to net densities but a plea has been made by J. R. James for them to pay greater attention, in the context of density and urban development, to gross densities which he describes as 'an important and useful planning concept. Within big urban sub-divisions, forming the appropriate envelope, standards of density can be set that permit the proper planning of housing with local facilities and ensure the economical use of our national stock of land.'[12]

Daylighting and sunlighting indicators

The daylighting indicator

This is a method recommended by the Ministry in their handbook *The Density of Residential Areas* for controlling the spacing of residential buildings on a site. It provides a quick and approximate means of ensuring that buildings are so placed in relation to each other that it would be possible to attain the daylighting standards recommended in the *British Standard Code of Practice* provided that in the design of the dwellings themselves the windows are properly positioned and of adequate size.[13]

Two basic types of indicator are employed, one for testing adequate daylight provision from surrounding streets and plot boundaries, and the other for testing from one building to

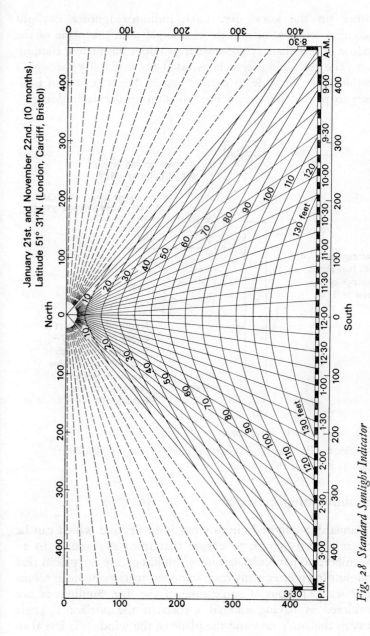

Fig. 28 Standard Sunlight Indicator

SOURCE: *Planning for Daylight and Sunlight* Planning Bulletin No. 5, HMSO, 1964

305

another on the same site. Each indicator ignores daylight reaching a window at a horizontal angle with the plane of the window of less than 45° because it provides insufficient illumination. The remaining light is assessed for suitability through a possible range of wide to narrow angles. Separate sets of indicators are provided for residential and non-residential buildings.

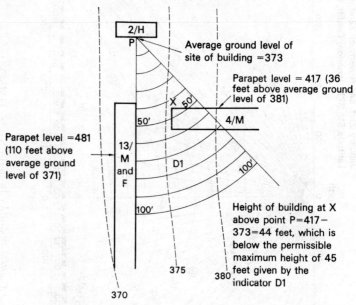

Fig. 29 The use of one of the range of daylight indicators
SOURCE: *Planning for Daylight and Sunlight* Planning Bulletin No. 5, HMSO, 1964

The sunlighting indicator

A Standard Sunlight Indicator has been devised which can be used as a ready check to ensure that from 21 January to 22 November, at particular latitudes, buildings are so placed that sunlight can enter as many main windows in as many main rooms for at least an hour at some time of the day. Sunlight is not considered as having entered a room if the horizontal angle between the sun's rays and the plane of the window is less than

306

22·5°, and if the sun has an altitude of less than 5° above the horizon.

Sets of indicators are available for latitudes 51° 30′N, approximately that of London, Cardiff and Bristol; 52° 30′N, approximately that of Birmingham; 53° 30′N, approximately that of Liverpool, Manchester, and Leeds, and 55°N, approximately that of Newcastle.

An explanation of exactly how both these indicators are applied in practice is beyond the scope of this book, but is lucidly described in the Ministry's Planning Bulletin Number 5, *Planning for Daylight and Sunlight*. They appear to have provided a valuable tool at the preliminary design stage of site layout.

Noise

In an age dominated by urban motorways and traffic congestion a great deal of research has been directed towards the measurement of traffic noise, the establishment of acceptable standards, and the means of reducing the level of intrusion. Statutory control of vehicle noise was introduced by the Ministry of Transport in 1968 under the Motor Vehicles (Construction and Use) Amendment Regulations whereby new vehicles are limited to a noise level of 92 dB(A), which represents decibels (dB) weighted on a special scale (A) for use in assessing traffic noise. On this weighting an increase of 10 dB(A) corresponds approximately to a doubling of loudness.

With regard to the total amount of noise produced by traffic on urban roads, there is currently no outdoor environmental noise standard, but the Greater London Council have adopted the recommendations of the Wilson Committee on the problem of noise in respect of acceptable indoor noise levels that should not be exceeded for more than 10% of either day-time or night-time. The following table lists suggested standards for various building types. When compared to typical noise levels in Inner London as described in Table 4 it can be seen that a great deal of work remains to be done in terms of reducing traffic noise. Both the Building Research Station and the National Physical Laboratory have carried out experimental work on constructing indices to measure noise pollution. Further, as an aid to the land use and transportation planner the Greater London Council has created a set of transparent protractors that assist in calculating the effect of distance and screening in reducing noise levels.

Table 3

Indoor noise standards for various buildings types

	Maximum indoor 10% noise level dB(A)	
	Day	Night
Quiet suburban areas	45	35
Busy urban areas	50	35
Lecture theatres	30	
New classrooms	45	
Private offices	45–50	
General offices	55–60	

Source: *GLC Urban Design Bulletin on Traffic Noise*, 1970

Table 4

Typical noise levels in Inner London

	10% noise level dB(A)	
Area	Day	Night
Residential	65	53
Industrial	66	54
Shopping	76	58
Offices	69	58

Source: *GLC Urban Design Bulletin on Traffic Noise*, 1970

The above standards are relatively simple to use, and give a fair indication of the annoyance caused, but they do not take into account the frequency of noise, the difference between peak foreground noise and general background noise, and they cannot be applied to aircraft or railway noise.

308

Car parking standards

To any motor vehicle owner it scarcely requires stating that the urban areas, and in particular the town centres, of this country are facing a crisis regarding traffic congestion and the ever-increasing demand for parking space. In controlling development it is incumbent upon the planner to decide how much parking space each individual development should provide, where, and of what kind.

It has long been established that with residential development each house should have at least one car parking space and a further proportion should be set aside throughout the estate for visitors' parking. The Parker Morris Report in 1961 suggested that an extra 25% should be provided for visitors' cars, but the Road Research Laboratory estimate that by 1980 there will be an average of one car per family, or almost three times the number of cars on the road. There is also an increase in the ownership of bicycles, scooters, boats and caravans, all of which must be catered for and stored. Most local planning authorities are therefore insisting upon one visitors' space per dwelling in addition to the household space.

There exists a great disparity between authorities regarding the standards they impose, particularly in respect of non-residential development. The following list should be taken as an indication only:

Table 5

Land use	Parking spaces	
Residential	2	per dwelling
Offices	1	per 350 square feet of gross floorspace
Central area shops	5·75	per 1000 square feet of gross floorspace
Suburban shops	5	per 1000 square feet of gross floorspace
Out-of-town shops	8·5	per 1000 square feet of gross floorspace
City hotels	1	per 10 bedrooms
Other hotels	1	per 3 bedrooms
Hospitals	1	per 12 beds
Theatres	1	per 30 seats
Restaurants	1	per 10 seats
Industrial	1	per 500 square feet of floorspace

Cars are such space-hungry devices that all these standards are probably insufficient. The crude application of standards can also lead to a haphazard distribution of small, privately owned, poorly located, under-utilised car parks. It is far better strategically to site fewer but larger public car parks available at all times to all people. For this reason local authorities conclude arrangements with developers whereby the latter make financial contributions towards the cost of providing spaces in public car parks as an alternative to supplying parking on the particular site which is to be developed.[14]

Parking standards, as such, tend to be inflexible in practice if discretion is not exercised on the part of the planning authority concerned. Some developments require very much less provision than other but may well fall within a general category of control. What is perhaps required is a complete revolution in urban transportation and parking policy. The imposition of flexible discriminatory road pricing and the wider introduction of park-and-ride schemes may not be far off.

Open space

The various recommended standards for individual activities such as rugby, cricket, parks, allotments, school playing fields and incidental spaces are detailed elsewhere.[15] They have changed little over the years but recent research has indicated that if anything they tend to be over-generous. At any rate the character of leisure and recreation is changing to such an extent that a demand is growing for completely different facilities.

The old Greater London Plan proposals in 1944 recommended that for every 1000 population there should be 10 acres of open space, 6 for playing fields, 1 for parkland, and 3 attached to schools. Based upon extensive survey work undertaken by Essex County Council in 1965 it has been suggested that, excluding land attached to schools, only 3·5 acres of open space would be sufficient in built-up areas as opposed to 7 acres previously proposed.[16]

In Table 6 there are some interesting contrasts between American cities in their provision of community open space.

Table 6

Cities	Open Space %	Gross population density	Net population density
Detroit	5·5	16·1 p.p.a.	35·2
Pittsburgh	6·1	7·6 p.p.a.	14·8
Philadelphia	8·6	14·3 p.p.a.	27·4
Los Angeles	9·1	7·9 p.p.a.	20·6
Cleveland	14·8	10·6 p.p.a.	23·9
Chicago	20·5	14·4 p.p.a.	44·7
New York	28·0	10·6 p.p.a.	26·1

A roughly similar survey was undertaken by F. T. Burnett during 1966 of ten of the established English new towns which demonstrated amazing discrepancies in the provision of major open space, ranging from 5·9 acres per 1000 population in Basildon to a staggering 39·2 acres in Peterlee. The latter due mainly to a high proportion of woodland within the designated area of the town. The average provision was in the region of 18 acres per 1000 population.

These broad figures in isolation do not portray a true picture of the quality and usefulness of the open space. It might not be accessible to large sections of the community, or it might be heavily wooded or liable to subsidence or flooding. In a period of worsening urban pressures, greater concentration of development, and increasing leisure time, it is imperative that further consideration should be given to the nature, form and distribution of open space and the standards that control it.

Planning standards—references

1 Ministry of Housing and Local Government, *The Density of Residential Areas*, HMSO (1952).
2 Ministry of Housing and Local Government, *Residential Areas: Higher Densities,* HMSO (1963).
3 Hall, P., *London 2000*, Faber (1969).
4 Wibberley, G. P., *Agriculture and urban growth: a study of the competition for urban land*, Michael Joseph (1959).
5 James, J. R., Paper given to the Town and Country Planning Association 1967. Conference on Residential Densities and Housing Layouts.

6 Keeble, L., 'Town Planning at the Crossroads', *Town Planning Institute Journal*, August, 1961.

7 James, *op. cit.*

8 Keeble, *op. cit.*

9 M. of H. and L.G., *Planning Bulletin Number 2: Residential Areas, Higher Densities*, HMSO (1963).

10 Rosenburg, G., 'A standard for the control of building bulk in business areas', *Town Planning Institute Journal*, September, 1969.

11 *Land Planning Bulletin Number 7*, United States Department of Housing and Urban Development.

12 James, *op. cit.*

13 Ministry of Housing and Local Government, *Houses and Flats*, HMSO (1958).

14 Strachan, A., 'Car Parks and Shopping', *Estates Gazette*, October, 1971.

15 Keeble, L., 'Principles and Practice of Town and Country Planning', *Estates Gazette* (1969).

16 Winterbottom, D., 'How much space do you need?', *Town Planning Institute Journal* (1967).

22   Site layout and development

The preparation of detailed site plans at the local scale is an expertise which appears to attract ever-diminishing attention from town planners in both training and practice. The stigma of 'physical determinism' discourages great premium being placed upon this part of the planning process. Admittedly, in the past, perhaps too much weight was attached to the design and layout of buildings, and the conformity to regulations and standards, but any policy for the social and economic development of a particular community must inevitably possess a physical expression. The determination of the precise form of the physical environment draws upon a variety of skills including those of the architect, engineer, surveyor, economist, landscape architect, lawyer, sociologist and town planner. It is unreasonable to expect one individual discipline to maintain a comprehensive view of the whole, whilst practising a specialist role in all parts. It is necessary, however, for the town planner to have an understanding of the principal factors that influence the method of site planning. Only in this way can he effectively fulfil his responsibilities regarding the control of development implicit in the implementation of his policy. In this context, it is worth remembering that a considerable proportion of a local authority's time and resources in respect of their town planning duties is taken up with the processing of applications for planning permission of a detailed and local nature.

Site planning has been described as 'the art of arranging the external physical environment to support human behaviour . . . Site plans locate structures and activities in three-dimensional space and, when appropriate, in time'.[1] The preparation or consideration of a site plan will often relate to a detailed design for a specific use such as housing, shops, or offices in a particular area. Sometimes it might involve mixed development, but always the nature of the use and the form of its layout will be governed by the relevant provisions of the development plan, the general accessibility and location of the area, the requirements of the client and the topography and characteristics of the site.

The experience of the author and confines of the text preclude any profound appraisal of design techniques or architectural merit, the general purpose is to outline some of the factors that warrant attention in assessing development.

Residential

Of paramount importance in deciding the form and layout of any site plan is an understanding of the exact needs and desires of the client for whom it is being prepared or considered. The nature of the plan will almost certainly vary according to whether the proposed development is public or private, high or low income, central, suburban or rural. Although each site and every situation will deserve individual treatment, broad elements that are common to all can be identified.

(A) Density

The various ways in which the density of residential development is measured, dwellings, persons, habitable rooms, and bedspaces per hectare, is fully discussed elsewhere.[2] It remains, however, a useful concept in assessing the intensity of development and regulating the impact in respect of the provision of community services and facilities. As in all other planning matters it provides a quantitative measure permitting comparison, judgement and control, it says little, however, about the actual coverage or use

314

of land. The most appropriate density for a particular site is determined by, first, the provisions of the development plan, any amendment amounting to a 'substantial departure' might require ministerial confirmation; second, the area itself and the character of surrounding development; third, the nature of the site, its topography and landscape; fourth, the prevailing demand regarding income, design, and size; and fifth, the availability of services, because scattered low density layout can prove extremely expensive to service.

Having examined these factors, various types of construction possess their own density margins. Detached housing rarely exceeds 20 dwellings per hectare, semi-detached 30, and terraced 50. To achieve levels above this, elements of high-rise housing types in the form of maisonettes or flats are required. In this connection, density standards can be employed as a gauge of performance; for example, above 30 dwellings per hectare problems of noise and loss of privacy emerge: as a general rule at about 50 dwellings per hectare the returns derived from private development reach a 'break-even' point, above this the provision of adequate space and amenity combined with low-rise construction becomes incompatible; in excess of 100 dwellings per hectare the process of design becomes difficult and costly; and over 200 dwellings per hectare everything becomes congested and almost overriding problems of lack of space for recreation, parking and servicing are encountered, even accommodation becomes cramped.

In deciding suitable levels of residential development a certain variation in the needs, and consequent size, of constituent households should be allowed for. A certain proportion, perhaps 10%, of one-bedroom dwellings should be provided, similarly about 20% two-bedroom and another 10% four-bedroom dwellings would more closely approximate to real household demand as opposed to the universal supply of the standardised three-bedroom 'family' house. Given the current conditions of the housing market, especially the methods of financing individual purchase, it is unlikely that the private sector developer would would be able to cater for this range of choice. Nevertheless, there remain many thousands of households who live in dwellings which are either too big or too small for their requirements.

(B) Dwelling types

Closely associated with the density of residential development
is the type of development involved, each possessing its own
peculiar characteristics, whether they be laid out in courts,
avenues, or *cul-de-sacs*, on a rectangular, Radburn, or patio
basis.

Fig. 30 Alternative detached housing layouts

SOURCE: Lewis Keeble, 'Principles and Practice of Town
and Country Planning', *Estates Gazette*, 1970

The advantages of detached houses are almost too obvious to
state, they form the ideal unit to which most people aspire,
having both light and access all round, the minimum of noise
and intrusion, and possessing independent support. On the other
hand they impose low densities of around 10 dwellings per
hectare. Requiring a frontage over 35 feet they contribute greatly
towards urban sprawl, and, with ever-increasing pressures upon
land for various uses, are rapidly becoming an impracticable
form of development in this country. They are at their best,
however, when individual treatment can be afforded to their
design and layout, and whilst they tend to be visually unrelated,
unless built at high densities, coherence and unity can be achieved
with careful landscaping by way of fairly dense planting or open-
frontage layout.

The characteristic semi-detached residence which epitomises so much of British suburban development also typifies the renowned art of compromise. They are comparatively cheap to build, give the illusion of being detached, and have reasonable access and orientation, but with frontages of 40 to 50 feet for a pair of houses, and a height of around 30 feet, their layout is considered to 'lack repose through the absence of long horizontal lines' and when 'ranged in a row, have very ragged and irregular shaped spaces between them producing the effect known as tooth-and-gap'.[3]

The growing preference for terraced housing is as much a matter of expedience, through force of economic circumstance, as it is a reflection of taste or fashion. Nevertheless, their facility for unity and continuity of design frequently bestow a most acceptable and satisfying form of urban development. The expression 'terraced' includes any three or more dwellings joined together with frontages of anything upwards of 18 feet. Their individual design can be identical or dissimilar. Even some of the famous Georgian terraces provided for different styles in the same row, achieving unity by ensuring that each was kept in proportion to the whole, with the storey and window line running through the block and the materials and style remaining constant. Their public image is again improving, perhaps the title 'town house' has helped. Having few external walls they provide the most space at the least cost, heat loss is reduced, advanced acoustic insulation has ameliorated the problem of noise, and the ease and flexibility of layout that their design allows readily appeals to the planning and architectural professions. The difficulty of private covered parking is overcome either by the popular, but unsightly, apparent return to 'mews living' with the car occupying the ground floor, or by the provision of communal garage courts conveniently situated nearby.

Variations on these low-rise dwelling themes are possible. Chain houses can be constructed whereby dwellings and garages are staggered alternately, thus affording a better visual rhythm than tooth-and-gap semis, and permitting the valuable estate agents description of detached. Mediterranean style patio houses can be developed allowing densities of up to 300 persons per

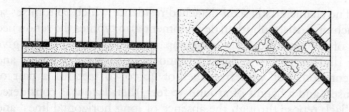

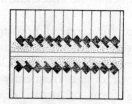

Fig. 31 *Alternative terraced housing layouts*
SOURCE: Lewis Keeble, 'Principles and Practice of
Town and Country Planning', *Estates Gazette*, 1970

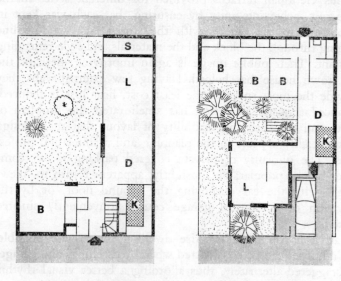

Single entry two storey   **Dual entry single storey**
Fig. 32(a) *Some alternative forms of patio layout—Internal*

318

hectare to be attained, but producing formidable problems of orientation, access, and privacy.

To accomplish higher densities over and above 250 persons or 185 habitable rooms per hectare some proportion of the dwellings must be provided in the form of flats. Judging by their selection of residence in the private sector of the housing market, the vast

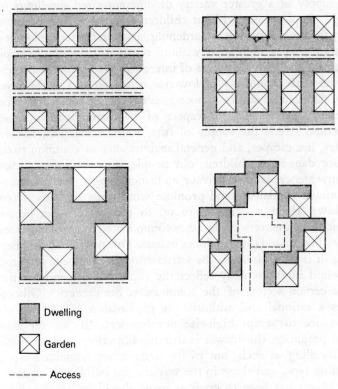

Fig. 32(b) Some alternative forms of patio layout—External

majority of the population of this country display a marked disdain of flatted accommodation. This is in distinct contrast to the custom and conditions prevailing on the Continent, where in many cities upwards of 80% of the population are housed in apartment buildings of one kind or another.

Characteristic advantages and disadvantages of flat development are immediately apparent. On the one hand they provide a compact arrangement of dwellings; a considerable saving of land up to certain levels; permit more people to live in proximity to central areas; allow for a convenient grouping of social facilities; encourage collective and economic provision of such services as central heating, hot water, and refuse disposal; favour the supply of a greater variety of different sized dwellings for single people, those without children and those who prefer to deny themselves the joy of gardening; assist in the redevelopment of high density slum areas without resort to excessive overspill schemes; and provide points of interest in the skyline that break up the drab monotony of low-rise urban areas. On the other hand flats can be said to impose greater costs of construction per dwelling, particularly in respect of combating the increased structural stress, the supply of lifts, sound insulation, rubbish chutes, fire escapes, and general maintenance of common parts; induce danger to children, old people, and the infirm; cause inconvenience, lack of privacy and, increasingly, mental stress; encourage vandalism, and promote wind traps and unwelcome shadows. Even at densities of up to 300 persons per hectare about three-quarters could be accommodated in two- and three-storey houses and the remainder in flats. This provides a balanced form of layout, assists in the satisfactory development of corner sites and might actually reflect the supressed demand for flats from certain sectors of the community. Sir Frederick Gibberd gives a rational and authoritative explanation of the national reluctance to accept high-rise development. 'If we set aside blind prejudice, the answer is that the objections are not to the flat dwelling as such, but to its abuse when combined into a building type, and abuse in the way the flat building is sited . . . The object has been to cram as many dwellings on the site as possible, irrespective of light, air, and amenities of planning.'[4]

There are two principal forms of high-rise flat development, the point and the slab block. The point block can be used to great advantage as a focus of attention in urban development, particularly for exaggerating the effect of natural contours and for minimising the impact of building upon open space. Their full effect is often lost if they are dispersed haphazardly throughout a town, far better that they should be clustered 'into bold groups in contrast to a horizontal setting and, with such groupings, there is also the interplay of one form against another in space which, even with two towers, has more than twice the significance of a single block'.[5] The slab block can be employed to surround and give definition to areas, to open out and provide perspective to areas, and also to give shelter. The wide variety of flatted accommodation, the scope, layout and design, is fully described in Sir Frederick Gibberd's outstanding book *Town Design*.

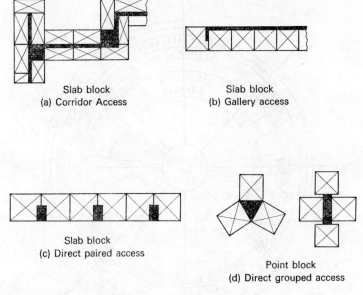

Slab block
(a) Corridor Access

Slab block
(b) Gallery access

Slab block
(c) Direct paired access

Point block
(d) Direct grouped access

Fig. 33 Some forms of flat development

(C) Space and orientation requirements

The placing of buildings in relation to one another, and with due regard to sun and wind, commands considerable attention in judging the layout of residential development. The traditional approach attempted to 'idealise' the orientation of dwellings, but in temperate climes and with modern designs a greater flexibility can be allowed for. The objective in respect of sunlight and daylight is to maximise the amount of light penetrating into the dwelling. In estate development this entails a certain amount of compromise to ensure that this prerogative is shared amongst the whole community. Neverthless, as a general rule of thumb, a layout which attempts to align the frontages on the dwellings in an approximately north to south direction is infinitely preferable to one whose orientation is west to east. In this way both the back and the front of the buildings will receive sunlight, one in the morning, the other in the afternoon and early evening.

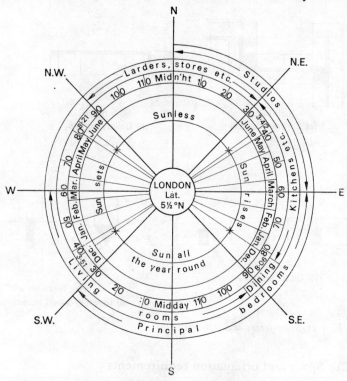

Fig. 34 Orientation for residential layout and design

The light in the south at midday is not really lost, because it has least penetration owing to its elevation in the sky. The internal arrangement of the house should aim to get as much sunlight into as many rooms as possible, as indicated in Figure 34, but in any event should take account of popular preference for early morning sun in the kitchen. In circumstances where it is not possible to secure north to south road layouts the use of house situated in echelon, or the introduction of courts or cul-de-sacs leading off, will often secure a satisfactory aspect. Although not a matter of great moment in this country, the prevailing wind should also be considered in selecting the most propitious plan.

This factor of orientation assumes even more importance in the location of high-rise, high-density development where not only the penetration of sunlight but also the effect of shadow and wind become significant. This is especially so where slab blocks of flats are under consideration for, often having only one central corridor, the individual flats will necessarily have only one aspect. Correct siting is therefore critical.

The degree of daylight and sunlight received by a dwelling is also affected by the space between buildings. To ensure adequate provision in this direction the government publication *Design of Residential Areas*, produced as long ago as 1952, sets down particularly useful guidelines. It estimates that proper penetration is only secured where there is an uninterrupted sight line of 25° from the horizontal. As demonstrated in Figure 35 this

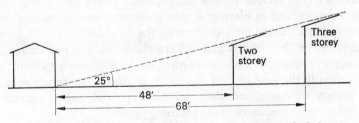

Fig. 35 Space required between buildings to allow adequate daylight

produces minimum distances of 48 feet between two-storey houses and 68 feet between three-storey houses. This is supplemented by the time-honoured '70 foot rule' which is selected as a satisfactory separation of dwellings, asserting that at this distance the outline of the human body becomes blurred and actions indistinguishable, thus preserving personal privacy. Perhaps the radical notion of curtains, by no means a modern invention, might permit a certain flexibility in the interpretation of this rule. It still serves, however, as practical indication for the spacing of buildings.

In this context another standard which regulates the layout of development is the 'building line'. This prescribes a line at a given distance from the middle of the road beyond which the erection of buildings is normally prohibited. Although it is sometimes varied to allow for outstanding features, it is inclined to produce a rather drab, uniform, and monotonous perspective if rigidly applied. Many of the New Towns adopted a more imaginative approach towards the control space requirements and either ignored or waived the adherence to building lines.

One final element of orientation that is frequently overlooked is the opportune and skilful use of existing features of note or views worth preserving and enhancing.

(D) Road layout

The layout of roads in residential areas not only provides the framework for development and the channels of communication between respective land uses, but also carries the facilities and utilities that service the dwellings, both above and below the ground, as well as playing a prominent part in determining the very character and environment of the neighbourhood. It is an element of the overall plan where the town planner exercises extensive control and although the detailed construction is essentially the province of the traffic engineer, the function and location of roads and their relationship with other activities is of great consequence in the planning process.

Different roads obviously fulfil different purposes and the individual design and the general layout should take account of and reflect this. The concern here is for local roads in residential areas. Two extreme forms of site layout present themselves. Firstly, the old-fashioned grid network where the land is divided up into squares or rectangles of approximately the same size. Whilst this leads to an economic use of building land it also gives rise to a large number of intersections between roads of equal importance which pose great accident hazards. The overriding uniformity also creates extremely monotonous vistas, disregard

324

of topography, lack of differentiation between roads and despite the blocking-off of certain links in the grid and the formation of *cul-de-sacs* the network remains inefficient and dangerous. Secondly, an alternative form of layout is developed in which roads radiate or branch out from a single distributor road, again forming a large number of rather long *cul-de-sacs*. This system is comparatively rigid and dictates a single direction of movement and whilst the problem of through traffic is eliminated it is at unnecessary cost to the provision of services, which must be run longer distances, and the uneconomic delivery of goods. For these reasons the city of Philadelphia has forbidden the creation of *cul-de-sacs* more than 150 metres long[6] and in this country 180 metres is considered a maximum length. Although no ideal form of layout can be established for comprehensive application, each site has unique characteristics and deserves special treatment. Certain guidelines common to all residential estates can be suggested:

1. it is important to seek the development of an 'environmental area' through which no extraneous traffic flows, the principle of which is illustrated in Figure 36
2. the road layout should discourage short cuts being taken through the area
3. long straight stretches of road which might lend themselves as racetracks should be avoided either by a constantly changing road pattern or by the use of 'speed bumps' built into the surface
4. crossroads should be excluded, particularly at the intersection of roads comparable in the hierarchy. The use of 'T' junctions is preferable
5. junctions should be staggered wherever possible, a suitable distance between neighbouring junctions being about 45 metres
6. roads should intersect at right angles to ensure adequate vision and safety
7. whilst depending upon the design speed of the roads, the sight lines provided at intersections should normally allow 90 metres of clear unobstructed vision from 9 metres at the junction of a local access road with a distributor and 60 metres at the junction of two access roads

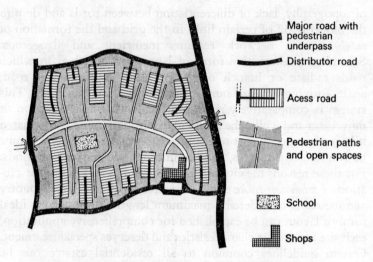

Major road with pedestrian underpass

Distributor road

Acess road

Pedestrian paths and open spaces

School

Shops

(a) The principle of traffic separation

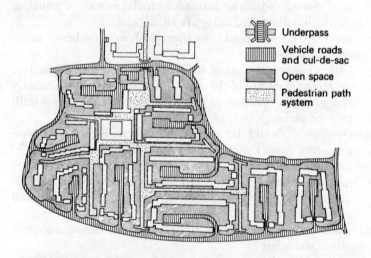

Underpass

Vehicle roads and cul-de-sac

Open space

Pedestrian path system

(b) An example of traffic segregation at Beeston, Notts.

Fig. 36 Traffic segregation

SOURCE: Design Bulletin 10—*Cars in Housing*, HMSO

8. the total length of roads should be kept to a minimum in the interests of economy, thus an attempt should always be made to secure a double frontage of dwellings

9. to ensure satisfying perspectives and vistas the views at the ends of roads should be 'closed' by the skilful positioning of interesting features such as churches or trees, or the careful layout of houses square to the road alignment

10. roads with house frontages are best designed in a north to south direction to permit satisfactory orientation

11. the length of *cul-de-sacs* should be kept within reasonable limits and never more than 180 metres long. Similarly, care must be taken not to inadvertently create a *cul-de-sac* out of a network of access roads. Most estates of any significant size should always provide more than one entrance and exit

12. the construction of houses fronting on to distributor roads should be avoided

13. the segregation of motor traffic and pedestrians should be considered

14. the overall layout of the road system should not be too complex, so that visitors and delivery vehicles can find their way around the estate

15. plot shapes should be kept as regular as possible

16. in low-rise residential development the provision of ample private open space in the form of back gardens should be given precedence over the supply of public open space and front gardens

17. the treatment of corner plots should merit special attention, the requirement for adequate vision often necessitates the setting back or total restriction of development and subsequent loss of developable frontage. This can often be overcome by the construction of small blocks of flats, maisonettes, or old peoples' bungalows where the demands for private open space are not so pressing

18. to ensure adequate drainage throughout the road system. there must be a minimum gradient of 1:200 everywhere A slope of over 1:10 becomes dangerous when freezing occurs and one in excess of 1:17 precludes use by service vehicles of any size

327

The actual nature and dimensions of the respective estate roads warrants some consideration. The distributor roads which convey traffic around the residential area should be about 7 metres wide and flanked with pavements about 3 metres wide the access roads which carry vehicles to the various individual dwellings require to be 5 metres wide with pavements 2 metres wide; the *cul-de-sacs*, which by their very nature carry no through traffic, need only be 4 metres wide with pavement again 2 metres wide. At the end of *cul-de-sacs* turning points will need to be provided which are big enough to accept the largest of service vehicles, turning circles are out-of-date and wasteful of land, the tendency being to employ hammer heads. If a great deal of kerbside parking is anticipated it might prove necessary to provide a separate parking lane which can be of a lighter construction, about 2·5 metres wide and designed in bays approximately 6 metres long so that it is only used for the desired purpose and vehicles park singly.

The use of grass verges separating the road and pavement is not just for convenience, safety and visual relief but can also accommodate services and utilities below the ground in an economic and accessible manner that causes least disturbance. Where laid, these verges should be at the very least 1 metre and where trees and bushes are planted, 2 metres wide. At any point where poles are placed on the kerbside for street lighting, telephone wires, or bus stops, they should ideally be placed 0·75 metres back from the kerb; regrettably, however, it is often less.

Another feature that is rarely incorporated into residential estate layout in this country is the cycleway. The merits of this form of transport are said to include 'quietness, economy, no pollution, good exercise, ease of parking and safety to others'.[7] When provided they should be approximately 4 metres wide with a generally curving alignment, easy gradients, and can be combined with separate pedestrian ways.

(E) Parking

The phenomenal increase in private car ownership over recent years has placed a great responsibility upon residential estate

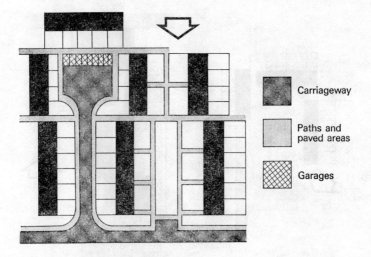

Carriageway

Paths and
paved areas

Garages

(a) The vehicle cul-de-sac

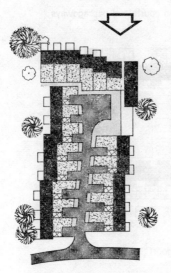

(b) The vehicle cul-de-sac
with individual garages

Fig. 37 (a, b)

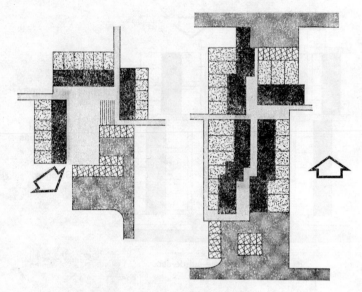

(c) Pedestrian courts and passageways

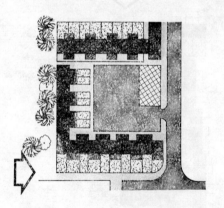

(d) Garage court (Laindon, Essex)

Fig. 37 (cont.)

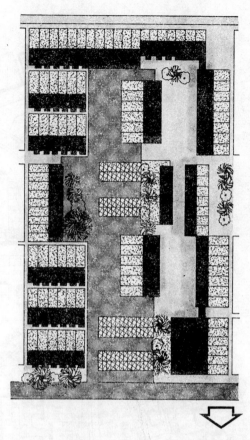

(e) Pedestrian and garage courts (Hook proposed new town)

Fig. 37 Examples of Radburn layout groupings

SOURCE: Design Bulletin 10—*Cars in Housing*, HMSO

developers and local planning authorities in ensuring that as many vehicles as possible are attracted off the already congested and cluttered roads when stationary. Although on-street parking is convenient for the householder during the day, and inevitable for the delivery of goods and supply of certain services, it should be realised that apart from being a constant source of danger to children, hindering refuse collection and street cleaning, one parked vehicle reduces the capacity of a road for 90 metres in both directions; this can restrict the flow of traffic in a residential

331

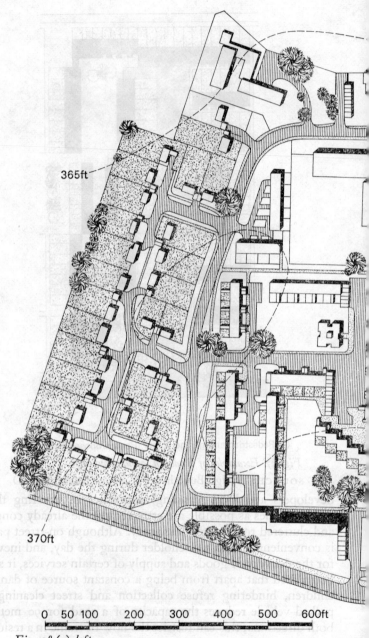

365ft

370ft

0 50 100   200   300   400   500   600ft

Fig. 38 (a) left

Fig. 38 Housing estate layout at Warley Essex illustrating various forms

SOURCE: Design Bulletin 10—*Cars in Housing*, HMSO

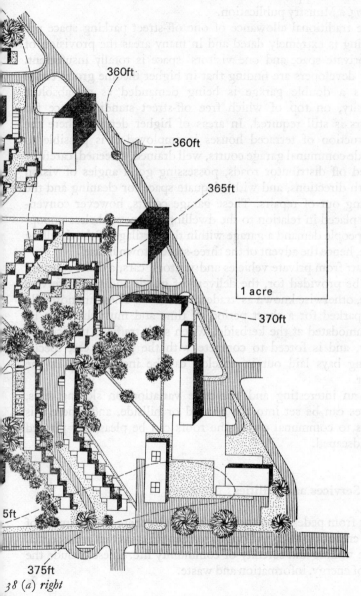

360ft

360ft

365ft

370ft

1 acre

5ft

375ft

38 (a) right

...ential development and different kinds of car parking treatment

area at peak hours by over 50%. Although the provision of parking spaces sometimes appears inadequate, Figure 37 portrays a variety of approaches to the problem selected from *Cars in Housing*, a Ministry publication.

The traditional allowance of one off-street parking space per dwelling is extremely dated and in many areas the provision of one private space and one visitors' space is totally insufficient. Many developers are finding that in higher income group estate houses a double garage is being demanded as an absolute necessity, on top of which free off-street standing space for visitors is still required. In areas of higher density where the construction of terraced houses is employed it is possible to provide communal garage courts, well drained, screened, carefully located off distributor roads, possessing good angles of vision in both directions, and with adequate space for cleaning and the carrying out of repairs. These garage courts, however conveniently placed in relation to the dwelling, are nevertheless unpopular; people demand a garage within the curtilage of the dwelling house, hence the advent of the three-storey 'town house'.

Apart from private vehicles and visitors' cars, a third category must be provided for, the delivery of goods and public service traffic, otherwise known as 'tradesmen traffic'. These are normally only parked for a short period of time and must therefore be accommodated at the kerbside. When such traffic is particularly heavy, and is forced to compete with the private car, special parking bays laid out in echelon can be incorporated in the layout.

As an interesting and attractive variation on sloping sites, garages can be set into the ground or hillside, and where this relates to communal courts the roofs can be pleasantly planted or landscaped.

(F) Services and utilities

Apart from pedestrians and motor vehicles there are a number of other critical flows in and out of residential areas that are essential to the welfare and serenity of community life. These include the flow of energy, information and waste.

Drains and sewers

Drains are essentially those pipes, channels and culverts within the individual property boundary which convey water and waste to local authority sewers. There are three basic systems of waste disposal: *combined*, which takes all domestic waste and surplus water together; *separate*, in which one pipe carries domestic waste and another surface water; and *partially separate*, where one pipe carries all domestic waste and surplus water from on and around the dwelling whilst another receives all other surface water. The separate and partially separate systems provide a more assured method of catering for excessive surface water imposed by rainstorms. Theoretically all land surfaces should be designed in such a way as to permit the flow of water away to drains and sewers. The appropriate gradient around residential dwellings to ensure this process is 1:50 but on other open spaces it can decrease to 1:100 and even 1:200 on specially constructed and engineered surfaces such as roads. In order to introduce a satisfactory system a knowledge of the total amount of water naturally entering a site, its possible velocity and its capacity to drain are prerequisities to the planner and engineer. The general configuration and geology of the site will govern the nature of the most appropriate system of drainage and sewerage. This is a major factor, albeit one of several, that should be taken into account in establishing the pattern of roads. The ideal situation is found where the roads can run along broad, gently sloping valleys along the line of natural fall. Roads which run parallel with the contours will cause problems because dwellings both sides of the same street will not be able to naturally drain into intermediate sewers, pipes will have to be laid through the intervening plots. Roads which run at right angles to the contours might facilitate the disposal of sewage but surface drainage is often difficult.

All sewers must be buried to prevent damage, the actual depth varies according to the potentiality of the area and the soil to freezing. Naturally the deeper they are laid the more expensive becomes both the initial operation and any possible future inspection and repair. As a general rule 1 to 2 metres is considered sufficient, below about 3 metres the task becomes very costly. At the same time, however, it must be recognised that

335

the main sewers must be laid at a sufficient depth to allow the flow of waste from neighbouring houses. In this country sewesr must be laid in straight lines, although more advanced systems in the United States are laid in gentle horizontal curves with a radius of never less than 30 metres.[8] In their vertical alignment the sewer pipes must have a minimum grade to maintain constant flow and permit self-cleansing. As always, it is more economic to take advantage of the natural contours of the site and the ideal gradient largely depends upon the size of the pipe and the expected flow. In most circumstances a slope of 1:200 will ensure a flow of 1 metre per second when operating at maximum capacity which is satisfactory. The minimum acceptable gradient is about 1:300, while at the other extreme the velocity should never exceed 3 metres per second, otherwise damage to the pipe as a result of scouring might occur. For uneven ground or extreme slopes, sudden changes in gradient can be made at manholes performing roughly the same function as locks on a canal. In any event these should be placed at intervals of between 90 to 150 metres in order to facilitate inspection, entry, repair, and cleansing.

The size of pipe varies according to the function it performs and the number of dwellings it serves. In practice 'run-off coefficients' and other formulae are used to calculate the requisite diameter, but as a rough guide it can be said that domestic pipes are approximately 100mm to 150mm wide and main sewers start at around 200mm, being sufficient to serve an estate of 100 houses, and for each additional 100 houses an extra 75mm in the width is required. In this context another important rule is that pipes must always discharge into larger ones, for fairly obvious reasons.

In assessing a site for residential development, flat or swampy land can cause serious problems. Pumping is always possible but is extremely costly. If the surface water is merely localised 'ponding' the planting of moisture-absorbing plants can ease the situation.

Water

The quantity, quality, pressure, and general availability of water exercises a material control over the feasibility of residential development. Whilst, however, it plays a prominent part in determining location it is not such an important influence over layout, although it is the most susceptible pipe to frost. Because it is distributed under pressure a much greater degree of flexibility can be introduced in respect of gradients, curves, and overall design. The size of pipe is normally about 200mm in diameter and, to equate the maintenance of a minimum of pressure with maximum of potential demand, a pressure of approximately 137 880 newtons per square metre at the hydrant or house is required. There are two basic methods or systems of piping water: firstly, like branches of a tree running off from a main stem which minimises overall length and is therefore cheaper to install, and secondly, as a series of loops, which is initially more expensive but virtually eliminates extensive reduction in pressure owing to breakage and subsequent interruption of the whole system to effect repair.

Electricity

On a national basis electricity is distributed at high voltage, being 'stepped down' for local use at transformers and connected from there with dwellings at low voltage. These low voltage secondary lines are wasteful and costly, therefore their length must be kept to a minimum, preferably about 120 metres.[9] It is this location of transformer stations that concerns the site planner at the local scale, although considerable discretion and flexibility can be exercised in their exact positioning. It is often the case that in any residential estate development there will be small, irregular and awkwardly shaped plots of land left over within the layout. These readily lend themselves for use as transformer sub-stations. They should have access to the road system and be suitably screened.

Electricity cables, whether for power or telephone, are best situated underground. This operation is initially more expensive but breaks are less frequent, although when damage does occur repairs are very costly to effect. There is marked tendency, especially in new town development, to erect one communal television aerial to which everybody has access and prohibit the use of separate individual antennae, a practice to be applauded and encouraged.

337

Gas

The provision of gas is based on approximately the same principle as that of water, with either a branching or loop system of distribution. The pipes, however, are considerably smaller and almost the only matter of concern for the site planner is to ensure that, because of the great danger caused by leakage, electricity and gas pipes are not laid in the same conduit.

Refuse disposal

Naturally provision must be made in the overall layout and internal design of the buildings for the collection of domestic refuse. The estate roads must be of sufficient dimensions to allow the service vehicles access and facility to turn. The actual areas set aside for dustbins should be well drained, adequately sheltered, conveniently situated for collection, having no steep gradients and with the route preferably paved.

Due to the propensity for damage and leakage and the consequent need for inspection and repair, all pipes and cables should, wherever possible, be laid under a public right of way so that they are readily accessible and cause the minimum amount of inconvenience, delay and expense. To this end the arrangement of conduits under grass verges flanking the road network supplies an admirable solution.

In assessing the relative qualities of urban residential development it should be recognised that the respective services, utilities and facilities that combine in producing a satisfactory 'life support system' also give rise to the unsightly clutter of poles, wires, aerials, lights, power lines and other such apparatus. There is no reason why the design and detail of these essential accoutrements of urban living should not attract greater attention in the process of site planning, and why a greater harmony between them and their relation to the general environment should not be achieved. A more eloquent plea is made by Lynch. 'Because of the prevalent ugliness of much of our circulation equipment, we consider roads and utilities as regretfully necessary things that must be supplied but should be hidden . . . we should demand an even clearer expression of the essential elements of this system instead of camouflaging them. Power lines and highways can be an expressive component of the landscape; exposed pipes can be handsome.'[10]

Landscape and planting

To achieve unity in design and coherence in layout it is necessary to supplement the bare form of buildings with a more natural and visually pleasing environment. The skill employed by the landscape architect in planning the composition and character of open spaces can be divided into two broad categories, the site itself, and the purpose to which it is put.

The site

When surveying a particular site in the preparation of a separate landscape plan it is important to take into consideration the following features:

1. an appraisal should be made of the existing vegetation, some of which might be suitable for retention or even replanting. Healthy mature trees are always worth preserving and featuring

2. the availability of natural water on the site plays a large part in determining the amount and kind of landscaping that can be provided. The purity of the water should also be tested, as should the level of the water table and the possible effect the proposed development might have upon it. Seasonal variations in the supply of water might prove significant and should also be recorded

3. an analysis of the micro-climate should be undertaken, examining the rainfall, temperature and amount of sunshine, together with any proclivity towards mist, fog or freakish winds. The orientation of slopes should also be noted as this affects the performance of certain species

4. the type of bedrock and the nature and condition of the soil can influence the approach towards landscaping. Although artificial fertilisation can be employed it is much better if the right kind of soil is matched to the most appropriate form of vegetation

5. any assessment of the site should also include an appreciation of the surrounding area. It might prove necessary to screen unsightly, noisy, or noxious neighbouring activities. On the

other hand, buildings of architectural and historic interest or views of particular beauty can be opened up and used to advantage in siting the residential development

The purpose

Landscaping can play a positive role in assisting the plan to fulfil its function. The following are examples of the way in which this might be achieved:

1. in an attempt to reduce the visual impact of the motor car, car parks can be screened and hidden
2. the segregation of pedestrian and motor vehicle can be obtained by expert planting even where the two channels of communication run almost alongside. A moderately meandering pathway flanked with trees and bushes and separated by only a few metres from the road can be both convenient and pleasant
3. undesired movement can be discouraged by the use of hard, rough but visually attractive surfaces such as cobblestones
4. in residential areas of low density where development is comparatively scattered landscaping can both ensure effective use of excess open space and act as a visual, and even physical, link between dwellings. In areas of medium density it can be used simply to break the monotony of uniform estate layout. In areas of high density it provides tremendous relief and contrast, but great care must be exercised in the choice of materials owing to the fact that such open space as does exist is subjected to intensive wear
5. landscaping can also be applied as a safety precaution regarding dangerous roads and water hazards

It can, therefore, be seen that the landscape architect should be brought in at an early stage in the planning and layout of residential areas. His art is not confined, as is the popular misconception, to providing the 'icing on the cake' for in its widest context the expertise is required from inception to completion of estate development.

Tree planting

The planting of trees and the retention of existing vegetation within a residential estate fulfils a number of functions, it gives shelter and protection against wind, noise and fumes; screens undesirable views and safeguards privacy, directs attention to and from buildings and other objects, acts as a visual link between development, demarcate boundaries, influences pedestrian circulation, accommodates changes in ground level, creates and defines external spaces and generally supplies visual contrast and relief. The great art of preparing and implementing a satisfactory tree planting programme lies in the ability to reconcile a number of conflicting factors such as:

1. The placing of trees close to buildings or underground services can cause extensive damage, not only directly by root growth, but also indirectly by causing moisture changes and therefore instability in the soil. Most roots lie within about a metre of the surface and can extend very approximately one-third as far again as the height of the tree; in dry soils, however, this can be even further. It should also be remembered that most trees require an enormous amount of water; a poplar may consume as much as 12 000 gallons in a year, although a conifer might only use 2000 gallons.

2. The right tree must be selected for the right site. Certain species are particularly suitable for use in towns, being more resistant to the polluted atmosphere, such as poplar, plane, elm and cherry. Others are especially tolerant to coastal conditions and salt spray, including certain types of elm and oak. Some varieties, such as alder and willow, demand a waterside location.

3. The nature of the soil is important, ash, lime and elm prefer a light alkaline soil, whereas chestnut, oak and pine are happier in sandier, more acid conditions. Most varieties grow well in a medium loam which has a neutral character.

4. Drainage might have to be provided in retentive subsoils such as clay. Porous formations such as sand, limestone and chalk are normally sufficiently self-draining.

5. Frequently quick results are called for and fast-growing species such as ash, birch, willow, alder or cypress must be incorporated within the layout.

6. Strongly coloured trees, such as purple maple, copper beech and golden false acacia, should be sited with great care,

341

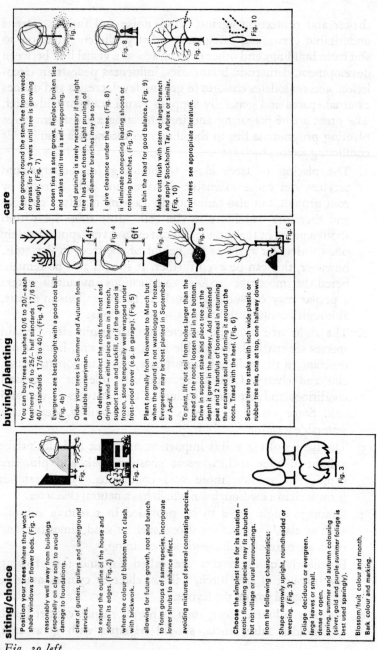

siting/choice

Position your trees where they won't shade windows or flower beds. (Fig. 1)

reasonably well away from buildings (especially on clay soil) to avoid damage to foundations.

clear of gutters, gulleys and underground services.

to extend the outline of the house and soften its edges. (Fig. 2)

where the colour of blossom won't clash with brickwork.

allowing for future growth, root and branch

to form groups of same species, incorporate lower shrubs to enhance effect.

avoiding mixtures of several contrasting species.

Choose the simplest tree for its situation – exotic flowering species may fit suburban but not village or rural surroundings.

from the following characteristics:

Shape narrowly upright, roundheaded or weeping. (Fig. 3)

Foliage deciduous or evergreen.
large leaves or small.
dense or open.
spring, summer and autumn colouring (silver, gold and purple *summer* foliage is best used sparingly).

Blossom/fruit colour and month.

Bark colour and marking.

buying/planting

You can buy trees as bushes 10/6 to 20/– each feathered 7/6 to 25/– half standards 17/6 to 40/– standards 17/6 to 40/–. (Fig. 4)

Evergreens are best bought with a good root ball. (Fig. 4b)

Order your trees in Summer and Autumn from a reliable nurseryman.

On delivery protect the roots from frost and drying wind – either place them in a trench, support stem and backfill, or if the ground is frozen, store temporarily well wrapped under frost-proof cover (e.g. in garage). (Fig. 5).

Plant normally from November to March but when the ground is not waterlogged or frozen. Evergreens may be best planted in September or April.

To plant, lift out soil from holes larger than the spread of the roots, loosen soil in the bottom. Drive in support stake and place tree at the depth it grew in the nursery. Add moistened peat and 2 handfuls of bonemeal in returning the excavated soil and firming it around the roots. Tread with the heel. (Fig. 6)

Secure tree to stake with inch wide plastic or rubber tree ties, one at top, one halfway down.

care

Keep ground round the stem free from weeds or grass for 2–3 years until tree is growing strongly. (Fig. 7)

Loosen ties as stem grows. Replace broken ties and stakes until tree is self-supporting.

Hard pruning is rarely necessary if the right tree has been chosen. Light pruning of small diameter branches may be to:

i give clearance under the tree. (Fig. 8)

ii eliminate competing leading shoots or crossing branches. (Fig. 9)

iii thin the head for good balance. (Fig. 9)

Make cuts flush with stem or larger branch and apply Stockholm Tar, Arbrex or similar. (Fig. 10)

Fruit trees **see appropriate literature.**

Fig. 39 left
Fig. 39 Trees in Estate layout

SOURCE: Michael Kennett, 'Safeguarding our trees', *Official Architect and Planner*, September, 1968

342

Botanical Name	Common Name	Special Characteristics	Eventual size in feet on good site		Remarks	Form (Evergreens shaded)
			Height	Spread		
Acer negundo	Box Elder	Fresh green summer foliage	40	× 25-30	Variety variegatum has white and green leaves	
Amelanchier canadensis	June Berry	April – white blossom Autumn colour	20-30	× 20-30		
Betula pendula	Silver Birch	Small leaves – gold in Autumn – silver stem	40-60	× 25	Fast growing on light soils. Plant small.	
Betula pendula youngii	Weeping Silver Birch	Slow growing	20-30	× 30-35	Slow growing	
Chamaecyparis lawsoniana	Lawson's Cypress and Varieties	Green, grey or gold-foliaged varieties	15-60	× 6-20	Some varieties not for smoky areas	
Crataegus oxyacantha plena	Double White Thorn	Double flowers in May. No fruit	20-25	× 20-25	Also pink and crimson varieties	
Crataegus X carrieri	Hybrid Thorn	White blossom, June. Large leaves and orange red berries into New Year	20-25	× 18-20		
Ilex aquifolium and varieties	Holly	Foliage and winter berry	40	× 25-30	Slow growing	
Laburnum alpinum and L. vossii	Laburnum	May–June – yellow blossom	20-30	× 20-25	Seeds poisonous. The variety watereri has fewer seeds	
Malus floribunda	Flowering Crab Apple	April-May – profuse apple blossom. Densely twiggy habit	20-25	× 25-35	Accommodating as to soil and situation	
Picea omorika	Serbian Spruce	Slender elegant evergreen. Good as a Christmas tree	60-80	× 20	Best on loam. Plant against dark background	
Prunus amygdalis	Almond	Pink blossom in March before the leaves	20-25	× 20-25		
Prunus cerasifera nigra	Purple Leaf Plum	Pink blossom in March before the leaves. Purple Summer foliage	20-25	× 20-25	Not for smoky areas	
Prunus cerasus rhexii	Flowering Cherry	Beautiful double white flowers – April–May	20-25	× 20-25	Also single white variety P. serrulata affinis	
Prunus hillieri spire	Flowering Cherry	Soft pink blossom April–May Autumn tints	25-30	× 6 – 8		
Prunus X Okame	Flowering Cherry	April – small rosy pink flowers	18-25	× 18-25		
Prunus rosea pendula	Cheal's Weeping Cherry	April–May. Double pink blossom on arching branches	15-20	× 15-20	Also known under Shidare-zakura	
Prunus subhirtella autumnalis	Winter Flowering Cherry	Semi-double white flowers in mild Winter periods	20-25	× 25-30		
Prunus padus and the variety Watereri	Bird Cherry	May – fragrant white flowers in long racemes	30-40	× 25-30	Accommodating as to soil and situation	
Pyrus salicifolia pendula	Weeping Pear	Dense silver grey foliage on arching branches	15-25	× 15-25	Willow-like leaves	
Robinia pseudoacacia fastigiata	Fastigiate Locust	Feathery foliage, bright green throughout Summer	25-30	× 6 – 8	Good on light soils	
Sorbus aucuparia and variety asplenifolia	Rowan or Mountain Ash	May–June. White blossom– red berries. Autumn tints	30-50	× 25-40		
Sorbus discolor	form of Mountain Ash	Similar, with fine Autumn colour	25-35	× 25-35		
Sorbys pinnatifida gibbsii	Hybrid Service Tree	Grey green leaves – bright red berries	20-30	× 10-15		

Fig. 39 right

preferably singly as a focal point contrasting with their background.

7. Trees should always be in proportion to surrounding developments.

8. The cost of planting, although small in comparison to other facets of development, is critical and therefore every precaution to preserve existing trees, to avoid inappropriate species that require excessive pruning, fertilising and drainage, and the introduction of young saplings as well as mature trees, must be taken.

9. Some species, such as poplar and ash, are exceptionally invasive with excessive root growth, whilst others shed vast amounts of foliage which can cause dangerous slippery surfaces and clog drainage systems. Both types must be sited with great care.

Industrial estates

The scale, location and condition of industrial estates play a large part in determining the character and tone of urban areas. The squalor of some sprawling nineteenth-century developments has a depressant effect upon a whole town or region, whilst the savage forms of some industrial buildings possess a certain splendour all of their own, enhancing the quality of an area.

(a) *Location*
Most industrial activities form only a part of a complete process, and a major locational factor becomes the proximity and accessibility to other related activities. This complementarity and demand for continuity can be extended beyond production and applied to the sharing of services and facilities as well as the desire for prestige location. Extractive industries, by their very nature, must be sited on the source of their raw materials. Others, such as shipbuilding, are also inextricably bound to particular locations. The need for water in vast quantities is a principal requirement in a number of other processes, demanding sites alongside rivers and canals. These include paper mills, bleach and dye works, and tanneries, which form a kind of incursive riverside ribbon development.

Although the demand for labour and the call for urban concentration suggest the need to establish industrial estates in the approximate vicinity of residential areas, great care must be taken to ensure that the traffic to work does not conflict with the rush-hour traffic travelling to the town centre. Some degree of separation is also occasioned because of the noise, fumes and unsightly appearance often associated with such development. With the prevailing wind in this country blowing from the south-west it is common practice to locate industry in the north-east sector of a town, especially where noxious operations such as brick and cement works are concerned, unless variations in topography or local micro-climate dictate otherwise.

Another principal factor influencing industrial location is accessibility. The use of rail has largely given way to road transport with only about 20% of industrial concerns requiring access to the railway network. As these tend to be the bigger concerns the presence of railway sidings is no longer a prerequisite to the siting of smaller industrial estates, although such a facility is always an advantage. It has recently been discovered that even airports attract certain specialised light industry; however, as yet, no direct runway links have been formed as occurs in the United States. One of the problems that has to be faced wherever an industrial estate is placed is the sudden disgorgement of vehicles on to the public road system at certain hours. If possible the most satisfactory method of dispersal is by way of several exits on to a number of secondary roads, but where this cannot be effected peak-hour traffic control at major intersections must be introduced.

One of the greatest misconceptions in respect of industrial location is the fact that not all operations are automatically non-conforming and must therefore be isolated from residential areas. Certain activities can be beneficially mixed with other uses including housing, the criteria being that 'they should not be detrimental to the amenity of the area by reason of noise, vibration, smell, fumes, smoke, soot, ash, dust or grit'.[11]

(b) *Layout*
It is impossible to lay down a format that governs the preparation of all plans for industrial estates in all circumstances. A number

of simple rules common to most layouts can, however, be identified:

1. The size of industrial estates varies considerably, from as little as 10 hectares to well over 200 hectares. A crude but convenient way of assessing the appropriate size for a particular urban area is to adopt a figure of 1·5 hectares per 1000 population. This produces an estate of 100 hectares for a theoretical New Town of around 65 000, which represents what appears to be a reasonable provision.[12]

2. Another method of calculating the size of estates, but more usually employed to regulate the extent of industrial development, is the application of the relevant density standards. In this country levels of between 125 and 175 workers per hectare have prevailed, but in recent years there has been a marked tendency towards lower levels of around 75 to 125 workers per hectare.

3. The intensity of development and ground coverage can be controlled by the use of the Floor Space Index, more popularly applied in office development. This relates the permitted amount of industrial floor area to the total plot size with some allowance for surrounding roads and is commonly put at around 0·5.

4. The site should be as flat as possible and under no circumstances have a slope in excess of 1:20.

5. The size of individual plots should vary to accommodate factories from 200 square metres to over 20 000 square metres.

6. The shape of plots and the provision of services should be so designed as to permit consolidation if necessary.

7. The most suitable plot shape is usually square or rectangular, served by a gridiron or loop network of access roads. The principal system of access roads should preferably be one-way with a number of cul-de-sacs branching off to individual plots or groups of plots.

8. A generous provision of land should be reserved for any future potential expansion both on individual plots and throughout the overall layout.

9. The roads should be of liberal proportions to allow for the continual passing of heavy vehicles. Each traffic lane requires to be about 3·5 metres wide, good sight lines are

346

required, a clear indication of the entrance and exit to the estate should be provided, extra lanes for accelerating and decelerating should be supplied on neighbouring arterial roads, the minor access roads within the estate should intersect at 'T' junctions, and the more important ones at roundabouts.

10. Heavy delivery and service traffic should be separated from employees' private cars.

11. If the construction of factory premises is undertaken they should permit flexibility of use with ample service and delivery bays. Single-storey straight-line buildings are more popular than multi-storey developments, having more uniform and effective natural lighting, less structural obstruction, being cheaper to erect, and easier to re-let or sell. Certain concentrated processes such as confectionery and flour milling are best suited to multi-storey buildings, but they are rare.

12. Industrial concerns having the same characteristics or requirements should be grouped together. In this way noxious or noisy activities can be segregated, and parking, canteen, medical and recreational facilities can be shared.

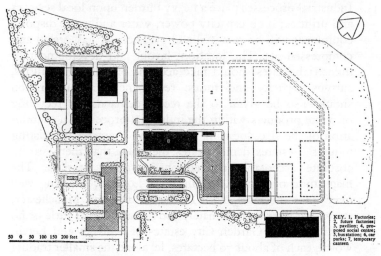

KEY. 1, Factories; 2, future factories; 3, pavilion; 4, proposed social centre; 5, bus station; 6, car parks; 7, temporary canteen

50 0 50 100 150 200 feet

Fig. 40 North Tees Industrial Estate
SOURCE: Frederick Gibberd, *Town Design*

13. Sports fields surrounding industrial estates not only provide a physical or spatial barrier but are also compatible uses in that sporting pursuits and industrial production often take place at different times, thus not impinging upon one another and permitting the sharing of parking facilities.

14. The amount of parking space provided in connection with industrial premises must obviously be related to the number of workers employed, the availability of public transport and the frequency and duration of delivery trips. The number of spaces supplied should normally be between 0·75 and 1·0 per worker, this allows for the overlapping of shifts. This is an ideal and perhaps excessive requirement. The number of spaces is usually related to the amount of factory floorspace, a crude and arbitrary standard, and varies enormously throughout the country, averaging approximately one space for every 25–30 square metres up to 250 and closer to one space for every 100 square metres beyond that. As workers know where their destination is, and will remain parked for up to 8 hours, it is reasonable to expect them to walk up to 100 metres. In this way central parking facilities can be provided for small concerns.

15. Industrial processes place a heavy burden upon local services and utilities; high capacity power, water and waste disposal equipment will be required and occasionally gas, steam and compressed air. The location, layout and development of industrial estates should take account of existing facilities, surplus capacity and future requirements. Consideration should also be given to the recent demands for recycling of waste products within the industrial process. An examination of the size, location, density and character of existing industrial estates demonstrates the point that there are no absolute acceptable conventions currently applied. The magnitude of Park Royal in West London, covering well over 1000 hectares, and Trafford Park near Manchester, stretching over approximately 500 hectares, bears little or no relation to the Garden City estates of Welwyn and Letchworth, each of about 70 hectares, let alone the smaller trading estates associated with so many urban areas today. It has been suggested that the most suitable size for such estates

348

lies between 20 and 60 hectares, below which only very small concerns will be attracted and the benefits of scale will be lost, above which it is difficult to relate to other areas of the town. There is no reason why small estates should not be designed in conjunction with overall residential and neighbourhood layout, not as a substitute for the larger industrial estate of the town but in addition to it. These sites need only be about 6 hectares in size and accommodate small single-storey factories, preferably those which employ a high proportion of women who could then work close to their homes. Such a development was planned as an integral part of the Caldwell Estate at Nuneaton.[13]

One further aspect of industrial layout and design is the need to introduce a more positive approach towards landscape and environmental quality. In the past control has tended to be of a negative kind, directed at layout, density, and materials to the virtual exclusion of all else. There is a need to create a planned landscape structure as with all other forms of development, because, as Lynch, asserts 'Industrial areas, like roads, are not simply unpleasant necessities to be kept as neat and reticent as possible. Roads, dams, bridges, pylons, cooling towers, stacks, quarries and even spoil heaps are magnificent objects if well shaped. They are big enough and meaningful enough to take their place in large landscapes. They explain the industrial basis of our civilisation; they contrast handsomely with hills, trees and lakes.'[14]

Neighbourhood shopping centres

Over the last ten years a minor revolution in shopping habits has taken place. The ascendant success of the supermarket, the movement out-of-town, the advent of discount trading, the beginnings of bulk buying and the creation of the modern covered centre. Despite these developments there remains a need for convenient local retail facilities grouped together with other community services and forming a neighbourhood centre. The dominant activity of the neighbourhood centre will continue to be shopping, therefore the most suitable location will be determined by the retailing potential which is heavily dependent upon the available catchment area. Thus, in selecting a site for locating a neighbourhood centre, it is necessary to consider the size, age and character of the local population, the capacity of existing utilities, the availability of public transport facilities, the nature of the surrounding road system, the direction and pattern of the pedestrian network and the proximity of competing centres. Accessibility is all-important. Although a support population of 5000 is sufficient to warrant the existence of a small centre, one of 10 000 will permit the introduction of a wider range of trades and even a certain element of competition.

Layout

In brief the material considerations which govern the layout of neighbourhood shopping centres are as follows:

1. The size of the site depends entirely upon the locational factors and the economics of demand. With the greater mobility conferred upon shoppers by increased car ownership the tendency in neighbourhood centres is likely to be towards fewer shops and smaller sites. To give some indication, however, a centre of twelve to fifteen shops plus ancillary services and adequate car parking would require something just less than 1 hectare of land.

2. As with all other forms of development, sites with excessive slopes should be avoided. Greater flexibility does exist in this respect, however, with shopping layouts, careful, and for that matter interesting, designs can be introduced whereby split level basements can be constructed and used for extra selling space, storage or car parking. If car parks are laid out on sloping ground it is imperative that the parking spaces lie across the slope, not up and down.

3. The site should be a focal point in both the road and pedestrian network.

4. Good visibility and sight lines are required, not only for reasons of safety and circulation but also to attract passing custom.

5. The shops can be laid out as a 'strip' running alongside an existing road, with or without a front service road. Before the Second World War this was the traditional form

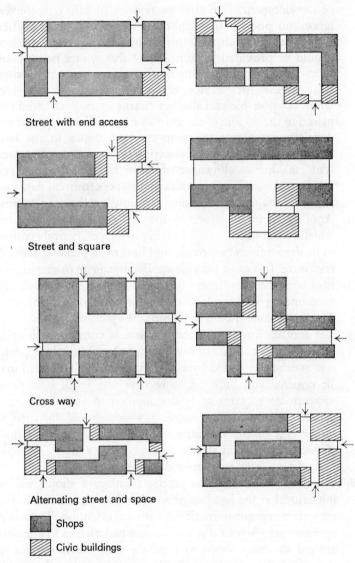

Street with end access

Street and square

Cross way

Alternating street and space

■ Shops

▨ Civic buildings

Fig. 41 Some examples of neighbourhood shopping form

SOURCE: Frederick Gibberd, *Town Design*

of development. For obvious reasons of safety, inconvenience and poor visual quality, it is to be avoided. Where local conditions dictate this approach, however, parking should be provided in front of the shops, care being taken to avoid dangerous turning or reversing on to a main road. Rear access for service deliveries should be provided wherever possible and the key tenant or magnet should be placed in the middle of the strip. A more suitable form of this development places the strip at right angles to the road with the shops facing the direction of the source of greatest trade, making an allowance of about 15 metres for rear servicing and ensuring that walking distances from car parks are kept to a reasonable minimum, certainly less than 120 metres.

6. Another form of layout is the 'U' or 'L' shaped centre which reduces the overall walking distances, permits custom to be drawn from two roads, and bestows a pleasing sense of enclosure. It is most suitably applied to square or rectangular sites with the shop fronts facing away from main roads and surrounding an open landscaped forecourt or parking area. The key tenants should be placed at the junctions.

7. Yet another form is the construction of compact pedestrian 'malls' which consists of two lines of shops directly opposite one another separated by a narrow pathway. This mall may be covered and built on more than one level. It is more appropriate to large-scale development where there are a number of competing magnets which should be sited at either end of the pedestrian way to stimulate circulation. These malls may in fact be arranged in a variety of shapes according to site, market or design requirements.

8. The distribution, mix and precise location of shops, whilst, not critical at the local neighbourhood level, is nevertheless important enough to merit the planners attention. The aim is to construct a layout that encourages pedestrians to circulate around as many shops as possible with the minimum of inconvenience. At this scale the supermarket will provide the main attraction and should be positioned so as to create the greatest movement around the centre.

9. In the above context the siting of car parks and their access

to the shops, the placing of the bus stop and the design of any staircases within the centre can be all-important.

10. Although the size of different shops varies according to their respective trades, the average neighbourhood unit in this country has a frontage of between 5 and 7 metres with a depth of about 12 to 15 metres. The supermarket might require anything from 300 to 800 square metres depending upon the local market with a frontage of not less than 12 metres, and readily lending itself to an internal corner site.

11. Rear access to each shop for deliveries and other services is almost essential, as is adequate staff parking and turning space.

12. The movement of private cars, service vehicles, and pedestrians requires thoughtful planning and segregation.

13. Car parks should be well signposted, with good lines of vision from the entrance and exit and no dangerous turns

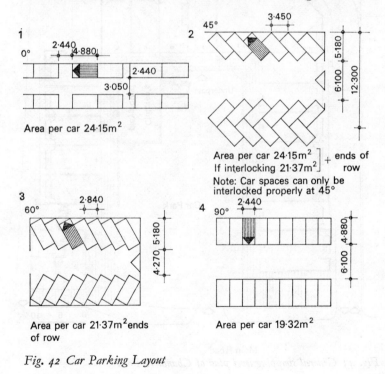

Fig. 42 Car Parking Layout

or junctions on to the neighbouring roads. The circulation should ideally be one-way, in which case a 45° herringbone layout of spaces can be provided which maximises space, otherwise bays must be laid out at 90° angles. The amount of parking space required largely depends upon the availability and frequency of public transport, although a standard provision of 3 to 5 spaces for every hundred square metres of selling space has been suggested. The car parks should be designed to cater for maximum peak-hour capacity and because of the rapid turnover an efficient circulation system, separate entrance and exit, and generously sized bays should be supplied.

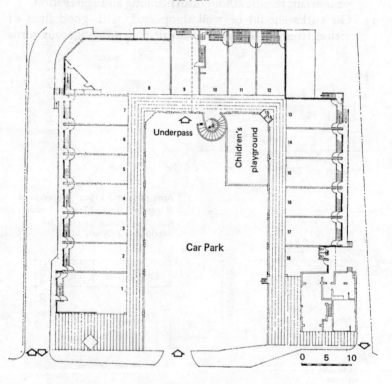

Fig. 43 *General shopping level plan of Chandlers Ford*

354

14. It must be remembered that a neighbourhood centre is intended to fulfil a social and community, as well as a retail, function. To achieve this the planner should consider the incorporation of a clinic, church, public house, café, bank, library, cinema, hall and public lavatory within his layout, taking account of the peculiar locational and servicing requirements of each. The centre should also provide telephones, a pram park, perhaps a crèche and seats.

15. As with all other forms of urban development the various services of drainage, electricity, gas, water and refuse

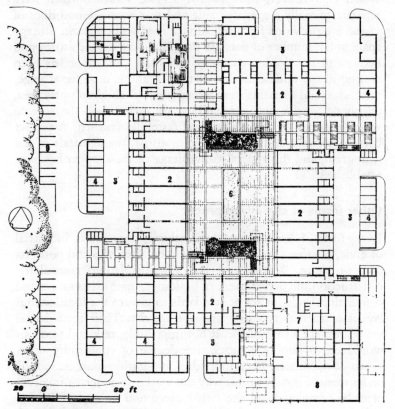

Fig. 44 Neighbourhood Shopping Precinct

1. Public buildings
2. Shops
3. Delivery area
4. Garages
5. Patio
6. Ornamental pond
7. Clinic
8. Offices
9. Visitors' car parking

disposal must all be provided and the orientation and aspect of the layout taken into account.

An object lesson in obtaining a simple inexpensive yet highly effective neighbourhood layout can be seen halfway between Winchester and Southampton in the Fryern Arcade at Chandler's Ford. Eighteen shops are grouped in a 'U' formation on a site of 0·8 hectare with the open end facing the road and enclosing a one-way circulation car park as shown in Figure 42. The site slopes away from the road and an overflow car park is provided at the rear with an access tunnel in the middle of the development which is, however, too low for service vehicles which have separate partially segregated side and rear access. Good lines of vision are provided from the service road and car park. Storage space and a number of flats are provided on a second storey and because of the sloping nature of the site a third floor has been created in the middle section of the 'U' and is used for storage, lavatories, and a tenants' conference room. A children's play area, telephone kiosks, and a restaurant are included in the scheme which is superbly constructed and tastefully finished. A perfect balance between the needs of the motorist, the demands of the pedestrian, and the general convenience of the shopper has been established.

Other forms of site development

Every form of development, be it private, commercial, industrial or civic, possesses its own particular characteristics and poses its own problems. Whereas the Building Regulations control the construction and performance of buildings, there exists no general convention, code, or set of standards to govern the location and layout of various types of land use activity. Their formulation would present a formidable, if not impossible, task and to do so would be to impose an excessive degree of conformity upon urban development. Each individual application must be judged on its merits for only in this way can vital private sector involvement be stimulated and the rich pattern and variety of British townscape be preserved. Certain proposals, however, are endowed with common elements that influence the nature of their siting. To illustrate the matters that might warrant consideration by a local authority planning committee in assessing an application for planning permission a brief outline of several different kinds of development and their distinctive features is included. It must be remembered, however, that no hard and fast rules can be laid down, for circumstances alter cases.

Service industry

This type of operation represents those very small commercial and industrial concerns catering for the needs of a neighbourhood and concerned with the maintenance, repair, and servicing requirements of that community. It includes shoe repairs, bakery, laundry, car repairs, builders, decorators, plumbers, window cleaners and even scrap merchants.

1. They do not need to be in the middle of a residential area but they do require to be accessible to it. Approximately 1 hectare of land for a neighbourhood of 10 000 persons is sufficient space for service industry.

2. They occupy fairly substantial sites which often tend to be rather untidy. For this reason, and the call for accessibility, they are best located adjacent to the neighbourhood shopping centre ideally on the rear service road.

3. Some degree of separation from the immediate vicinity of residential dwellings is required, a certain amount of disturbance being inevitable.

4. The volume and type of traffic associated with the particular service industry commands attention. The frequency should not be excessive, the surrounding roads should be of suitable construction and sufficient dimension to permit convenient access, and the lines of vision at entrances and junctions should be adequate.

5. Provision for parking employees, clients and delivery vehicles should be made.

6. The amount of noise, fumes and vibration should be taken into account, as well as the times of incidence. A baker's, for instance, might commence work and delivery at 3 or 4 o'clock in the morning and apart from the clamour even the smell of freshly baked bread can begin to pall.

7. Because of their frequent proximity to residential areas the control of advertisements demands special consideration.

Petrol filling stations

1. The major considerations governing site layout relate to matters of traffic flow and road safety. The final solution is nearly always an uneasy compromise between commercial viability and satisfactory planning.

2. From an economic point of view an ideal location is the intersection of major traffic routes. The greater the flow the better the business. The prime position, however, must be at a spot where the flow is comparatively slow, in order to attract the attention and entice the custom of passing motorists.

3. From a satisfactory planning point of view a petrol station should not be sited opposite a break in a central reservation between dual carriageways as it is likely to encourage traffic to cross the road, nor should it be close to a road junction or roundabout but it could with advantage be placed where traffic is already slowing down provided it does not interfere with turning or weaving traffic.[15] The encouragement of right turns is generally to be avoided.

4. A service road layout provides an acceptable solution with two points of access and possibly more than one station. Ideally, stations should be paired on opposite sides of the road to serve traffic from both directions and so located that the nearside station comes into view first.

5. A petrol filling station should be designed to cater for customers well away from the road. The entrance and exit should both give clear lines of vision, a one-way system of service is preferable, a deceleration lane is a great advantage, and plenty of space should be allowed for queuing during peak periods.

6. Apart from traffic considerations extra control might have to be exercised over ancillary activities that are associated with petrol filling stations, such as car repairs and the sale of goods. These can often cause additional disturbance and congestion inappropriate to a particular area.

7. The design and appearance of a station are important, not only in its structure and layout but also in the display of advertisements which with this type of development can reach absurd and visually disastrous proportions.

Over the last decade tourism has developed as a major growth industry but the provision of accommodation to cater for the rise in tourists has consistantly lagged behind the demand for hotel space. Great pressure is being exerted upon local planning authorities, not only in London but throughout the country, to release land for hotel construction, and a vast number of applications for planning permission are continually being received. Certain factors common to most applications can be discerned.

1. As a general rule hotel developers seek to obtain sites that optimise their position in terms of accessibility. They wish to be as close as possible to transport terminii, entertainment facilities, shopping centres and places of interest. Naturally these are also the areas of greatest congestion and conflict between other activities.

2. Adequate provision must be made for car parking. One space for every five beds and a further space for every forty daily visitors, depending upon the amount of conference and banqueting facilities, is considered to be sufficient. In central areas, however, with increased dependence upon public transport these standards are found to be extravagant.

3. One of the major problems in determining hotel location is assessing and controlling the amount of traffic generated by the proposed development. Congestion of varying degrees is likely to be caused throughout the day with exceptional peaks at particular times. This problem is again further aggravated where public room facilities are provided. In a traffic survey of the Hilton Hotel in London well over 1000 vehicles were counted setting down and picking up passengers during a twelve-hour period. Although hotel staff generate little traffic, tending to live close to work and travel in off-peak hours, the amount of service vehicles visiting hotels, whilst varying considerably, can cause great pressures on the transport network. The same Hilton Hotel survey indicated 60 vans and 40 lorries calling within the twelve-hour period. Another serious aspect is the growing volume of coach traffic associated with hotels, for few establishments have off-street facilities for parking and disembarking.

4. The control over the intensity of hotel development is

exercised by way of plot ratio. Most central area zones permit densities of between only 2:1 and 4:1. This level is proving increasingly uneconomic for many developers and it is worth noting in this context that established hotels such as the Grosvenor and the Cumberland have plot ratios of approximately 11:1. Some flexibility in the exercise of density regulations is probably required.

5. Another contentious element that has emerged in recent years is the creeping or surreptitious development of hotel accommodation whereby existing purpose-built blocks of residential flats, having certain communal facilities and common entrance hall, have been gradually converted into hotels. A number of enforcement notices alleging a material change of use without planning permission have been served during the last few years.

6. In the case of large-scale hotel development the effect of staff moving into a particular area might have a debilitating effect upon local conditions, especially the provision of low cost housing. Conversely hotels can act as great stimulants within the local economy, providing a valuable source of trade for service and entertainment industries. Furthermore, with careful planning and design a dual use can be made of hotel facilities for conference or university accommodation during off-peak seasons, thus promoting productivity and protecting local employment.

Site layout and development—references

1 Lynch, K., *Site Planning*, M.I.T. (1971).
2 See page 293.
3 Gibbard, F., *Town Design*, Architectural Press (1970).
4 *Ibid*. p. 297
5 *Ibid*. p. 310.
6 Leibbrand, K., *Transportation and Planning*, Leonard Hill (1970).
7 Lynch, *op. cit.*, p. 139.
8 *Ibid*. p. 169.
9 *Ibid*. p. 184.
10 *Ibid*. p. 133.
11 Ministry of Housing and Local Government Development Control Policy Notes, *Industrial and Commerical Development*, HMSO (1969).

12 Keeble, L., 'Principles and Practice of Town and Country Planning', *Estates Gazette* (1969).
13 Gibberd, *op. cit.*, p. 225.
14 Lynch, *op. cit.*, p. 343.
15 Ministry of Housing and Local Government, *op. cit.*, Petrol Filling Stations.

To be truly effective, any administrative system that seeks to plan the nation's resources and regulate the use and development of land requires the full rigour of a statutory code to ensure compliance and control. The history and administration of town planning and the responsibility for the preparation of development plans have already been described. These tend to accentuate the functions of central and local government, and the respective duties with which they are charged. To permit the proper and efficient execution of planning policy, however, it is necessary to devise and enforce a competent method of planning control. Thankfully the law relating to town planning has largely been consolidated in the 1971 Town and Country Planning Act.

General planning control

Generally speaking all development requires planning permission which can be obtained from the local planning authority. The definition of what actually constitutes 'development' is at the very nub of planning control and is described in Section 22 of the Act as 'the carrying out of building, engineering, mining or other operations in, on, over, or under land, or the making of any material change in the use of any buildings or other land'. Thus there are basically two broad categories of development,

362

firstly, anything in the nature of a building operation, and secondly, any material change of use. Problems naturally arise in determining whether or not certain activities on land fall within these categories and thus require planning permission. To assist in clarifying the position the Act expressly states that:

1. *The following are development* (Section 22)

    a The use of one house for two or more dwellings

    b The depositing of refuse on an existing dump if the area is enlarged or the height increased above surrounding land

    c The display of advertisements on the outside of a building not normally so used

2. *The following are not development* (Section 22)

    a Works of improvement, alteration, or repair, except for building below ground level, which do not materially affect the external appearance of the building

    b Maintenance or improvement of existing highways, sewers, pipes, and cables undertaken by the local authority or other statutory undertakers

    c The use of any buildings or land within the boundary of a house for any purpose incidental to the enjoyment of the house as a house

    d The use of land for agriculture, forestry, and associated buildings

3. *The following may be development but do not require planning permission* (Section 23)

    a The resumption before 6 December 1968 of the normal use of land which was temporarily used for another purpose on 1 July 1948, when planning control commenced

    b The occasional use of land for a purpose apart from its normal use, so long as there has been at least one such occasional use before 6 December 1968

    c The use of land unoccupied on 1 July 1948 for the purpose last used before that date but after 7 January 1937

    d The resumption to a previous use on the expiration of a limited planning permission or enforcement notice provided that use is not itself in contravention of planning control

    e The display of certain types of advertisement for which planning permission is deemed to be granted under the

Town and Country Planning (Control of Advertisements) Regulations 1969, as amended

f Certain development by local authorities and statutory undertakers sanctioned by central government under a development order

Apart from town and country planning legislation, a vast body of case law has been decided in an attempt to further define the act of development. A building operation has been held to mean work normally undertaken by a builder, such as rebuilding, alteration, and addition to any structure or erection excluding plant and machinery. This has included the construction of Bekonscot model village[1] and even the demolition of part of a building.[2] The expression 'material change of use' is nowhere defined as such, but the change must be substantial.[3] This can be caused by the nature, intensification or frequency of the change. A full discussion of the relevant case law is beyond the scope of this text.[4] Statute has, however, sought to provide some guidance in the form of the 1963 Use Classes Order, as amended. This order sets out nineteen classes of land use activity such as Shops, Class One; Offices, Class Two; Light Industry, Class Three; General Industry, Class Four; certain Chemical operations, Class Five; and so on; when, in the event of a change of use taking place from one use to another falling within the same use class, it does not amount to a 'material' change of use, and does not constitute an act of development, and therefore does not require planning permission. It says no more. It does not make any statement regarding a change of use from one use class to another, this may or may not constitute development according to the individual circumstances. Exemptions are made in certain Classes, such as the sale of fried fish and motor cars in Class One, and expressions such as 'shop' and 'office' are further defined in both statute and case law; a shop, for example, is a building used for retail trade and includes a hairdresser, undertaker and ticket agency but not a betting office, garage, hotel, or public house.

Development control

As previously mentioned most acts of development require prior consent from the relevant local planning authority. If any

364

doubt exists in the potential developer's mind whether a particular act constitutes development or not, the matter may be determined by an application to the local planning authority under Section 53 of the 1971 Town and Country Planning Act. One notable exception to the general requirement to obtain planning permission is the power conferred upon the Secretary of State under Section 24 of the 1971 Act to introduce 'development orders' which automatically grant permission to particular kinds of development known as 'permitted development'. These are introduced in an attempt to rid the public and the planning authorities alike of the mundane trivia that might otherwise clog the planning machine. The most important of these orders is the General Development Order 1963, as amended by that of 1969. These set down twenty-three categories of development for which planning permission is automatically granted, and include the enlargement of existing dwelling houses within prescribed limits, the construction of fences and walls to certain heights, the external painting of buildings, the erection of selected temporary buildings, and specified material changes of use. There are certain standard conditions relating to highways and road traffic which apply to all categories. Moreover, if for any special reason permitted development is thought inappropriate the Secretary of State may direct or approve the withdrawal of deemed permission, either for a particular category or for a chosen area. This is done by issuing an Article 4 Direction and is accepted practice in areas of outstanding natural beauty. The General Development Order also lays down the procedure involved in applying for planning permission.

Application for planning permission

Application must be made to the local planning authority on the forms provided, and to save unnecessary expenditure outline planning permission can be sought prior to a detailed submission. Once outline permission is granted the authority are obliged to allow the development in some form or other but may reserve their judgement on such matters as siting, layout and design. An applicant does not have to possess an interest in the land, but in such circumstances he is required to serve notice of his intention upon the owners and complete certain certificates to this effect in accordance with Section 27 of the 1971 Act. Certain classes of 'bad neighbour' development such as knackers yards, public conveniences, cinemas, dance halls and refuse disposal operations must be publicised in the local press, and by a notice on the site, to enable third parties to make representations for consideration by the local planning authority when coming to their decision. Under Section 28 this provision also now applies to proposals that might affect the character of a conservation area.

Having received the application the local planning authority must notify the applicant of receipt and make their decision within two months, unless a trunk road is affected, in which case the period is three months. These periods may, however, be extended by agreement between the parties. If no decision is reached within this time the application is deemed to be refused. To expedite the procedure of planning control in this country some critics favour the adoption of the French system whereby permission is deemed to be granted after the effluxion of the statutory time limit.

In making their decision the local planning authority must have regard to the provisions of the development plan and any other considerations thought material. The decision itself must be made in writing and may refuse permission, grant it uncon- ditionally, or grant it subject to conditions. If permission is refused or conditions are imposed reasons must be given. A register of all applications and decisions is kept by the authority and is open for public inspection. Since 1968 certain decisions may now be given by a named officer of the local planning auth- ority if the authority has delegated the power to him so to do. In exceptional circumstances where matters of national concern or extreme controversy are involved the Minister may under Section 35 of the 1971 Act 'call-in' an application and determine it himself.

Duration of planning permission

Under Section 41 of the 1971 Act all planning permissions are subject to a time limit of five years, although this may be extended or reduced in individual cases. Outline permission, however, is only valid for three years and development must be started within two years of any reserved matters being dealt with. The beginning of development is defined in Section 43 of the 1971 Act. These provisions limiting the duration of planning permission were introduced to facilitate the process of development control, combat the speculative holding of land off the market, and prevent a number of out-of-date permissions from accumulating upon a piece of land which might involve considerable compensation to revoke. In the same context the ability to limit the time allowed for the completion of development has been conferred upon local planning authorities who are now empowered to serve a Completion Notice. This terminates the permission relating to development already begun but which has not been finished within the time specified by the permission, and which appears unlikely to be completed within a reasonable time. The Notice, which is served upon the owner and occupier, must be confirmed by the Minister and allows twelve months for completion before the planning permission ceases. Any development finished before that date is considered permissible.

Conditional planning permission

The local planning authority may impose such conditions 'as they think fit' upon a permission, Section 30. These may relate to the regulation of any land within the control of the applicant, the removal of buildings and discontinuance of use at the end of a specified period, the length of the permission and the time by which it must be started as well as the design, layout, and materials of any buildings. Any condition must, however, be 'fit' from a planning point of view. It must be reasonably certain, intelligently and sensibly related to the particular planning scheme and the prevailing policy for the area, made in good faith, and not attached for an ulterior motive. The condition restricting occupation of cottages to agricultural workers has been held valid[5], but the obligation to construct a road which was not just for service but gave a public right of way,[6] the payment of of money as security against fulfilment of conditions, and the restriction of occupation of industrial premises to firms already within the county,[7] have all been held to be invalid. If a condition is invalid it is a matter of common sense whether or not it strikes at the root of the whole permission and thus renders it

367

invalid. If it is incidental and not fundamental to the decision then the original planning permission can still be valid.

Appeal

Appeal against refusal of permission or the imposition of conditions lies to the Secretary of State under Section 36 and must be made within six months of receipt of the decision. The Secretary of State may reject or allow the appeal, or may alter the terms of the conditions, but before doing so he must afford both sides, if they so desire, either a private hearing or a local public enquiry before one of his Inspectors. To save the expense of a hearing, appeal proceedings can be conducted by way of written submissions. To expedite matters certain appeals are not only heard by the Secretary of State's Inspector but may also be determined by him. The Secretary of State is further empowered to refer an appeal relating to the design or external appearance of a particular building to an independent tribunal by way of a development order. Certain matters of exceptional importance may be referred to a Planning Inquiry Commission consisting of a Chairman and several other members. All appeals to the Secretary of State are otherwise final except on a point of law which lies to the High Court and must be made within six weeks of the appeal decision.

Revocation and modification

If, due to a change of policy, circumstance, or even error, a local planning authority wishes to retract or alter a planning permission they have previously granted they may do so by means of an order made under Section 45 of the 1971 Act. Such a revocation or modification order must be served before any change of use has taken place or any building operations have been finished and does not affect completed work. Unless the orders are unopposed or unlikely to give rise to claims for compensation the Secretary of State's consent to the service of the order is required. Compensation is payable for any abortive expenditure incurred such as the preparation of maps and plans and for any loss directly attributable to the order.

If a local planning authority desires the removal or alteration of an existing authorised, but non-conforming, development they must serve a Discontinuance Order under Section 51 which again requires confirmation by the Secretary of State and attracts full compensation for any loss and disturbance caused by the service of the order.

Control of advertisements

Due to the large number of applications and their special nature, a separate code has been devised for the control of outdoor advertisements under the Town and Country Planning (Control of Advertisements) Regulations (1969), now authorised by Section 63 of the Town and Country Planning Act (1971). Although the display of advertisements is considered to be a building operation thus constituting an act of development requiring planning permission, the regulations confer a wide range of 'deemed consent'. Among those included within these classes of permitted development or deemed consent are temporary advertisements such as 'for sale' boards, the functional advertisements of local authorities and statutory undertakers such as bus stops and street name plates, those relating to certain business premises such as trade signs or professional plates, and flags bearing the emblem or name of the person occupying the building over which they fly. Certain standard conditions are laid down in the regulations which apply to all these categories in respect of siting, dimension, safety and cleanliness. It can be seen that the definition of the term 'advertisement' is fairly broad, it applies to 'any word, letter, model, sign, placard, board, notice, device or representation, whether illuminated or not, in the nature of and employed wholly or in part for the purposes of advertise-ment, announcement or direction'. The regulations do not apply, however, to those advertisements which are not readily visible to the public, are inside a building and more than one metre away from any opening, form part of the fabric of a building or are carried on a vehicle. Where other proposed advertisements do not fall within the classes of permitted development they naturally require planning permission.

If it is thought appropriate a local planning authority can require that advertisements currently displayed with deemed consent should be made subject to control by the authority and 'express consent' obtained from them in order to secure continued display. This practice is known as the 'challenge procedure' and is operated in the interests of amenity or public safety. Any such grant of express consent must be for a fixed term of not more than five years.

Stricter control over the display of advertisements is exercised in areas of special control which are normally designated in the development plan or created by means of an order confirmed by the Secretary of State. The general rule is that no advertisements should be displayed in these Areas apart from essential public signs, those that are permitted are treated as exceptions to the rule. Over one third of the country is now covered by Special Area Control.

Control of caravans
Because of the inordinate amount of litigation caused by this particular form of development in the years proceeding the 1947 Town and Country Planning Act, the general code of law relating to the control of caravans was reinforced by the Caravan Sites and Control of Development Act (1960). In general, the development of land for the siting of caravans requires both planning permission and a site licence. Application for planning permission is made to the local planning authority and must be obtained before a site licence can be granted. The site licence is issued by the local borough or district council who are obliged to grant one if planning permission has been obtained. They may, however impose conditions which they consider to be necessary or desirable in the interests of both the caravan dwellers and the public at large. These conditions may relate to the number of caravans permitted, their size, layout, state of repair; and the sanitation, safety and amenity of the site. Appeal against the conditions attached to a site licence lies to the Magistrates Court and must be made within twenty-eight days of issue.

There are a number of circumstances in which exemption for a caravan site from the provisions of the 1960 Act is given, these include the use of land within the curtilage of a house so long as it is incidental to the enjoyment of the house; the use of land for not more than twenty-eight days in the year for a single caravan not exceeding two nights at any one time; the use of more than five acres of land for not more than three caravans at any one time for a period not exceeding twenty-eight days in the year; and the use of land for exempted caravan organisations, agricultural, construction, and entertainment workers.

Another provision relating to caravans and concerning town planning, albeit somewhat peripherally, is the Caravan Sites Act (1968), which places a responsibility upon local planning authorities to consider the provision of caravan sites for, and protect the interests of, 'gypsies and other persons of nomadic habit'.

Control of office and industrial premises

Both the development of offices and factories is governed by the Control of Office and Industrial Development Act (1965) largely re-enacted in the Town and Country Planning Act (1971). To combat London's growing congestion, and encourage the decentralisation of offices, it is not only necessary to obtain planning permission but if the proposed development is in the the Greater London or the South East area an office development permit is also required. This provision only applies to premises over a certain size, the limit currently being 10 000 square feet. Both the limits and the areas to which they apply are subject to change. The permit is issued by the Department of the Environment and should be obtained prior to making application for planning permission. Any permission granted without such authority is invalid. The Department may attach any conditions which they consider 'necessary or expedient' and these must be included by a local planning authority in any subsequent planning permission. There is no appeal against the refusal of an office development permit or the imposition of conditions, nor is there any provision for compensation upon restriction. The Act carefully defines the nature of office work, and applies to the extension, alteration, and conversion of other buildings and the change of use of other buildings, to office purposes, as well as the construction of new premises.

A roughly similar system of control exists in respect of industrial premises whereby any such proposed development outside a Development Area, of over 10 000 square feet in the Greater London and South East areas, and 15 000 square feet elsewhere, requires an industrial development certificate from the Secretary of State prior to, and as an essential part of, planning permission. Again the limits and the areas to which they apply are subject to change. As in the case of office development conditions may be attached to the certificate which must be incorporated in any subsequent planning permission and against which there is no appeal. Unlike office development permits, however, a purchase notice may be served upon the refusal of a certificate, and compensation possibly payable, if the local planning authority state that permission would have been refused even if a certificate were granted.

Protection of trees and woodland

Under Section 59 of the 1971 Act a tree preservation order can be served by the local planning authority on an individual tree, groups of trees, or woodlands, the only criterion being that it is 'expedient so to do in the interests of amenity'. The confirmation of the Secretary of State is required unless no objection is raised, and in any event no order can be made on Forestry Commission or Crown land without their consent. The procedure for making an order is laid down in the Town and Country Planning (Tree Preservation Order) Regulations (1969) and covers the form of the notice, the persons to be served, and time limitations regarding appeal. Once in operation a tree preservation order prohibits the cutting down, topping, or destruction of protected trees without the consent of the authority unless they are dead, dying, diseased or dangerous. Even then it is possible that the owner may be required to replace the felled trees.

If certain trees appear to be in imminent danger the local planning authority are empowered under the Civic Amenities Act 1967 to issue a provisional Tree Preservation Order operative for six months which takes immediate effect. This same Act has introduced fines of up to £250 or twice the value of the tree, whichever is the greater, for contravention of an Order.

Protection of buildings

The Secretary of State for the Department of the Environment is charged under Section 54 of the 1971 Town and Country

Planning Act with compiling a list of buildings of special architectural and historic interest. A copy of the list is sent to the local planning authority and made available for inspection. Notification of listing is also sent to individual owners and occupiers of the respective buildings; they are not, however, consulted beforehand. Once listed, any demolition, alteration, or extension of a building which would affect its character requires 'listed building consent' from the local planning authority unless it is urgently required in the interests of safety or health. Any act that might otherwise damage a listed building can upon summary conviction result in a fine of up to £250 or a term of imprisonment, or both. Upon conviction on indictment the term of imprisonment can be up to one year and the fine can take account of any financial gain resulting from the offence.

Because of the expense that is often involved in consequence of listing, the Department of the Environment are permitted to make grants and loans towards preserving the building. If any contravention of listed building control is suspected, the local Planning authority are authorised in accordance with Section 96 of the 1971 Act to serve a 'listed building enforcement notice' specifying the alleged contravention and demanding a remedy. They are also allowed to serve a repairs notice to ensure proper preservation and if this is not complied with compulsory purchase powers are available; moreover, if urgent works are required they may even enter the premises, undertake the works, and recover the cost. If a building is not included on the list and the local planning authority consider it to be of special architectural or historic interest they may themselves serve a Building Preservation Order which has the effect of temporary listing for six months during which time the building can be considered for addition to the Secretary's list. If he does not accept its addition the Order ceases to have any effect, compensation might be payable, and no further Order can be served for the next twelve months.

If whole areas, because of their special character and general environment, merit protection, there is provision under the 1967 Civic Amenities Act to designate them as Conservation Areas. If any development is proposed within such an area the application for planning permission must be advertised in both the local press and by way of site notices, and any representations received from the public must be taken into account by the local planning authority in making their decision.

Enforcement of planning control

If a local planning authority consider that any development has been carried out without the grant of planning permission, or that any condition or limitation to which such permission was subject has not been complied with, an Enforcement Notice can be served in accordance with Section 87 of the 1971 Town and Country Planning Act. The Notice can also be served by the Secretary of State for the Department of the Environment. It must be served on both the owner and the occupier, and, if the authority think fit, on any other person having an interest in the land who might be affected. If the alleged breach of planning control is a building operation, or a change of use to a single residential dwelling house, the Notice must be served within four years of the breach occurring. If the breach amounts to any other material change of use a Notice may be served at any future time. Since the four-year rule also used to apply in cases alleging a material change of use and was only abolished in 1968, a person having an interest in land which was subject to a change of use taking place before 1964, and still continuing, may apply to the local planning authority for a Certificate of Established Use which if granted precludes subsequent enforcement proceedings.

Although there is no prescribed form for an Enforcement Notice it must specify the alleged breach, describe the steps required to remedy the breach, the time allowed for the necessary steps to be taken and the date from which the Notice becomes effective, not being less than twenty-eight days. It must be served to take effect on all the parties at the same time. Care must be taken in the preparation and service of an enforcement notice because, although the Secretary of State can correct any informality, defect or error which is not material on appeal, a false statement of fact as the basis upon which the Notice is served can render it a nullity.

Within the twenty-eight days before the Notice takes effect an appeal may be lodged with the Secretary of State who, if the appellant or the local planning authority desire, must afford each an opportunity of appearing before an Inspector appointed by him. An appeal can only be made on certain grounds, which are, that Planning permission for the alleged breach ought to be granted, has been granted, is not required, the time limit has expired, no development is involved, the requirements of the notice are excessive or that the period of compliance is too short. The notification of appeal need only indicate the general grounds upon which it is made, in fact for safety all can be stated, but the Secretary of State discourages mere recital and usually requests amplification. Unlike most other planning appeal proceedings the burden of proof is placed firmly upon the appellant and evidence is usually given under oath. The Secretary of State has a wide discretion to allow or reject the appeal, grant planning permission, or vary attached conditions, and except on a point of law where further appeal lies to the High Court, his decision is final. Once the appeal has been rejected the Notice immediately becomes effective. If the terms are not then complied with several other remedies are available to the local planning authority; in certain circumstances they may enter the property to ensure compliance and recover expenses, apply to the High Court for an injunction against persistent breach, and even prosecute the occupier of the land when he is not directly responsible, who may himself in turn make recovery from the owner at fault.

Because development in contravention of planning control was frequently pursued during appeal proceedings, to the general detriment of the public interest, a new procedure called a Stop Notice was introduced in 1968, now re-enacted in Section 90 of the 1971 Act, which has the effect of halting the alleged breach almost immediately. This notice can be served by the local planning authority upon any person who appears either to have an interest in the land or be concerned with carrying out the alleged breach. It can only be issued following the service of an Enforcement Notice and in respect of a building operation or the deposit of refuse specifying the date from which it is to take effect, not being less than three days and not more than fourteen. Failure to observe the notice is a criminal offence punishable by a fine. If, however, the Enforcement Notice to which it relates is subsequently withdrawn or quashed on appeal the Stop Notice automatically ceases to have effect and full compensation for any loss incurred can be claimed.

Compensation for planning restrictions and proposals

As a general rule the circumstances in which compensation is available for refusal of planning permission or the imposition of onerous conditions are severely curtailed. In respect of 'new development', which is defined as any development not falling within the 8th Schedule of the 1971 Act, compensation is limited under Part 7 of the Act to those applications where an 'unexpended balance of established development value' is attached to the land. This refers to the established claim made under the 1947 Town and Country Planning Act as amended by the 1953 and 1954 Acts and reduced by the value of any subsequent development. Even if this condition is fulfilled compensation is still not available in accordance with Section 147 of the 1971 Act if the refusal or condition relates to a material change of use, access to a highway, the working of minerals, the display of advertisements, the number, design or layout of dwellings, premature development, development of land liable to subsidence or flooding, or where permission exists for residential, commercial or industrial development. This precludes payment in the vast majority of cases. Compensation does, however, arise when restrictions apply to development that falls within Part 2 of the eighth Schedule, often referred to as 'existing use rights'. It may also be claimed, as previously intimated, in situations where planning permission has been revoked, modified, or discontinued.

The other main categories in which compensation becomes payable are when individuals suffer as a result of an adverse planning decision or proposal and are able to compel the local planning authority to purchase their interest. Where planning permission is refused or onerous conditions are attached which 'render the land incapable of reasonable beneficial use in its existing state' an aggrieved owner may within twelve months of the decision, under Section 180 of the 1971 Act, serve a Purchase Notice on the local authority requiring them to acquire the land affected by the decision. The Notice may only apply to the land in the original application, not more and not less. The local authority must serve a counter notice within three months either accepting, in which case notice to treat is deemed to be served, or refusing, giving reasons which must be communicated to the Secretary of State. He can confirm or reject the Notice, with or without modifications, confirm the original planning permission, grant alternative planning permission, or substitute an alternative purchaser, notifying the parties accordingly and affording them an opportunity of a hearing before an Inspector. Apart from the refusal of planning permission or imposition of onerous conditions, a Purchase Notice can also be served in connection with revocation, modification, discontinuance, and tree preservation orders as well as the control of advertisements, listed buildings and industrial premises.

If an individual is affected by an adverse planning proposal, as opposed to decision, he may serve a Blight Notice upon the local planning authority in accordance with Section 192 of the 1971 Act, so long as the land concerned is indicated in a statutory plan as being required for one of the purposes described in the Act. These include highway development, compulsory purchase, public facilities and services. In other words, the eventual loss of the land is a prerequisite to serving a Purchase Notice. The class of owner who can claim is, however, restricted to resident owner occupiers of residential dwelling houses, owner occupiers of farms, and non-resident owner occupiers of hereditaments with an annual value below £750. Before the owner can serve a Blight Notice he must show that he has made reasonable attempts to sell his interest and has been unable to do so except at a price substantially below the normal market value. The authority upon whom the notice is served may, within two months, serve a counter notice under Section 194 denying blight, refuting the owners' attempts to sell, or claiming that they do not propose to compulsorily acquire the land for at least fifteen years, which exempts them from purchase. Appeal lies within a further two months to the Lands Tribunal.

Town planning law—references

1 Buckinghamshire County Council v Callingham.
2 Coleshill and District Investment Co. Ltd. v Ministry of Health and Local Government (1968).
3 Palser v Grinling (1948).
4 See Heap, D., 'An Outline of Planning Law', *Estates Gazette* (1969).
5 Fawcett Properties Ltd. v Buckinghamshire County Council (1959).
6 Hall and Co. Ltd. v Shoreham-by-Sea Urban District Council (1964).
7 Allnat London Properties Ltd. v Middlesex County Council (1964).

Further recommended reading

Encyclopaedia of Law and Planning, *Estates Gazette*.
Telling, A. E., *Planning Law and Procedure*, Butterworth (1970).